PLACES OF LEARNING

PLACES OF LEARNING

MEDIA   ARCHITECTURE   PEDAGOGY

ELIZABETH ELLSWORTH

RoutledgeFalmer

NEW YORK AND LONDON

Published in 2005 by
Routledge
Taylor & Francis Group
270 Madison Avenue
New York, NY 10016
www.routledge-ny.com

Published in Great Britain by
Routledge
Taylor & Francis Group
2 Park Square
Milton Park, Abingdon
Oxon OX14 4RN
www.routledge.co.uk

10 9 8 7 6 5 4 3 2 1

Library of Congress Cataloging-in-Publication Data

Ellsworth, Elizabeth Ann.
    Places of learning : media, architecture, pedagogy / Elizabeth
Ellsworth.
        p. cm.
    Includes bibliographical references and index.
    ISBN 0-415-93158-4 (hc : alk. paper) —
    ISBN 0-415-93159-2 (pb : alk. paper)
    1. Place-based education. 2. Self-culture. I. Title.
    LC239.E44 2004
    370.11'5--dc22

                                                        2004008581

Cover art: "Thoreau's Aperture," by Sarah Ellsworth.

Contents

Acknowledgments

I wish to thank the editors of *Symploke* for permission to include here, as Chapter 5, work that first appeared in a special issue of the journal, entitled "The Sites of Pedagogy." As a Visiting Fellow at the U.S. Holocaust Memorial Museum, I conducted the research that informs that article under a Research Grant from the Memorial Foundation for Jewish Culture. I thank the Foundation and the Museum for their kind assistance and generous support.

I also wish to thank Arthur Levine, President, and Darlyne Bailey, Vice President for Academic Affairs and Dean of the College, Teachers College, Columbia University, for the honor and opportunity to serve as the Julius and Rosa Sachs Distinguished Lecturer, 2002–2003. During that year, I presented three public lectures that formed the basis for this book's Chapters 2 through 4. I also thank President Levine and Dean Bailey, as well as Ruth Vinz, Enid and Lester Morse Professor in Teacher Education, for the invaluable opportunity to think out loud with students in the several seminars that I taught while at Teachers College and to learn from their insightful comments and criticisms. I thank those students for their patience and for their interest in working with me on ideas as they were still emerging.

My gratitude goes to those at the New School University who attended a work-in-progress lecture based on what has become Chapter 6. Their special appreciation for questions of how aesthetic experience relates to pedagogy helped me to refine and extend arguments that I had not yet fully articulated. The support that colleagues in the New School's Media Studies Program extended to me during my first two years as Core Faculty in that Program — which were also the last two years of writing this book — made its completion possible. Even then, I delivered the manuscript to Routledge editor Catherine Bernard well past its due date. I thank her for her unflagging support of the project and especially for the editorial comments and suggestions that helped me to clarify and strengthen what I was trying to say.

Sarah Ellsworth, a graduate student in architecture, took days out of her deadline-filled student life to offer line-by-line editorial suggestions for most of the chapters in this book. Her excellent skills as a writer and her experiences and perspectives as a student of architecture allowed me to see what I had written in fresh ways and from new angles.

My octogenarian parents continue to prove that passions for noncompliant learning know no bounds of age or physical ability. I learn and am inspired by them daily and thank them for their apparently endless love and support.

Janet Miller knows like no other how difficult the writing process got at times. She did for me what she does every day for her students — she listened to my thoughts as they were in the making and then offered them back as something that I still recognized as my own — except now that "something" was inflected by her brilliance. She does the same with all that I am privileged to share with her.

Introduction

… what is it today to think or to imagine, to construct or to design, in relation not to "things made" but to "things in the making"? … To think about things in the making is … to think, and think of ourselves, "experimentally."

—John Rajchman

What really exists is not things made but things in the making. Once made, they are dead….

—William James

Knowledge, once it is defined, taught and used as a "thing made," is dead. It has been forced to give up that which "really exists": its nature when it is a thing in the making, continuously evolving through our understanding of the world and our own bodies' experience of and participation in that world.

When taught and used as a thing made, knowledge, the trafficked commodity of educators and producers of educational media, becomes nothing more than the decomposed by-product of something that has already happened to us. What has already happened was once very much alive: the *thinking–feeling*, the embodied sensation of *making sense*, the *lived experience* of our learning selves that make the thing we call knowledge. Thinking and feeling our selves as they *make sense* is more than merely the sensation of knowledge in the making. It is a sensing of our selves in the making, and is that not the root of what we call learning?

Places of Learning explores what it might mean to think of pedagogy not in relation to knowledge as a thing made but to knowledge in the making. By focusing on the means and conditions, the environments and events of knowledge in the making, it opens an exploration into the experience of the learning self. *Places of Learning* reconsiders pedagogy as the impetus behind the particular movements, sensations, and affects of bodies/mind/brains in the midst of learning, and it explores the embodied experiences that pedagogy elicits and plays host to: experiences of being radically in relation to one's self, to others, and to the world.

This book does not look at individuals' personal or subjective experiences of schools or of teaching strategies. This is not, and could not be, an ethnography of teaching and learning. If the experience of knowledge in the making is also the experience of our selves in the making, then there is no self who preexists a learning experience. Rather, the "self" is what emerges from that learning experience. We must look for the *experience of the learning self* in what comes before the self and in what cannot be reduced to the self who learns. We have to look for the experience of the learning self in the times and places of knowledge in the making, which are also the times and places of the learning self in the making.

Educators and social and cultural theorists alike grapple with the difficulties of talking about the times and places in which we encounter the learning self. To think of pedagogy in relation to knowledge in the making rather than to knowledge as a thing made is to think of something that cannot be easily captured in language. When my self and what I know are simultaneously in the making, my body/brain/mind is participating in an event that exists outside the realm of language. As a nonlinguistic event, the experience of knowledge and self as simultaneously in the making can even be said to preexist cognition.

To think and to speak about aspects of learning that exceed the realm of language presents educators and educational media producers with special difficulties. It challenges many of our assumptions and practices. In the wake of these difficulties and challenges, the following question remains desperately under-theorized: How does the fact of human embodiment affect activities of teaching and learning? Modern linguistics, semiology, sociology, and, of course, cognitive psychology have dominated theories that inform the current generation of educators and educational media producers. Few of these domains of knowledge encouraged investigation into "experience" understood as the non- or prelinguistic ground on which meaning, images, knowledge — and selves — are formed. They have schooled us instead to be suspicious of experience because it is "under-theorized" and easily "contaminated" by naïve subjectivity. Non- and prelinguistic ways of making sense of the world are an embarrassment to the social sciences because they put them up against the limitations of their scientific, philosophical, and political assumptions and practices. They especially challenge those assumptions and practices whose histories have privileged language over sensation, objects of experience over subjects of experience, the rational over the affective, and knowledge as a tool for prediction and control over learning as play and pleasure. Concurrently, with its connection to body, emotion, subjectivity, and the realm of the ephemeral, experience has often been attributed qualities of the feminine, and therefore has been easily dismissed.

But things are changing. Intriguing developments in cultural studies, media studies, architecture, science studies, and aesthetics are now shifting the terms in which theorists and critics pose questions of experience, study it, and design for it. Recent developments in brain research and the life sciences are throwing into crisis long-held assumptions about such fundamental human activities as cognition, perception, sensation, and action. They are shifting our understandings about embodiment in ways that make it more and more difficult to maintain the philosophical or practical distinctions between reason and sensation, the body as material and the mind as immaterial (Massumi, 2002). Some theories about human agency and social change that we thought were powerful enough to account for cultural and political events and capable of guiding progressive social and cultural action have failed, in troubling ways, to do either. New developments in media, technology, intelligent artificial environments, and the massive global exchanges of people, cultures, products, and ideas now disrupt "progressive" discourses that were forged under very different circumstances and in relation to very different objects of study.

Such events have provoked a sense of urgency in the search for new mindsets capable of moving away from the strict binary discourses of self/other, real/virtual, reason/emotion, mind/body, natural/artificial, inside/outside, thinking/feeling, irony/humor. Contemporary social, cultural, and aesthetic theories are marked by the search for ways to rethink the terms of these binaries that have been so strategic to social, political, and educational thought. The search is on to create concepts and languages that release and redirect the forces now locked up in such binaries by addressing them not as separate and in relations of opposition but rather as complex, moving webs of interrelationalities (Kennedy, 2003).

In subsequent chapters, we will see how this search brings a number of theorists, designers, and practitioners back to the question of experience. They are revisiting theories of experience generated by American pragmatisms which they see as "ripe today for recontextualization" (Ockman, 2000, p. 19) from new angles and perspectives made visible by the developments I mentioned above. They re-read Henri Bergson, William James, and C.S. Peirce not to reinvigorate them or to put forward any one pragmatist line but to use them as catalysts for departure to somewhere else in our understandings of experience — somewhere that offers a fresh perspective on experience that would allow us to undo some of the damage left in the wake of binary thinking and use new understandings of experience to create concepts and pedagogies capable of making more of the experience of the learning self.

To think experimentally about "important cultural transformations still very much 'in the making'" (Ockman, 2000, p. 22), we need concepts and languages that will grasp, without freezing or collapsing, the fluid, continuous, dynamic, multiple, uncertain, nondecomposable qualities of *experience in the making*. Attempts to invent such a language have generated efforts to speak of experience, for example, as an event of force and sensation. Watching a film, according to this mindset, becomes an event that melds the matter of mind/brain and body with the matter of film, sound, sensation as movement, and the "in between" of cognitions (Kennedy, 2003, p. 5). In this mind/brain/body meld with objects, spaces, and times, the self is understood as a becoming, an emergence, and as continually in the making. This, one theorist says, moves us beyond a contemporary politics of difference based in semiotics and linguistics toward an experimental "pragmatics of becoming" based on making and doing (Kennedy, 2003, p. 6).

All of this is an attempt to think relationally — an attempt to understand and talk about the nature of reality in a way that acknowledges that to be alive and to inhabit a body is to be continuously and radically in relation with the world, with others, and with what we make of them.

Experience, of course, presupposes bodies — not inert bodies, but living bodies that take up and lay down space by their continuous, unfolding movement and that take up and lay down time as they go on being. When we begin to think of experience as an event in time that also takes place, we can see why a number of contemporary theorists are using media and architecture to help them structure their concepts about experience. While both media and architecture can be said to communicate ideas, sensibilities, assumptions, and sometimes hidden power relations to their users and viewers, our experiences of the cinema or of a building exceed merely reading or decoding their signs and meanings. The visual experience of watching a film entails not only representation. It has a material nature that involves biological and molecular events taking place in the body of the viewer and in the physical and imagined space between the viewer and the film. Affect and sensation are *material* and part of that engagement (Kennedy, 2003, p. 16).

Likewise, architecture consists not only in the uses and meanings of buildings and spaces. In architectural spaces, bodies have "affective somatic responses" (Grosz & Eisenman, 2003, p. xiv), and these responses arise out of the "assemblage" (mind/brain/body/building) that is the time and space of a building's inhabitation. Our experiences of a building arise not only out of our cognitive interpretations of the building's allusions to historical or aesthetic meanings but also out of the corporeality of the body's time/space as it exists in relation to the building.

Like media and architecture, pedagogy involves us in experiences of the corporeality of the body's time and space. Bodies have affective somatic responses as they inhabit a pedagogy's time and space. Specific to pedagogy is the experience of the corporeality of the body's time and space when it is in the midst of learning. Because this experience arises out of an assemblage of mind/brain/body with the time and space of pedagogy, we must approach an investigation into the experience of the learning self through that assemblage. How, then, might we think about knowledge in the making? How might we think of pedagogy experimentally?

Pedagogy and Experience

The purpose of this book is to invite interested readers into an experiment in thinking about pedagogy in terms that are quite different from, say, an ethnography of various individuals' reported and observed learning experiences. It is an experiment that promises, as a consequence, quite different opportunities and challenges for students and teachers alike.

I offer for consideration here a number of places of learning ranging from multimedia projections onto urban buildings to public events as performance art involving teachers, students, and their community's police. Each of them presents emergent pedagogical qualities and elements that I see to be still very much in the making (Ockman, 2000, p. 23). In each of these places of learning, we will locate those qualities and design elements that seem to constitute its pedagogical force. I hope that any insight our experiment offers may become a catalyst for generating new thought about pedagogy and its force in the experience of the learning self.

Like all experiments, ours is fueled by a fundamental curiosity about things and processes — in this instance, emergent pedagogical elements and qualities — that we do not yet understand and that provoke us to think or imagine in new ways. The most provocative and promising places in which to begin our investigation, in other words, are anomalous places of learning: peculiar, irregular, abnormal, or difficult to classify pedagogical phenomena. Like all anomalies, the places I have chosen appear to be peculiar only when we look at them from a particular angle of view. In astronomy, an anomaly is an apparent angular deviation of the orbit of a planet around the sun, *as seen from the sun*. The pedagogical anomalies that form the impetus for this book are difficult to see as *pedagogy* only when we view them from the "center" of dominant educational discourses and practices — a position that takes knowledge to be a thing already made and learning to be an experience already known. But, when viewing them in relation to the multiple and potentially eccentric connotations of the phrase "the experience of a learning self in the making," their force as *pedagogy* becomes more apparent.

We could picture most educators and educational researchers as attempting to center pedagogical practices in schools in a close and regular orbit around curricular goals and objectives, as well as measurable, verifiable educational outcomes. We could picture the pedagogical anomalies that we will work and play with here as orbiting the practices in schools and the discourses in the field of education in elliptical paths that sometimes swing quite far from the schools as centers of learning. We would then see students and teachers follow the deviating orbits of some of these anomalies away from school as they set off on field trips to museums, galleries, or other public spaces. Others might appear at first glance to take us to the outer fringes of education's charted solar system and beyond, escaping the gravity of conventionally defined education and flying off into other systems of practice and thought: into media, architecture, entertainment, art, social engineering, or politics.

In the spirit of thinking experimentally about pedagogy, our goal is not to engage with these anomalies for the purpose of bringing them back into education's familiar orbit. We will not try to make them into something that we, as educators already made, would recognize as pedagogy. Instead, in an attempt to take on what Rajchman calls an "experimentalist relation to the future," we are going to use these anomalies not to predict or program the future of pedagogy but rather, paraphrasing Rajchman, to diagnose the unknown or unforeseen [pedagogical] forces knocking at the door (Rajchman, 2000b, p. 14). We are going to look at these anomalies as harboring and expressing forces and processes of pedagogies "as yet unmade, that provoke us to think or imagine new [pedagogies] in new ways" (Rajchman, 2000b, p. 15).

In the following chapters, we will look for the various qualities and design elements that seem to constitute the pedagogical force of each place of learning. We will try to find, in other words, those elements that seem designed specifically to "assemble with" their visitors', users', and viewers' *learning selves*, and we will watch these qualities and elements interact with, elaborate upon, and challenge each other.

So, just what are these pedagogical anomalies that might sustain and reward such an experiment? Which qualities and elements of our anomalous pedagogies promise to interact with each other and with more familiar pedagogies in ways that "complicate definition and give room for the possibility of creatively mated taxonomies and their wildly unpredictable offspring" (Williams, 1991, p. 11)?

Architects, artists, performers, media producers, and designers of content-based experiences, museum exhibitions, and public spaces are inventing "processual paths," "communicative instruments," urban "critical vehicles," theatrical performances, provocative interactive encounters, architectural spaces, and mediated cityscapes — with pedagogical intent, and they are doing so in ways that emphasize noncognitive, nonrepresentational processes and events such as movement, sensation, intensity, rhythm, passage, and self-augmenting change. They seem to aim their designs at involving their users in ways that exceed psychical mechanisms such as memory, recognition, or cognition.

Such places of learning implicate *bodies in pedagogy* in ways that the field of education has seldom explored. As they do this, they encourage and challenge us to move away from understanding the learning self merely through notions of cognition, psychology, or phenomenology or as being subjected to ideology. Such notions are underwritten by assumptions that there is an identifiable self, a locatable point of view or subject position from which meanings are made and through which experience is organized and held together, but the anomalous places of learning that we will consider here refuse to be contained by an understanding of pedagogy as the mere construction or representation of objects (for example, concepts, bodies of knowledge, curriculum, events in the world) for or to subjects (learners). The learning self that these anomalous places of learning invite to participate in attempts to invent new ways to see and new things to say does not preexist its involvement.

Rather, in these places, the *learning self* of the *experience of the learning self* is invented in and through its engagement with pedagogy's force. This self emerges along with the new concepts that its participation in a particular pedagogy helps to create and the new challenges that its participation helps to pose. Given the terms of their invitations, these pedagogical innovations must not address their students as already presumed, diagnosed, or assessed within the prevailing educational approaches or agendas. Instead, they must find ways to address a student that is not coincident with herself, but only with her change. They must figure out how to address a learning self that is in motion. To do that, they must set the concept of pedagogy itself in motion into interdisciplinary spaces between the cognitive sciences, cultural studies, aesthetics, psychology, media studies, architecture, and the biological sciences.

Material Tales of Pedagogy

In *Art Matters*, Peter de Bolla explores the singular nature and value of experiences with artworks — especially those that move us profoundly. He chooses four artworks to use in his attempts to make his own aesthetic responses more visible to himself. His criteria for his choices: works that generated in him "varied, sustained, polyphonic" responses that were "deeply felt." If a work generated in him responses that were "uniform, monotonous, weakly felt, or trivial," it was out of the running (de Bolla, 2001, p. 17).

Pedagogy, like painting, sculpture, or music, can be magical in its artful manipulation of inner ways of knowing into a mutually transforming relation with outer events, selves, objects, and ideas. Or, it can be used to simply manipulate, through congealed forms, unresponsive shapes, and derivative logics. The specific places of learning that I address here were chosen not only because of the qualities of the sensations of learning that they generated in me but also because of what appeared to me to be the qualities of their pedagogical volition. I animate the chapters that follow, that is, with pedagogical designs chosen because my encounters with them and my (re)readings of those encounters through the writers that I draw upon here have opened the future of my own practice as an educator.

When de Bolla meditates on the several works of art that he considers key to what he calls his aesthetic education, he asks what it is that those works "know" and how it is that, in his encounters with them, he simultaneously learns *from* them and creates his *own* understandings in relation to them. In each of his extended descriptions of his encounters with a painting, a sculpture, a musical performance, and a poem, his aesthetic experience morphs into something else, into his experience of his own learnings in the making. This moment arises in de Bolla when he senses that the artwork "knows" something that he himself is uncertain of. What it knows, he says, is something that cannot be explained, made certain, or authenticated through the language of proposition or linear logic. This, he concludes, is because sculptural "knowings" of the world and of the self, as well poetic, painterly, or musical "knowings," arise from a place more elemental than intellectualization. They arise from the "frisson of the physical encounter" and "immediate somatic response" (de Bolla, 2001, p. 2). Such knowings arise, in other words, from a place that can be neither accessed nor authenticated through propositional or referential language. Nevertheless, de Bolla insists, frissons of physical encounter and immediacies of somatic responses have their own "unknowable authenticity" (de Bolla, 2001, p. 128).

When I read de Bolla's detailed descriptions of his responses to four artworks, I am drawn to specific moments in his accounts. Those are the moments when he explores his own somatic experiences: the frissons of his physical encounters with the artworks and his senses of being filled with something other than "representation" and "more elemental than a process of intellectualization" (de Bolla, 2001, p. 2). I am drawn to these moments in his accounts because it is there that he says his bodily sensations sometimes "quickly give way" or "rapidly mutate" into a "variety" or "jumble of thoughts" (de Bolla 2001, p. 2). I believe that such moments, these instants of the "giving way" itself and the duration of the "rapid mutation" of sensations and movements into jumbles and varieties of thought, mark the *time* of the learning self.

What places are capable of acting as this moment's "hinge?" What environments and experiences are capable of acting as the pedagogical pivot point between movement/sensation and thought? At the beginning of his project, de Bolla poses questions about the specificity of aesthetic experiences. He asks: "What is an aesthetic experience? ... What would such an experience be *of*? What might keep [aesthetic experience] in the realm of the aesthetic, or allow it to be open to ... other registers or forms of experience?" (de Bolla, 2001, p. 5).

My project in the course of this book is to pose similar questions about the specificity of the experience of learning. What is an experience of the learning self? What would such an experience be of? I address these questions, in part, by inflecting de Bolla's third question toward the experience of the learning self. It thus becomes: What might allow aesthetic experience to open to the registers or forms of experience that we call teaching and learning? The wager of this book is, in part, that the pedagogically charged events, environments, and objects I have chosen to consider here *constitute a series of "whats" that do indeed open the aesthetic in new and unprecedented ways to teaching and learning,* and they do so in ways that invite teaching and learning to open in return to the aesthetic in terms that are largely unexplored by the official literature of educational research.

In no way do I intend to present these places of learning as examples, blueprints, prototypes, or utopian visions. That would fly in the face of their own pedagogical volition. They never offer themselves as didactic models of the future, nor do they present themselves as objects to be consumed uncritically. Instead, they gesture beyond themselves. They are investigations more than they are models.

In other words, my aim here is not to argue that Maya Lin's memorials or Frank Gehry's architecture should be seen as prototypes for classroom pedagogies, as if such designs could be made feasible in the space, time, or economics of public schools. Instead, I am going to follow Anthony Dunne's argument that the process of design itself holds potential for cultural critique and social innovation (Dunne, 1999). With him, I am going to suggest that we take up these non-examples as "conceptual machines that engage the imagination" and highlight the "boundaries that limit everyday experience." By refusing to accede to the demands of "miserable reality," they "remain defiantly conceptual" (Dunne, 1999, p. 72).

The fields of architecture and product design have long-standing traditions of idea competitions. Such competitions do not necessarily result in built form but instead offer an opportunity to publicly disseminate radical ideas about how architecture, and possibly the life it accommodates, might be differently conceived.

The field of education could benefit greatly from a similar speculative area in which to think experimentally about possible and impossible pedagogies. Creating room for speculation enables an educator to explore her understanding of the places in which people encounter enjoyable learning experiences and the means through which she, as an educator, could imagine making and using such places. Education needs "non-examples" to act as "conceptual machines" and "hypotheses for action" (Dunne, 1999, p. 13). It needs non-examples of "the material embodiment of [pedagogical] functions derived from alternative value systems" (Dunne, 1999, p. 14) outside of education — such as those currently shaping museum exhibitions, aesthetic practice, social action, and even entertainment. As "material tales," "conceptual test-pieces," and "poetic products," the anomalous pedagogical designs I work with here act as catalysts, not just to "visualize a 'better world,' but [to] arouse in the public a desire for one" (Dunne, 1999, p. 68). My intention is to open up such an area of speculation about pedagogy.

While it may seem risky to base experimental thinking upon poetic non-examples, the project of this book is to elaborate upon Dunne's theory by explaining how certain places of learning might be seen as genotypes "embodying the essence of an idea" (Dunne, 1999, p. 72). Because highly designed spaces do not conform to the economic or political realities of most public schools, it is tempting to dismiss them as utopian, technically useless to most schools except as valued sites for field trips, or, worse yet, elitist. Dunne says that such dismissals point out the difficulties of crossing over from aesthetic or gallery practices to different contexts in which the public can encounter design thinking.

But, the specific conceptual test pieces that I use here are powerful precisely because they *have* succeeded in crossing over. These popular and widely used (often by school groups) museum exhibitions, public spaces, media types, and performances have successfully woven themselves into the fabric of everyday life to the extent that some have even been funded by school districts. Because people have become deeply involved with them as physical environments and embodied experiences, they have evolved well beyond Dunne's genotype stage and have entered the realm of lived events that can be experienced, critiqued, cherished, and/or debated. Why, then, have we so seldom involved ourselves with these genotypes as educational theorists or researchers interested in thinking experimentally about pedagogy as it is widely practiced in public schools?

Perhaps it is because these places of learning speak with a voice that is so different from our own as educators. Rather than articulating ideas about education through language, they "speak through" qualities and elements composed of multimedia, landscapes, sculpture, content-based experiences, architectural time and space, critical vehicles, public projections, and performance art. Designers, architects, and performers are neither educators nor educational researchers, and when discussing their own work they do not employ explicit references to teaching and learning. In interviews and writings regarding the intentions of their work, designers seldom make direct or clear connections between their work and particular educational perspectives and practices. While a designer's discourse can be invaluable for illuminating the role pedagogy plays in her work, it is through her designed landscapes, objects, spaces, and events that we will discern the most palpable evidence of her pedagogical intent. It is through the design vernacular — the orchestrations of space, time, duration, movement, sensation, sound, text, image, interaction, juxtaposition, and invitation to surprise — and not through language that these designers speak to, assemble with, and modulate the minds/brains and bodies of learning selves in the making.

Therein lies the power of the places, objects, and events that we consider here: They speak to and about pedagogy *indirectly* through design — a means that reaches beyond the limiting scope of language. The indirect ways that these places of learning address pedagogy create a space between that which pedagogy is and that which it could potentially be. These places of learning struggle to remain, themselves, *things in the making*. By framing the potential "outcomes" of our engagements with them as open and unprescriptive, they provide us with a "zone of historical indetermination" that allows room for experimentation (Rajchman, 2000b, p. 14). As things still in the making, these anomalous places of learning are highly charged event potentials that promise surprise and constantly challenge us with new and unexpected questions.

At the time of this writing, most of the places of learning that I discuss here are well documented on the Internet. I have decided not to offer a list of websites associated with each place because of the short lifespan of many web addresses; however, this book lends itself to being read side by side with the many online resources that refer to the places we will consider here and provide relevant images, videos, interviews, documentaries, and interactive sites. A simple search for the names of the designers, architects, media producers, exhibitions, performances, media texts, and public spaces and events that I work with here will point you to rich visual materials capable of augmenting both appreciations and critiques of the discussions I offer.

Thinking Experimentally About Pedagogy

In the following chapters, I stage a series of encounters among specific design elements and qualities that shape particular places of learning, and the inventive writings of Brian Massumi, Elizabeth Grosz, Peter de Bolla, Adam Phillips, Jessica Benjamin, Barbara Kennedy, Herbert Muschamp, and John Rajchman. Each of these writers is a participant in contemporary debates about how philosophy, aesthetic and cultural theory, and psychoanalysis might best be used to address current issues and problems concerning culture and power. Massumi, Grosz, Kennedy, and Rajchman base much of their work on that of Gilles Deleuze, Henri Bergson, and William James; Muschamp, Phillips, and Benjamin base their work on Freud and Winnicott; and de Bolla draws on the aesthetic theory of Kant.

Many readers would consider the sources that I use here to be "secondary sources." Secondary sources are always open to the suspicion that they may not provide valid interpretations of the primary source. Often they are regarded as being merely rhetorical, specifically if they use words and ideas from the originating thinkers to argue a point or persuade an audience as opposed to offering an "original" contribution to a field of study. Given the canon of Western thought, the distinction and hierarchy between primary and secondary sources effectively relegate most women and most of Western thought's non-Western others to the status of secondary sources.

In the same manner, the field of education suffers its lesser status, in part, because it can be considered secondary to the fields that make up the natural and social sciences and the humanities. Educators are easily reduced to the roles of the interpreters or explainers of the sciences and humanities — fields seen as authoring and originating the knowledge that educators then teach. A similar distinction exists within the field of education itself: The area of curriculum (the area supposedly concerned with knowledge itself) is often treated as primary, while the area of pedagogy (the area of instruction concerned with the teacherly description, explanation, and restatement of curricular knowledge) is often treated as secondary. Such hierarchies also perpetuate the gendered nature of educational work. Men continue to dominate the production and distribution of curriculum theory and educational philosophy in universities and professional organizations, while women primarily occupy teaching positions at all levels of education. This reinscribes, through long-embedded, gendered inequalities, the hierarchies between curriculum and pedagogy, knowledge and explanation, thought and action, theory and practice, mind and body, philosophy and the "other" disciplines.

While the sources I reference throughout this book base their thinking in the work of so-called primary sources, they do so in ways that transcend mere description or restatement. Through the inventive ways in which they put those borrowed ideas to use, they are able to bring their sources into relation with ideas, events, imperatives, people, questions, and practices that lie outside of those sources' original optics or lived realities. They refine ideas from primary sources in ways that render problematic — better yet, render useless and uninteresting — the whole idea of a primary source as something that requires the subordination of other sources as secondary. They employ the masters' ideas not to explain them — which is a way to embalm them unchanged and unchangeable — but to make something (else) of them.

In this sense, they mirror the project of this book: to make something else of pedagogy — not simply to make pedagogy's subordination to curriculum obsolete but to think pedagogy in ways that make pedagogy encompass curriculum. To think pedagogy, in other words, in ways that make a "new force visible" … a force ontologically prior to curriculum … a force out of which curriculum itself emerges … a force that "puts up something new to thought" (Rajchman, 2000a, p. 44); namely, the force of the experience of the learning self.

Reading Places of Learning

Places of Learning, then, circulates between pedagogical anomalies and what a number of contemporary (re)thinkings of experience are now making of theories about human subjects as embodied — as moving, sensing, acting agents in the world — specifically what these theories propose regarding the way we come *to know*. Like de Bolla's readings of artworks, I do not present pedagogical material tales alongside theories of experience for the purpose of criticism or analysis. My intent is not to appropriate concepts from architecture, media studies, or philosophy in order to apply them to the pedagogical innovations for the sole purpose of critique or evaluation. Rather, my hope is that any elucidation I offer here might be "instrumental, performed as a way of getting somewhere else on the way" to alternative understandings of pedagogy (de Bolla, 2001, p. 100). As Massumi does, I hope that such instrumental readings might "ramify the effects of an interdisciplinary encounter," in this case, among pedagogy, media, and architecture, and "scatter thoughts and images into different linkages or new alignments without destroying them" (Massumi, 2002, p. 19).

Thus, *Places of Learning* becomes an itinerary for an uncharted and experimental journey. It loosely maps one educator's tracings of the paths of scattering thoughts, angles of linkages, and trajectories of potential alignments experienced in the turbulence generated by interdisciplinary encounters with pedagogically charged times, spaces, and objects. It is both a retrospective chronicling of these movements and encounters as well as an attempt to ramify them for the purpose of my own and perhaps for others' future actions as educators.

Mirroring the practices of documentary film, which overlaps and juxtaposes film, video, sound, voice, text, interview, narrative, and music to create new linkages and alignments, the words and concepts of others have become my raw material. I have treated the quotes, observations, and examples drawn from the writings of others as if they were interviews with their authors. I "intercut" these "interviews" with my own accounts of pedagogical events, places, and objects. I excerpt intact the accounts and interpretations of places of learning offered by reviewers and critics in order to preserve the specific terms that commentators consider to be crucial to capturing their lived experiences of the events, places, and objects that they describe. Also in the spirit of documentary, my contribution to thinking pedagogy experimentally lies in this book's "through line" — the particular story that emerges from its assemblage.

One of the best ways I know to ramify and scatter thoughts and images into new and different alignments and practices is what some forms of documentary practice do so well. They juxtapose, complicate, and creatively mate their source materials in ways that overlap and "wildly mix" things that are supposed to be separate and never thought or seen together, and they complicate definition by opening up volatile spaces of difference between things and ideas that are often seen as being the same. They look at the same event from many different angles and experiences — sometimes all at once. They give materiality to abstract ideas or arguments by showing how they actually shape the lived experiences and stories of "real people." By turning all of this into a film or video, they attempt to make something new and different of what we already think we know.

I hope that a writing strategy informed by such documentary practices will leave me and this book's readers with the problem of "what in the world to do with it all" (Massumi, 2002, p. 19), because that, as Massumi suggests, is where our experimentation begins. The problem of what to do with it all spreads the potential for surprising and unexpected futures for pedagogy.

1

The Materiality of Pedagogy

Sensations Crucial to Understandings

The camera cuts to a close-up of a child's face. We see the *look* and witness the *moment* that has become the culmination of so many documentaries about successful schools. It is the dramatic turning point in countless news reports on effective teachers. It is the cause for celebration and the inspiration in scores of teacher education videotapes. This look is the climax in many educational documentaries as well as the exclamation point at the end of numerous dialogs concerning education.

When audiences — especially audiences of teachers — see this look, smiles and nods of recognition sweep the room: They have seen this look on the faces of many of their own students in all manner of contexts. Often, audiences murmur with appreciation: This is the look and the moment that many teachers and parents work for and value. Sometimes, audiences murmur with compassion: There is something naked and vulnerable about this look, even as it signals a child's powerful experience of intense self-presence.

The rhetorically loaded cutaway to this look has become a mainstay of media representations of teaching and learning. Directors have grown to regard it as convention. But, this particular expression, able to provoke both appreciation and compassion in educators, is not associated with just any experience of learning. As educators, we become familiar with a variety of expressions worn by children when they are participating in the experiences that count as learning. We see the look of deep absorption in the task at hand that we associate with students concentrating on step-by-step problem solving while engaging in projects, building things, preparing for tests, or gaining clearly defined skills. We see the look of "turning gears" — for example, on the faces of the youngsters in *Spellbound*, the award-winning documentary about America's national spelling bee, as they try to solve the puzzle before them ("Of all of the word lists and pronunciation keys I've studied, which one holds the key to spelling this word?"). And, we see the look that says "I've got it!" and speaks of satisfaction, relief, and triumph upon arriving at the end of a process and grasping something aimed at — usually the "right" answer. But, these familiar looks are not the one I am talking about here. Each of these other looks hinges on the comprehension of a particular kind of knowledge — a knowledge already gotten by someone else. For various social, political, economic, or pragmatic reasons, someone has deemed this knowledge to be in need of being grasped, passed on, and repeated yet again and in ways that are clearly mapped and understood.

These goal-oriented looks of concentration on a given task, of gears turning, of discovering a solution have too much to do with compliance for my interests here. My intention is to open a discussion regarding an experience of learning that has little to do with *learning as compliance*. I am concerned, instead, with the experience of learning that gives rise to that unmistakable, naked, vulnerable look of simultaneous absorption and self-presence. It is the look that has become, at the hands of media producers, the face of Learning with a big "L" — Learning itself. It is as if media producers sense that they have captured in that look the precious visual evidence of otherwise elusive events. While its poignant appearance in documentaries, news reports, or teacher education videos often substitutes for any further elaboration about what composes it, this look is merely the tip of a very deep iceberg. It signals the presence of complex occurrences in excess of and elsewhere than at the surfaces of cognition or awareness.

It is in the inaccessible-through-cognition-or-awareness events of mind/ brain and body that I will locate the experience of the learning self as a self not in compliance but *in transition* and *in motion* toward previously unknown ways of thinking and being in the world. The look on a child's face as she experiences learning in this sense — as the sensing of new and previously unthought or unfelt senses of self, others, and the world *in their process of emergence* — might now be a media convention, but that has made it no less momentous and no less enigmatic. It is the look of someone who is in the process of losing something of who she thought she was. Upon encountering something outside herself and her own ways of thinking, she is giving up thoughts she previously held as *known*, and as a consequence she is parting with a bit of her known self. The look of the learning self that concerns me here gives form to the sensation of simultaneously being with oneself *and* being in relation to things, people, or ideas outside oneself.

I have chosen the particular designed spaces, media, objects, and events that animate the coming chapters because they "materialize," in the forces and sensations that they offer, a particular pedagogical desire: the desire for this look and for experiences of learning as noncompliance and knowledge as in the making. The qualities and design elements that seem to constitute their pedagogical force invite sensations of being somewhere in between thinking and feeling, of being in motion through the space and time between knowing and not knowing, in the space and time of learning as a lived experience with an open, unforeseeable future. They invite the sensation of a mind/brain/body simultaneously in both suspension *and* animation in the interval of change from the person one has been to the person that one has yet to become.

In this chapter, we are going to take an initial look at several sometimes-fleeting moments in interviews, artist statements, and analytical reviews when designers and reviewers attempt to articulate the sensations out of which learning and understanding — in this sense — emerge. I see these moments as efforts to give expression to the events that give rise to the look that I am associating here with learning when it is noncompliant and in the making. These moments give us an opening sense of what it might mean to materialize pedagogical forces in and through places of learning.

We are going to then take that preliminary sense into a series of encounters with a constellation of ideas now emerging from interdisciplinary encounters among the fields of philosophy, cultural studies, science studies, architecture, and media studies. Those ideas, especially as put forth by Brian Massumi (1995) when he uses Henri Bergson and William James to explore what the body's movements and sensations mean for thought, *challenge educators to shift how we make bodies matter in pedagogy.* Some social theorists say that the ideas we will consider here and in subsequent chapters compose a "new pragmatism" or an "experimental pragmatics of becoming," building as they do on Gilles Deleuze's use of Bergson (especially his ideas about time, space, and experience) to approach thinking as experiment (Kennedy, 2003, pp. 5–6). The particular rethinkings of experience and becoming that we will engage here seem to be driving, as well, a renewed interest in D.W. Winnicott's notion of "transitional space" as the time and place out of which experiences of the learning emerge (Winnicott, 1989).

Read together, the efforts of designers of anomalous places of learning, their reviewers, and some contemporary theorists' efforts to implicate bodies in thought and learning present us with new ways of thinking about the experience of the learning self. Here, I will map some of those ideas and indicate how they draw from and build upon one another. I will then put these ideas to use in each of the remaining chapters to see what they make visible, thinkable, and possible as we look closely at the group of anomalous pedagogies that form the motivation for this book. By reading anomalous pedagogies through these emerging ways of thinking experience, I hope to contribute to efforts to reconfigure educators' conversations and actions about pedagogy as the force through which we come to have the surprising, incomplete knowings, ideas, and sensations that undo us and set us in motion toward an open future. How might we — can we — "set things up in such a way as to have this kind of experience" (de Bolla, 2001, p. 5)?

Experiences Crucial to Understandings

I turn first to designers and reviewers of several of the anomalous places of learning that we will revisit in more detail and from different angles in subsequent chapters. How do they articulate the sensations, movements, and experiences crucial to the experience of learning as noncompliance and in the making?

Maya Lin, best known for her design of the Vietnam Veterans Memorial in Washington, D.C., writes that she approaches the process of designing memorials and public spaces, in part, with a pedagogical intent. She says that her intent for a number of landscapes, sculptures, and memorials is that they teach about historical events. Her design for the Southern Poverty Law Center's Civil Rights Memorial in Montgomery, Alabama, for example, centers around a circular black granite "water table" twelve feet in diameter and engraved with a timeline that reveals "how often the act of a single person — often enough, a single death — was followed by a new and better law" (Lin, 2000, p. 4:28). In writing about such works, Lin declares that the "experience of the work is crucial to its understanding" (Lin, 2000, p. 3:11). In particular, she takes sensations of movement and duration to be crucial to understanding the concepts (for example, that individuals' actions can lead to new and better laws) that shape her designs (Lin, 2002, p. 2:07):

> Time is … a crucial element in how I see my architecture. I cannot see my architecture as a still moment but rather as a movement through space. I design the architecture more as an experiential path.

Here, we can see that, for Lin, our *sensations* of time and of space as we are put in motion along the "experiential path" — be it a building, landscape, or sculpture as memorial — are crucial to what we make of the history, people, or events that are memorialized.

Adrian Dannatt, art and architectural critic, implicitly agrees that the qualities of an *experience* of learning are crucial to *what* is learned. He describes how the entrance of the U.S. Holocaust Memorial Museum in Washington, D.C., shapes its visitors' movements and sensations in ways crucial to understanding the concept that the Holocaust is a historical event that has not yet come to rest. Dannatt writes (Dannatt & Hursley, 2002, p. 14):

> There are two rows of glass block lit along the floor, a path which ends between two stairways. Like being given a route to discover, it

leads to more choice, another directional dilemma. Neither stairway leads to the display if that is what one is, by now, looking for.... This glass trajectory crosses next to a public information counter, the only shelter in the empty plain, where people cluster less for advice than for protection from the dizzying agoraphobia of so much open space. The very idea of advice or assistance seems futile in such an environment.

For Dannatt, the sensations of being given a route to discover which leads only to more choices and directional dilemmas; of being lost in an environment that makes the "very idea of advice or assistance seem futile"; and of being refused The Answer that would presume to relieve him of the responsibility to create his own route through the museum's materials and his own responses to the Holocaust stake out the limits of pedagogy itself. Upon recognizing pedagogy's limits, we might shift our efforts from trying to "know" and then "teach" the Holocaust to engaging with it as an event that has not yet ended and to contemporaneously respond to it.

Witold Rybczynski, a professor of architecture, offers another attempt to articulate the relation between the materialities of movement and sensation, and learning. In his review of architect Henry Cobb's and exhibit designer Ralph Appelbaum's design of the National Constitution Center in Philadelphia, Rybczynski states the question that faced the design team: "What sort of building is a national schoolhouse?" He then goes on to describe how the designers "answered" this question in the form of an experiential path that is crucial to understanding the Constitution as an ongoing "event" (Rybczynski, 2003, p. 1):

At this point we find ourselves back in the lobby, but on an upper level, overlooking Independence Hall in the distance. It is hard not to be moved by this evocative view of its graceful Colonial spire against the crowded backdrop of downtown office buildings. It is a further example of how the felicitous collaboration of Mr. Cobb and Mr. Appelbaum provides a rich and seamless experience of learning about the past and experiencing the present. It turns what might have been heavy-handed lecturing, or simply boring lessons, into an occasion of considerable civic dignity and circumstance.

For Rybczynski, the *sensation* of past interfusing with present — gained not through heavy-handed lecturing or prescriptive lessons but felt via a lived encounter with the "rich and seamless" juxtaposition of colonial spires against crowded downtown offices — becomes an experience of learning about the past through its material impact on our inhabitations of the present. Such an experience, this design seems to say, is crucial to understanding the relevance of a centuries-old document to a modern citizen — namely, that this document affords citizens considerable dignity by involving them in the contemporary work of citizenship, work that is both shaped by this document and that reshapes it in response to present circumstances.

Herbert Muschamp, architectural critic for *The New York Times*, also agrees that pre- and nonlinguistic experiences of a place of learning are crucial to what is learned there. He describes his responses to his first visit to the Lois and Richard Rosenthal Center for Contemporary Art in Cincinnati, designed by Iraqi-born architect Zaha Hadid. It is a space, Muschamp implies, designed to invite the visitor into awareness of lived experience as an emergent event (Muschamp, 2003, p. 30):

> The building's power is fully disclosed only to those who engage it with their feet as well as their eyes.... Wandering through the building is like exploring the varied and unpredictable terrain of present time....
>
> I gave myself over to the finely tempered rhythm of spatial compression and expansion that draws a visitor through the building....
>
> Up the stairs, you gain the dream sensation of breaking through a solid membrane into an alternative world: the steps lead you up into a soaring atrium space suffused from above with natural light.

Muschamp describes the building's "play of geometric variations," its "artful arrangement of processional spaces," and its presentation of "a rhythm of multiple perspectives," as "roughly synchronized with the movements of bodies propelled by curious minds" (Muschamp, 2003c, p. 30). Through the powerful and indirect "disclosures" made by Hadid's architecture, Muschamp comes to a learning: The present time is varied and unpredictable, it is in a continuous unfolding emergence which makes "staring right into the present ... immensely more shocking than gazing at some corny crystal ball" (Muschamp, 2003c, p. 30). Muschamp both discovers and creates this understanding through his sensations of a "heightened mind–body connection," a connection heightened by the multiple perspectives he gains by walking through, wandering through, being drawn in through, and breaking through a membrane that is merely the imaginary barrier of habitual and conventional ways of perceiving, thinking, and being. For him, this building modulates the compression and expansion of space in a way that offers a material correlate for the experience of the learning self as in the making. It does so by powerfully synchronizing his body's movements with the propulsion of his curious mind toward a particular understanding of the present time.

Lawrence Halprin provides yet another example of a designer's attempt to give voice to the movements and sensations that he considers as being crucial to the pedagogy of a designed space. He says that his approach to designing the Franklin Delano Roosevelt Memorial in Washington, D.C., was shaped by his memories of other places that had affected him emotionally. Those places had several elements in common (Halprin, 1997, p. 7).

> They unfolded like voyages, based on movement along prescribed routes.... These processional paths always offered variations in pace through their design, yet there was always a consistent sense of physical and emotional choreography. Visitors were drawn on through a sequence of experiences — some calm, some intense — and there was a pervasive sense of drama. At the end of such experiences, I felt that in a profound way I emerged deeply changed. I felt that I had come through a focused slice of life that affected me intensely and emotionally.

Pervasive senses of drama, being physically drawn through spaces choreographed for variations in emotional intensity and profound, deep self-change — these are the experiences that Halprin deemed crucial to learning about history-making people and events. As central design elements in Halprin's memorial to FDR, they serve as pre- and nonlinguistic experiential analogs to an intellectual understanding: that this era changed people's lives profoundly.

The last example that I will offer of an attempt to articulate an experience felt as being crucial to an understanding comes from the more playful but no less meaningful recollections that some Baby Boomers report having of their grade-school experiences of their "learning selves." From 1956 to 1964, Bell Telephone Laboratories produced nine films as part of the Bell Labs Science Series. Part animation, part live action, they played for years in public school classrooms and auditoriums nationwide. Famed Hollywood director Frank Capra directed several of the films in the series, which included such subjects as the sun, blood, cosmic rays, and weather. In a newspaper account of some Baby Boomers' nostalgia for these films, Wallace Stevens, a former purchaser of educational materials for Southern California school districts, described their influence as "almost a subliminal one." He says he "still carries unshakable images from the films themselves, mainly the exposed hearts of animals and the booming voice of the animated Mr. Sun. ... It's almost like they've been absorbed into our subconscious mind while bypassing our memory" (Templeton, 1999).

Bill Cheswick, a Bell Labs worker, designed a website where he lists the fictional scientist who narrated several of the films (played by Dr. Frank Baxter) as his childhood hero. "When I was in school, I drank up and swallowed everything Dr. Baxter said," Cheswick recalls. "I remember seeing *Hemo the Magnificent* and running home to brag to my parents that I'd seen an open-heart operation" (Templeton, 1999). Cheswick found the old films in the archives at Bell Labs and began hosting lunchtime film festivals. "I was impressed by how many times I sat there thinking, 'Oh, yeah. I knew that. I guess I must have learned it from this movie — and remembered it for 30 years.' That's pretty cool" (Templeton, 1999). Templeton quotes one woman as saying, "*Mr. Sun* is my favorite. A very warm childhood memory .... The Bell Science films had such a sense of wonder that it stuck with me my entire life. My own sense of wonder about the world may have started right there" (Templeton, 1999).

If we could flash back to the faces of these adults as they watched *Our Mr. Sun* or *Hemo the Magnificent* as elementary-school children, we might see the expression that gives body to the experience of the learning self. It is the look that accompanies the almost subliminal experiences of having the unconscious addressed, of having memory bypassed, of drinking up and swallowing "facts" and "information" in a way that leaves "unshakable images" and ideas that can be remembered "warmly" for 30 years. It is the look that we might have seen on the faces of Lin, Muschamp, Halprin, Dannatt, and Rybczynski as they experienced the sensations they speak of: sensations of ideas being made futile by the environment surrounding them; sensations of being "in motion"; sensations of time and space, finely timed rhythms, and heightened mind–body connections; sensations of drama and of being "drawn through"; senses of wonder, of bypassed memory and cognition; awareness of self-change; and full body involvement.

The Materiality of Learning

As events, objects, and environments, the anomalous and "poetic" places of learning to which these designers and reviewers refer, as well as others that we will encounter in the coming chapters, materially and profoundly implicate minds/brains in the bodily sensations and movements that are crucial to what may potentially be understood. Their efforts to express how, when, where, and why pedagogically charged spaces and events invite such enfoldings of minds/brains and bodies have sent me in search of critical and analytical languages capable of expressing the power of such times and places and informing efforts to invent more of them.

That search led me to Peter de Bolla's *Art Matters* (2001), an account of his sustained effort to create a lexicon to deal with sensations and movements crucial to understandings. He locates his effort in the context of his own experiences with artworks — especially those that move him into and within what he calls a sense of wonder. His efforts are useful to me here because, for him, wonder is deeply interfused with the experience of learning. Like the attempts we considered above by designers and reviewers to make communicable to themselves and to others particular forms of experience that they consider as being crucial to particular understandings, de Bolla also strives to articulate how it is that specific forms of experience have composed his "aesthetic education" about various artworks. de Bolla's perspective on what makes an artwork "art" and what constitutes its "art component" is especially relevant to the question of the body's material implication in pedagogy. For de Bolla, the "art component" of an artwork is not something that we can point to in its content; rather, we can detect the "art component" of a work only through the nature of our response to the work. Our response, in effect, constitutes the "material" of the art-ness of an artwork.

The same can be said of pedagogy. Our lived experience of pedagogy is what makes its features *as pedagogy* visible and remarkable. The educational qualities or value of a pedagogical effort — what, in other words, counts as "educational" in that effort — exist only in our responses to it. The educational component of a pedagogy is knowable to us only in our response. Paraphrasing de Bolla, our experience of an event or occurrence of learning constitutes the materiality of its pedagogy (de Bolla, 2001, p. 18). And this makes our experience of pedagogy — our experiences of dwelling in and inhabiting a pedagogy — the proper object of our attention as educational researchers and practitioners (de Bolla, 2001, p. 18).

Not that educators have ignored the bodies of students. They have developed numerous (and often competing) ways to come to grips with the fact that students are not simply brains on tripods. Some take psycho-analytic approaches to questions of pedagogy and explore how our bodies' histories shape pleasure, desire, repression, and the unconscious and how these in turn shape students' knowledges and "ignore-ances," as well as the erotics and counter-transference of the pedagogical relation. Some use theories of ideology and discourse to understand how social, cultural, and sexual differences mark bodies and position them differentially within relations of power. These approaches have shown how some social dynamics make some bodies matter more than others, and that they make social and cultural differences figure in the human interests that shape the social construction of knowledge.

Other educational researchers explore links between bodies and cognition. They have developed pedagogies aimed at addressing aspects of cognition that seem to be enabled and enhanced by the kinesthetic, leading to hands-on, holistic, and project- or arts-based approaches to teaching. Some educators are concerned with the clinical bodies of learners. They focus on the relationship between the body's development and the brain's functioning, for example, or on the need to slow some bodies down through medication or pedagogical strategies aimed at increasing attention spans. Some are concerned with the relationship between nutrition, student achievement, and free lunches. Others are concerned with the pedagogical needs and interests of students with differing physical and mental abilities.

Bodies do figure in many discussions and practices that shape pedagogy, but the *terms* in which bodies figure in those discussions privilege approaching bodies as things we *have* (as in "we are minds with bodies"). Most school-based pedagogies focus their address on the mind even if they may sometimes approach it through the body. For the most part, when bodies figure in educational institutions and practices, they do so in terms that put them in the service of cognition and prefigured cognitive goals. Educational researchers and theorists rarely address pedagogy first and foremost as the occasion and opportunity for studying what de Bolla and others claim has ontological primacy over cognition. Namely, those "immediate somatic responses," those "frissons of physical encounter," and those "somethings" that are "more elemental than a process of intellectualization" (de Bolla, 2001, p. 2). Pedagogy is seldom engaged as an *event* in which the *materiality* of a time and place of learning impinges on the *materiality* of the learning self understood as a "processual engagement of duration and movement, articulated through webs of sensation across landscapes and panoramas of space, bodies, and time" (Kennedy, 2003, p. 4) and educational materials. Pedagogy is seldom made to be a question of the artful or banal orchestrations of its materials or of the orchestration of forces, sensations, stories, invitations, habits, media, time, space, ideas, language, objects, images, and sounds intended, precisely, to move the materiality of minds/brains and bodies into relation with other material elements of our world.

What might become possible and thinkable if we were to take pedagogy to be sensational? What if, as educators, we began to consider pedagogy to be a time and space designed to assemble "with the bodies [of learners] in a web of inter-relational flows in material ways" (Kennedy, 2003, p. 26)?

Pedagogy and the "New Pragmatism"

To engage these questions, I turn to the constellation of ideas now being developed by cultural critics and theorists, including Elizabeth Grosz, Barbara Kennedy, Brian Massumi, and John Rajchman, who are generating interesting and provocative discussions about "experience" as it can be rethought through what some call the "new pragmatism." Adam Phillips, an essayist and psychoanalyst, contributes to these discussions by offering a reading of Winnicott as a pragmatic empiricist in a way that renders Winnicott's notion of "transitional space" useful to this new pragmatism. Together, these theorists are providing a powerful set of concepts that I will use in efforts to better articulate and elaborate upon anomalous places of learning and the experiences of the learning self that they invite.

The authors listed above ground their discussions wholly or partially in attempts to understand "aesthetic experience." Grosz focuses on media and architecture; Kennedy on cinema; Massumi on performance, media, and architecture; Rachjman on the arts; and Phillips on aesthetic experience and creativity. Like de Bolla's reflections on his own "aesthetic education," I find it intriguing that these writers' concerns constantly spill over into the realms of thinking, knowing, and acting. The *terms* in which they see the aesthetic as impinging on thought and action are key to the project of this book and, I believe, to the future of pedagogy.

Their work suggests that the very possibility of thought is predicated upon our opportunities and capacities to encounter the *limits* of thinking and knowing and to engage with what cannot, solely through cognition, be known. Aesthetic practices and experiences provoke precisely such engagements and, to the extent that they are provocative of thought, they are crucial to understanding pedagogy. These theorists' discussions of experience challenge educators to approach the question of the experience of the learning self as a question of sensation. This is not a challenge to look for better understandings of the experience of the learning self within individuals' subjective experiences of learning; rather, this is a challenge, as Kennedy puts it, to explore "affect and sensation as … 'depth' or an 'intensity' which is felt primordially, in the body, but beyond subjectivity…" (Kennedy, 2003, p. 29).

Affect and sensation felt beyond, without, or prior to subjectivity — what might that mean? Kennedy uses the experience of watching the flight of a butterfly to explain what it is to "feel primordially, in the body" — not in the "psychic body" or in the "ordinary physical body, in its biological determinants" but in a body understood as a "complex set of intersecting forces" (Kennedy, 2003, p. 29). Her example of the butterfly's flight highlights how the "eye-brain" finds various forms of motion to be "more appealing, more alluring, more beautiful" (Kennedy, 2003, p. 116) than repetitive or predictable forms of motion:

> … the pathways of the flight of a butterfly will produce the most invigorating, beautiful and captivating pathways of motion, a cartography of visionary dance across the eye-brain…. The highly variable trajectory of the butterfly will make the brain continually break and form, break and form, breaking any symmetry…. The [rhythmic] "eternal return" of the eye-brain activity (and the butterfly) creates the kineasthetics, wherein the brain's activities are beyond the merely visual, but become tactile, fluid, in process. (As Massumi argues, "beauty pertains to a process, not to a form.")

In other words, we feel beauty, attraction, or allure not merely as affect or as intellection — we feel them materially as processes, as events of the body. They are something we do not merely observe; we live through them. For Kennedy, Massumi, Rajchman, de Bolla, and Grosz, sensation is not merely "subjective, involuntary feeling" that can be simply opposed to "objective, intentional thinking." Rather, sensation, according to Massumi (2002, pp. 97–98), is the…

> … immanent limit at which perception is eclipsed by a sheerness of experience, as yet unextended into analytically ordered, predictably reproducible, possible action. Sensation is a state in which action,

perception, and thought are so intensely, performatively mixed that their in-mixing falls out of itself. Sensation is ... pure mixture....A receding into a latency that is not just the absence of action but, intensely, a poising for more: an augmentation.

In other words, experience is not subjective in the sense that "I have" an experience. When we think of experience as a question of sensation, we remind ourselves that we do not *have* experiences. We *are* experiences. The "I" of an experience does not precede the experience. It emerges from it, or, as Massumi puts it, "the personal" (our sense of self and identity) is the "grand finale" (Massumi, 2002, pp. 190–191):

> From what does all individual awareness arise and return? Simply: matter. Brain-and-body matter: rumbling sea for the rainbow of experience.

Phenomenology has certainly been concerned with experience and awareness, but not in the sense that Massumi lays out here (Massumi, 2002, p. 191):

> For phenomenology, the personal is prefigured or "prereflected" in the world, in a closed loop of "intentionalty." The act of perception or cognition is a reflection of what is already "pre-" embedded in the world. It repeats the same structures, expressing where you already were. Every phenomenological event is like returning home. This is like *deja vu* without the portent of the new.

> [But] experience, normal or clinical, is never fully intentional. No matter how practiced the act, the result remains at least as involuntary as it is elicited.... The personal is not intentionally prefigured. It is rhythmically re-fused in a way that always brings something new and unexpected into the loop. The loop is always strangely open....

Following this thread of Massumi's thinking, I am going to suggest that the reason that the designed spaces, environments, and events that we look at here appear anomalous from within some approaches to pedagogy is because they invite and support *unintentional, involuntary* experiences of the learning self. They do so by attempting to move us through "sensations, prelinguistic and presubjective," that precede concepts, images, or recognitions as things made and promise to "bring something new and unexpected into the loop." If this is what makes them anomalous, it also makes them cause for celebration.

Sensational Pedagogies

The anomalous pedagogies addressed in this book stage learning as a "material process" that arises out of the imbrication of the *material* elements of mind/brain and body (Kennedy, 2003, p. 15). They are concerned with designing, building, and staging objects, mediated environments, events, performances, public projections, configured times, and spaces. They are concerned with making, for example, "prosessual paths" to be walked or "interrogative designs" to modulate and intensify the habits, dispositions, gestures, and speakings that make up the materiality of social relationships on an urban street. The resulting paths, juxtapositions, sounds, interruptions, durations, and rhythms "actually impinge on the body/mind/brain in a multiplicity of ways" (Kennedy, 2003, pp. 27–28) and attempt to provide sensations that create the conditions for potential learning experiences.

As I work through my own encounters with these pedagogically inflected times and spaces, I am not seeking a new sense of pedagogy; rather, my desire is to articulate and better understand *new pedagogies of sensation*. Such pedagogies do not address us as having bodies but rather address us *as bodies* whose movements and sensations are crucial to our understandings. Paraphrasing Kennedy, I consider these times and spaces as "sensation constructions," in which the "body" of the pedagogic environment, event, or media relates and assembles with the bodies of its users/viewers/observers "in a web of inter-relational flows in material ways" (Kennedy, 2003, p. 26).

The consequences of refiguring pedagogy in this way are far reaching. They encourage us to ask what pedagogy *does* rather than what it means or how it means. Pedagogy as "sensation construction" is no longer merely "representational." It is no longer a model that teachers use to set the terms in which already-known ideas, curriculums, or knowledges are put into relation; rather, to the extent that sensations are "conditions of possible experience," pedagogy as sensation construction is a condition of possible experiences of thinking. It becomes a force for thinking *as experimentation*. Paraphrasing Rajchman's reading of Deleuze on aesthetics, unlike pedagogues who are here "to save us or perfect us (or to damn or corrupt us)," the pedagogic assemblages we will consider in the following chapters set out to "complicate things." They set out to "create more complex nervous systems no longer subservient to the debilitating effects of clichés, to show and release the possibilities of a life" (Rajchman, 2000a, p. 138).

Regarding pedagogy as experimentation in thought rather than representation of knowledge as a thing already made creates a profound shift in how we think of pedagogical intent or volition — the will to teach. Considering Rachjman's readings of Deleuze on "aesthetic volition," it might be possible to think of the pedagogical intent, the will in pedagogy, as belonging *not* to a known or identifiable agent; rather, education and its pedagogical acts might be thought of as "many different people and disciplines talking and seeing in new ways at once, interfering and resonating with one another, thanks to some as-yet informed or uncoded material of expression" (Rajchman, 2000a, p. 121).

Consequently, we would not understand the will to teach as an individual teacher's desire for or pursuit of curricular goals and learning objectives, nor would the will to teach be explained by the teacher's altruism or personal love of learning. Rather, we might begin to think of pedagogical volition as a simultaneity of interfering and resonating desires distributed *across the social body* — across different people, practices, and disciplines such as art, performance, architecture, museum exhibition, and public events. The will to teach then becomes thinkable in terms of a distributed, emergent desire to innovate, design, and stage materials of expression and conditions of learning in which something new may arise. Teaching becomes not a "medium" for communicating the personal expression of a particular teacher's "artful" instructional skills or educational imagination, because that would make pedagogy a code or language for a preexistent subject, agent, or public; rather, teaching becomes the activity of participating in the "becoming pedagogical" of "expressive materials" distributed across many teachers, sites, events, and interactions (Rajchman, 2000a, p. 121).

Paraphrasing Rajchman, teachers who are drawn to and transformed by pedagogy in this sense or who invent ways to see and say new things through it do not preexist it but are rather invented in the process (Rajchman, 2000a, p. 121). Teachers, understood as being in the making themselves, would necessarily have to create places of learning in embodied terms and in ways that depart from the dominant perception of learning as the acquisition of knowledge driven by cognitive functions. Thinking of teachers as interfering and resonating with one another and with different disciplines in this way disburses the place of the teacher, and this recasts many of the problematic dynamics associated with the teacher–student relationship, such as the will to know, the desire for the one who knows, and the desire to teach what one knows.

What I sense in the anomalous places of learning that we will look at closely in the coming chapters are attempts to engage learning in the making. I consider their times and spaces to be encouragements and challenges to explore the ramifications of staging pedagogy as the field of emergence of the learning self. They provoke us to ask: What pedagogies, as sensation constructions, as forms of habitation, as modes of existence of the learning self in the making, as risk, will incite a "taste for fresh sensations and constructions of sensations" (Rajchman, 2000a, p. 142)? What pedagogies will incite a "belief in what we may yet become, and in the peculiar time and logic of its effectuation in ourselves and in our relations with one another" (Rajchman, 2000a, p. 142)? In the particular expressions of pedagogical volition that we will consider here, pedagogy becomes the time and space of the learning self *in the making.*

When thinking pedagogy through Deleuzian notions of sensation, experience, movement, and the logic of the in between, we find at stake the possibilities that "other paradigms of experience outside of language" might be reconceptualized and valorized in and for education: "For example ... the body, dance, movement, and process might be [rediscovered by education] as ways of articulating ideas, feelings, attitudes, and experiences in ways outside of written or oral language" (Kennedy, 2003, p. 32), but something even more disruptive to current educational institutions and practices is at stake. According to Kennedy (2003, p. 13), pedagogic engagements with the materiality of the brain/mind and body prior to language and subjectivity may provoke...

> ... new affectivites, new intensities between people [that] might provide a mutant sensibility which could prove more significant in changing people's experiences of themselves and the world than any macro-defined politics.

Such speculation turns many approaches to social and political change on their heads, especially those that would have us believe that meaningful and effective political change happens only or primarily at the macro-systemic level. And, it challenges assumptions that our reasons for initiating particular political action must be grounded in language-based knowledge claims. Rajchman extends these challenges in ways that are significant to those of us interested in pedagogy when he asserts that (Rajchman, 2000a, p. 38):

> [Thought] is free in its creations not when everyone agrees or plays by the rules, but on the contrary, when what the rules and who the players are is not given in advance, but instead emerges along with the new concepts created and the new problems posed.

What are we to make of Kennedy's "mutant sensibilities" and "new intensities" that exist between people and prior to "selves?" And, what might we make of Rajchman's "players" who do not play the game of thought but emerge, along with the rules of thought, from participation in the game itself?

The Materiality of the Learning Self in the Making

It has helped me to think of these questions alongside Winnicott's attempts to grapple, in different terms, with the paradoxes of selves in the making, of self-change, and of the self in creative dissolution and self-augmentation. Winnicott invented the idea of transitional space to help him do precisely that. As a clinical child psychologist, he tried to understand what happens when people creatively change how they relate to and "use" themselves, others, and the world. Some of the designers and cultural critics discussed here use Winnicott's notion of transitional space in order to explain the efficacy of the anomalous places of learning we are considering.

According to Winnicott, the transition at the heart of transitional space is a most difficult one. It is the transition from reacting to the outside world in habitual ways, based only on past experiences, traumas, fears, or senses of who we are and what we want — to responding to the oldness and newness of the outside world, contemporaneously, in the here and now. Winnicott's transitional space is what makes possible the difficult transition from a state of habitual ("natural" feeling) compliance with the outside world, with its expectations, traditions, structures, and knowledges, to a state of creatively putting those expectations, traditions, and structures to new uses.

In Winnicott's view, this event of inner transition is made possible only when we dare to move into relation with the outside worlds of things, other people, environments, and events. We must be able to access something external to our own projections and identifications; otherwise, our entire reality would consist of our own dreams or individual delusions. Our creative transformation of what exists independently from us distinguishes art or knowledge from dreams or individual delusion, but our encounters with the "outside" also necessitate our reengagements of the "inside," because creative transformation of what is given — outside — happens only by bringing something of our inner reality into the process (Flax, 1993, p. 121). Winnicott called this movement the never-ending work and play of keeping inside and outside both interrelated and separate. In order to learn things and in ways not given in advance, Winnicott believed, we need opportunities and capacities that allow us to be interrelated and separated at the same time. Thus, according to Winnicott, learning, changing, or becoming each requires opportunities and capacities for being (radically) in relation.

Kennedy uses language influenced by Deleuze and Bergson to describe what Winnicott called, in the language of psychology, transitional space. She enlists the help of Nobel Prize winning geneticist Barbara McClintock in an attempt to describe the "separate but interrelated" being in relation that is the experience of learning. McClintock's account of a "learning" gives body to Winnicott's notion of transitional space. For Kennedy (2003, p. 32), McClintock's particular experience of learning about chromosomes came about because McClintock had a capacity for...

> ...whole and total engagement with the molecular forces of being in the world. A complete depersonalisation is involved, where subjectivity is rendered subjectless. Barbara McClintock explains how this "depersonalisation" feels in describing her scientific work: "The more I worked with chromosomes the bigger and bigger they got, and when I was really working with them I wasn't outside, I was

down there. I was part of the system…. As you look at these things, they become part of you. And you forget yourself. The main thing is that you forget yourself." Rather than a feeling being felt then by some subjectivity, a feeling is not owned by a subject, but the subject is part of the feeling. In other words, the "subjective encounter" is experienced within the materiality of existence. "The world and I exist in difference, in encounter. In the feeling, being is in sensation."

McClintock's experience of existing "in difference" with the world and yet of existing "in encounter" with it, of being "*in* sensation," is what Massumi calls the "*felt reality of relation*" (Massumi, 2002, p. 16).

Getting to that space between self and other, self and world — a place that is neither self nor other but the reality of relation — requires a "withdrawal from oneself" (Rajchman, 2000a, p. 87). But, according to Rajchman (2000a, p. 86), this withdrawal, this…

…impersonality is not an alienation or an "inauthenticity" … but, on the contrary, the condition of … a lightening-up of life and its possibilities. It is not a generality that abolishes differences but, on the contrary, a condition that frees difference from the determinations of habit, memory, routine and the practices of recognition or identification within which we are caught, opening up other vital possibilities.

For Winnicott, withdrawal from self, the "depersonalization" that Kennedy credits for McClintock's inventive understanding and that Rajchman credits with the potential for invention, both requires and opens up a third space of simultaneous interrelation and separation that is neither self nor other, inner nor outer. Winnicott called this time and space of being in between, this interval of change, *transitional space*, a term that refers, in part, to the interval, the space of self-difference, and the process self change that opens up in the psyche when an experience of the learning self is in the making.

Pedagogy as the Materialization of Transitional Space

For Winnicott, Massumi, and Kennedy, transitional space is not simply a metaphor or theoretical abstraction. It has a materiality. For Winnicott, "inside" and "outside" are not simply metaphors for referring to the psyche and to "reality." They also refer to the inescapable materiality of embodiment. As Phillips (1988, p. 78) explains it, Winnicott places…

…the body at the root of development out of which a "psychosomatic partnership" evolved. The self was first and foremost a body self and the "psyche" of the partnership "means the imaginative elaboration of somatic parts, feelings and functions, that is, of physical aliveness."

The "self" that experiences the self-augmentation that takes place in transitional space is a psyche–soma couple. It is "the body creative." In it, "the aliveness of the body-tissues and the working of the body functions" are creatively and imaginatively elaborated into new ways of being in the world and making sense of it (Phillips, 1993, p. 135). Transitional space is the space where both real and imagined physical boundaries between the body's "inside" and "outside" are put into play.

Likewise, for Massumi, there is a materiality even to the psyche's self-change. Habit, he says, resides not only in conscious and unconscious senses of self. It also "resides in the flesh. Some say in matter. As acquired, it can be said to be 'cultural.' As automatic and material, it can pass for 'natural'" (Massumi, 2002, p. 11). Habit has an ambiguous double location within both culture and the materiality of the body, and this is what allows Massumi to call habit "an acquired automatic self-regulation" (Massumi, 2002, p. 11).

For Winnicott, the *material* qualities of transitional space and their impingements on our embodied experiences of being in relation were crucial to the event of learning. Frequently, he referred to transitional space as a "holding environment," and he gave much consideration to the environmental qualities that would make for spaces and times most likely to invite and support the "felt reality of relation." He saw this "holding environment" as a third zone that is the space of relationship between me and not me. This third zone is opened up when the body that I am is, in Massumi's words, "in a dissolve: out of what it is just ceasing to be [and] into what it will already have become by the time it registers that something has happened" (Massumi, 2002, p. 200). Winnicott's holding environment can be seen, in Massumi's mindset, as the space/time that "smudges" past and present (Massumi, 2002, p. 200).

According to Winnicott, the job of a "good-enough" holding environment is to "hold" without imposition our capacities to sense and creatively use our own processes of self-complication. When it manages to do that, it also holds the potential for our responsive engagement with what is different from our selves. An environment of interrelation holds the potential to become transitional space when it provides opportunities for us to both act in the world and to be acted upon by it — while at the same time offering us the flexible stability we need to risk allowing ourselves to be changed by that interaction. Stability may be offered in the form of limits, forms, traditions, expectations, or conventions. Formations of power may seek to impose stability by attempting to contain change.

Transitional space does not appear spontaneously or simply because we will it to, but it does exist always and everywhere as potential. Whether it is in fact actualized, whether it is "sprung" into a materiality, depends, in part, on how an environment holds stabilizing dynamics such as habit, foundations, and already-achieved "knowledge" with *flexibility*. A flexible, responsive holding environment meets the self-in-transition with curiosity and playfulness, and the good-enough holding environment is open to itself being changed in turn — as the result of having been in relation with a learning in the making.

Pedagogy, Transitional Space, and Fields of Emergence

Reading Winnicott side by side with recent writings by Massumi, Grosz, Kennedy, and Rajchman, his notion of transitional space begins to look like a psychologist's description of what Massumi, borrowing from mathematics and the natural sciences, calls a *field of emergence*. Massumi appropriates this concept for the humanities as a tool for thinking about agency and social change. We are able to employ it here to assist our experimental thinking about pedagogy and learning.

Like transitional space, a field of emergence, as Massumi explains it, is an "interaction in the making" — or, in other words, a *relation* (Massumi, 2002, p. 9). A field of emergence (of newness and self change) takes shape when our minds/brains and bodies pass through time, space, and events — and do so with *undetermined directions and outcomes*. What emerges from this uncertain passage are selves as well as social and cultural positions and determinations, including what are then retroactively encoded as subjectivities, genders, races, and knowledges (Massumi, 2002, p. 9):

> The field of emergence is not presocial. It is open-endedly social. It is social in a manner "prior to" the separating out of individuals and the identifiable groups that they end up boxing themselves into (positions in gridlock). A sociality without determinate borders: "'pure' sociality."

Massumi uses William James to make the point that relations are as real — and as material — as the social subjects and objects in relation (Massumi, 2002, pp. 230–231):

> Participation precedes recognition: being precedes cognition. The separately recognizable, speakable identities of the objects and subjects involved in the unfolding event come into definition only retrospectively. In the event, they are inseparable from the immediacy of the relation. Their coming together precedes their definition. And it is their definition that culminates the event.... As long as the event is ongoing, its outcome even slightly uncertain, [the contextual identity of subject and object are] open to amendment.

As in Winnicott's notion of transitional space, Massumi's descriptions of a field of emergence put the terms that make up binaries, such as inside/ outside, self/other, subject/object, into motion and interaction. Instead of opposing terms such as stasis/motion or inside/outside, as if they were logical binarisms, Massumi distinguishes them in a different sense. It is a distinction that "follows the modes by which realities pass into each other. 'Passing into' is not a binarism. 'Emerging' is not a binarism. They are dynamic unities" (Massumi, 2002, p. 8).

Looking at transitional space in these terms, and paraphrasing Massumi, when the continuous becoming that is the self experiences transitional space, "it" is under "qualitative transformation" (Massumi, 2002, p. 8). In these terms, then, the self, when it is "in" transitional space, is not a discrete entity positioned between a former self and a future self. The self in the midst of an experience of transitional space is in the immanent relation that is change itself. It is "simultaneous and consubstantial" with the "outside," with others, or with events. The self in transition is participating in the "unfounded and unmediated in-between of becoming" (Massumi, 2002, p. 71). The self who has participated in transitional space is not a separate entity, but a "differential emergence" from a "shared realm of relationality" (Massumi, 2002, p. 71).

The payoff for thinking of the self in terms of transitional space or field of emergence, rather than as "positioned" in relations of agreement (sameness) or opposition (difference), lies in the fact that change itself can then be seen as something other than opposition. It can be seen as "more or other than negation, deviation, rupture, or subversion" (Massumi, 2002, p. 70). Transitional space, as a field of emergence then, as *relationality*, consists in an interactive openness "to being affected by something new in a way that qualitatively changes its dynamic nature" (Massumi, 2002, p. 224).

What might it mean to think of the pedagogical relation in terms of Winnicott's space of transition or Massumi's field of emergence? We might begin to consider pedagogy as an address to a self who is in the process of withdrawing from that self, someone who is in a dissolve out of what she or he is just ceasing to be and into what she or he will already have become by the time she or he registers something has happened. In transitional space, this someone is in a deeply interfused encounter with and at the same time in a "differential emergence" from the materiality of the world. The time of that emergence, and pedagogy's involvement in it, is a time where the past and the future "smudge." A space/time of learning becomes "more like a Doppler effect than a point: a movement that registers [learning's] arrival as an echo of its having just past" (Massumi, 2002, p. 200).

The environments, objects, and events that motivate the following chapters strive to address "learning selves" within exactly such a time and space. They seek to mobilize, simultaneously, perception, cognition, sensation, emotion, and imagination in an "anexact way, never prefiguring" what might emerge, twisting away "from addressing [or representing] preexisting forms and functions toward operating directly as *technologies of emergent experience*" (Massumi, 2002, p. 192). Their "pedagogical strategy" is not to represent, construct, or incarnate a life world but rather to present us with "strange constructs" that we can "inhabit only through transmutation and or self-experimentation, or from which we emerge refreshed as if endowed with a new optic or nervous system" (Rajchman, 2000a, p. 135).

The Force of Pedagogy

The experience of the learning self is not composed of the steps up a curricular scaffold of objectives or cognitive schemas, nor is it composed of the standardized tests used to supposedly "measure" its progress, retrospectively, after it has already occurred. The only material evidence we have of what makes a curriculum or pedagogy "educational" is that lived experience. Like an arrow in flight, the lived experience of a learning is "nondecomposable: a dynamic unity" (Massumi, 2002, p. 6). An arrow's path, Massumi points out, is not composed of positions, despite our attempts to "plot" its path as points on a grid.

One of the consequences of "fluidifying" (Massumi, 2002, p. 6) our approaches to teaching and learning is the realization that, when we look at test scores or curriculum content, we are looking at only one dimension of the reality of learning. That other dimension of learning's reality — its nondecomposable continuity of movement and sensation, its felt reality of the relation that is experience couched in matter — is as real as test scores or curriculum content. When we overlook *this* dimension of the reality of teaching and learning, we not only impoverish our understandings of what we do as teachers and students, but we also open ourselves, as teachers, to doing harm.

If, as Grosz reminds us through Irigaray, the futures of the self, of knowledges, and, I would add, of pedagogies are "to be made rather than foreseen or predicted," then we cannot program them in advance. But, we can attempt to bring them into existence (Grosz & Eisenman, 2001, p. 148). We can design pedagogies for and in this other reality of teaching and learning. We are about to see how some people are attempting to do just that.

The camera cuts to a close up of a child's face, and we see the look. The power of that look to elicit heartfelt responses from teachers — indeed, to keep teachers teaching — lies, in part, in the fact that no matter how familiar this look may be it never arrives as a cliché. The occasion of this look is at the same time unmistakable and unprecedented. This look never emerges in the same way twice. In its newness, it is comparable only to itself (Massumi, 2002, p. 175). It is singular, without model and without resemblance. "It resembles only itself" (Massumi, 2002, p. 163). It always appears on the scene of pedagogy as a surprise and elicits from teachers a sense of accomplishment and triumph: "It's working! This young person has gone into a dissolve and is on the way to becoming someone who will be a surprise to everyone." Surprising, uncontrollable moments of learning in the making like this are what authenticate pedagogy, but anxiety often follows on the heels of such excitement and feelings of accomplishment. There is something naked and vulnerable about this look, even as it signals an intense self-presence. What is our responsibility to this child as dissolve, this child as smudge in the space between its past and future? What will we educators make of this moment — of this child-become-open-ended potential, of this learning self as pure potentiality? Will we educators move *ourselves* to meet this look as, where, and when it emerges? What does addressing the learning self as a mind/brain/body in motion and in transition toward unforeseeable understandings and uses of self, others, and the world do to education?

Unlike other activities that we often call "learning" — activities such as memorization, puzzle solving, compliance, or achieving high test scores — a pedagogy that invites the experience of the learning self as a newness in the making raises questions such as these. That is its power and its promise. It forces the question: "What will we allow anomalous, sensational pedagogies to make of us, as educators?"

2
Pedagogy's Hinge
*Putting Inside and
Outside into Relation*

Designers of the anomalous places of learning we are about to encounter shape space, time, experience, and objects with pedagogical intent. They seek, in other words, new ways of knowing that also transform knowledge, self-experience, awareness, understanding, appreciation, memory, social relations, and the future. They incorporate into their primary medium — whether it is architecture, public projections, multimedia exhibitions, or performance — the force of pedagogy, a force with its own logics, materials, forms, and processes aimed at reforming what we think we know. They incorporate into their primary medium the force that creates the experience of the learning self, and the place that these designers give to pedagogy in their work is a powerful place. They locate pedagogy at and as a *pivot place*. When they talk about their spaces, events, objects, and pathways as pedagogical — as the vehicles through which we come to know differently — they all share in one way or another a concern with the ways that their work puts inside and outside into relation. Their work strives to create the experience of the learning self by putting inner thoughts, feelings, memories, fears, desires, and ideas in relation to outside others, events, history, culture, and socially constructed ideas. They see the power of their designs as residing in their abilities to invite self in relation in ways that activate the instability of the binary self/other. They see their designs as drawing attention to how we are made up on the inside of our neverending interactions with and constantly changing images of people, events, and experiences from the outside — which is itself shaped in turn by what we bring to it from our inner realities.

Designers of the anomalous places of learning we turn to now have created assemblages that incorporate pedagogical pivot points into whatever their primary medium might be. Architecture becomes pedagogical, pedagogy becomes architectural when together they create a fluid, moving pivot place that puts inside and outside, self and other, personal and social into relation. A performance becomes pedagogical, pedagogy becomes theater when together they create the potential to disrupt and refigure both inside and outside — both self and society. At the hands of these designers, pedagogy becomes a dynamic that creates the *experience* of an idea, of a way of making sense of self, the world, and self in the world. It becomes the force that sets interior self-experience in motion to encounter the outside "not me." Pedagogy stages encounters with the unthought — encounters with the future as in the making.

In this chapter, I take a closer look at a number of anomalous places of learning. I use concepts introduced in Chapter 1 to locate qualities and design elements that constitute the pedagogical force of these places and times, their pedagogical pivot points — the times and places of *putting in relation* — that are central to these designs. Then, in Chapter 3, I ask what exactly is happening in these pivot places? Who or what do we find at pedagogy's hinge, inviting us into relation? Once there, where are we? And what might we make of our time there?

Speaking of Pedagogy Through the Vernacular of Design

Instead of articulating concepts and approaches to pedagogy through language, the places of learning that ground this and subsequent chapters "speak" indirectly of pedagogy through multimedia designs; pedagogically charged orchestrations of the experience of walking through, past, within, and around text, photography, film, video, artifacts, other people, audio soundscapes, and one's own memory; public events that teach; walkable pathways that instruct and offer insight; designs of buildings that are analogous to the operations of memory and teaching; museum exhibitions analogous to the sensory range and cognitive register of great writers and visual artists; landscapes designed to facilitate encounters between history and memory; and communication instruments and critical vehicles designed to assist immigrants, strangers, and outsiders to survive and transform the conditions of their social existence.

Before I use the analytical concept of a pedagogical pivot place to discern what the qualities and design elements of anomalous places of learning might be saying to and about pedagogy, I want to clarify what I mean when I say that the places and events I work with here incorporate pedagogy into their primary medium. We do not usually think of public spaces or events, buildings themselves, or theatrical performances as being "pedagogical." Evidence of the pedagogical address of a particular memorial or museum exhibition may not be obvious. When journalists, critics, or promoters describe or evaluate the places that I refer to here, they seldom make peda-gogical qualities or intentions a focus, but, as we will see in the examples below, when we view them with an eye to how their designed times and spaces attempt to set interior self-experience in motion to encounter the outside "not me" (the unthought), their relevance to the project of thinking experimentally about pedagogy becomes apparent.

For example, in July 2002, the Civic Alliance To Rebuild Downtown New York organized a two-day "twenty-first-century town meeting" called "Lis-tening to the City," which gave voice to over 4500 downtown residents, workers, families, and survivors of the World Trade Center collapse, includ-ing emergency and rescue workers, business and property owners, inter-ested citizens and community leaders, civic leaders, and public officials. The Listening to the City website states that participants were charged with charting a "bold vision for Lower Manhattan while honoring those who lost their lives on September 11" (http://www.listeningtothecity.org/previous _event/). Preliminary proceedings called the events a "public conversation" and a "model for civic engagement." Newspaper accounts called it, vari-ously, a historic "exercise in the very principles of participatory democracy," a "city-wide conversation," and a "series of simultaneous jury delibera-tions." But, we can also see the design of this event as creating a fluid, mov-ing pivot place that puts inside and outside, self and other, personal and social *in relation* in the ways that it "married computer technology and the venerable concept of the town meeting," thus making "it possible for people to make real connections with each other despite the enormous size of the gathering" (Civic Alliance To Rebuild Downtown New York, 2002, p. 5). Participants seated at 500 tables of up to ten people could see their groups' ideas and votes "flashed on giant screens as the sessions progressed, allow-ing the large and diverse group to discuss an array of issues and make its feelings known almost instantly" (Civic Alliance To Rebuild Downtown New York, 2002, p. 5). A network of laptop computers recorded the ideas generated during the discussions. The input of each table was instantly transmitted to a "theme team … that identified the strongest concepts from the discussions and reported them back to all participants." The theme team developed priorities and questions that were posed to the partici-pants on large screens throughout the meeting hall, "allowing people to receive immediate feedback about where their perspectives fit within the thinking of the larger group." Each participant used a wireless polling key-pad to vote on proposals, and results were immediately displayed on the media screens. This allowed the agenda to be modified to correspond closely to the tenor of the discussions (Civic Alliance To Rebuild Down-town New York, 2002, p. 7). The success of the event has been attributed to several factors: to the diversity of the participants, the form and quality of their engagement, and the resultant fact that the ideas generated by the event directly influenced the next steps of reimagining and rebuilding downtown. We might also attribute its success to how, as an anomalous place of learning, the qualities and elements of its designed space and time created the potential for participants to think and communicate in many different "new ways at once, interfering and resonating with one another, thanks to some as-yet informed or uncoded material of expression" (Rajchman, 2000a, p. 121).

Memorials are not often thought of in terms of pedagogy, but Maya Lin's commission to design a civil rights memorial in Montgomery, Alabama, called for a memorial that would encourage reflection and provide the opportunity for education. In response, she designed a sculpture that is also a walkable pathway. When visitors, the majority of whom are school children, gather at the cite, they circumnavigate a black granite timetable, described in the website of the Southern Poverty Law Center as a "powerful lesson written in stone" that chronicles the times, places, and events that cost the lives of "ordinary people in the struggle for justice and equality" (http://t3.preservice.org/T0300238/crmArticle.htm). Lin (2000, p. 4:28) describes how she sees the formal elements of design itself, not merely its "content," as being capable of "teaching" a concept:

> The memorial's design uses the idea of asymmetrical balances, aesthetically equal yet not identical ... the asymmetry is conceptually a very important aspect of the design. In choosing to break the symmetry of the existing building, I am conveying a simple conceptual message — things don't have to be or look identical in order to be balanced or equal.

Public and performance artworks are seldom discussed in terms of pedagogy. More often, they are spoken of as "political public art," "site-specific experimental art," or "public installations." In discussions that follow, however, we will also consider Shimon Attie's and Krzysztof Wodiczko's nighttime projections of photography, historic documentary film footage, and text onto public buildings and memorials as *pedagogical* interruptions in the experience of urban daily life. In his 1998 project for New York City's Lower East Side entitled *Between Dreams and History*, Attie projected, onto tenement exteriors, residents' "living memories" of their neighborhood's rich cultural history and fabric and visual records of its current evolution. In addition to documenting and researching the neighborhood's architectural and social histories, Attie asked Lower East Side residents to write down their recollections of the neighborhood, their experiences with other immigrant groups, and their childhood memories. Laser lights were then choreographed to inscribe neighborhood buildings with residents' words in their own handwriting. Visitors who walked through the neighborhood's streets encountered ghostly lasers that, as Creative Time's website (http://www.creativetime.org/between/) describes, wrote "each text onto building facades, letter by letter, echoing how memory unfolds with each retelling. In such a way neighborhood architecture is imbued with 'personality' and human experience while individual histories are made public for brief moments in time." In other words, the design of Attie's projection created the potential for it to operate as a pedagogical pivot place capable of putting individual memory, self, and the personal in a mutually transforming relation with collective history, others, and the social.

Wodiczko can be seen as working with and through similar pedagogical forces. He has projected photographs, text, and live and recorded video onto public monuments and monumental architecture in cities around the world. In 2001, for example, he evoked the experiences and conditions of undocumented workers who cross into the United States by projecting images of a Mexican worker with his hands clasped behind his head, as if being arrested by the Immigration and Naturalization Service, onto the exterior of the Centro Cultural Theater of Tijuana. Inside the theater, a documentary tracing the "official" history of Mexico is screened daily. Ten years earlier, soon after the beginning of the 1991 Gulf War, Wodiczko projected skeletal hands (one grasping an M-16 machine gun, the other a gas-pump nozzle) onto the triumphal arch celebrating the victory of Generalissimo Francisco Franco in the Spanish Civil War. One reviewer, on his Art for a Change website (http://www.art-for-a-change.com/Krzysztof/krzy.htm), gestures toward the pedagogical potential of Wodiczko's work when he says that Wodiczko's "ephemeral projection pieces last only a night or two, but they reclaim the city streets as places for discussion and heated debate."

In work that is related to his public projections in purpose and intent but takes a radically different form, Wodiczko incorporates pedagogical intent into what he calls "communicative instruments" and "critical vehicles." He designed a "homeless vehicle," for example, in response to his discussions with homeless people in New York City and modified it according to their criticisms and suggestions. The vehicle functions as a cart for collecting and transporting bottles and cans to redemption centers, it stores personal belongings, and it provides shelter and security. It was never intended as a temporary or permanent solution to the housing problem. Instead, Wodiczko says, it was designed to articulate the "fact that people are compelled to live on the street and that this is unacceptable" and to "call attention to the specific limitations and compromises imposed by urban nomadic existence" (Wodiczko, 1999, pp. 79–80). Wodiczko intends for his various critical vehicles to aide immigrants, strangers, and outsiders in their efforts to survive and transform the conditions of their social existence. His communicative instruments assemble with the force of pedagogy when they create the potential to disrupt habitual ways of inhabiting urban space and refigure ways of knowing both the inside and the outside — both self and society.

Finally, several of the anomalous places of learning that I have chosen to work with here are museum exhibitions. Like the places and events that I discussed earlier, they speak of pedagogy indirectly through the vernacular of design. Of course, museum exhibitions are regularly designed with explicit pedagogical intent, and museum educators have been more interested than most in the relation between learning and the embodied experiences of designed spaces and events. Partnerships between museums and schools have generated innovative programs and pedagogies nationwide. Some might therefore question why I regard the several museum exhibitions that I work with here as *anomalous* places of learning and include them in this project. The exhibitions that I include here are anomalous in that the qualities and elements of their designs set them apart even from most other museum exhibitions. Their pedagogical force is concentrated in an address to visitors as *bodies* whose *movements* and *sensations* are crucial to their understandings of the exhibitions. The force of their pedagogies resides as much or more in "sensation construction" as it does in the merely representational. More than many other exhibitions, the pedagogical address of those that I consider here appeals to noncognitive, nonrepresentational processes and events of minds/brains/bodies, and they do so by configuring time and space in ways that modulate intensity, rhythm, passage through space, duration through time, aesthetic experience, and spatial expansion and compression.

We will see, then, how the designs of some contemporary museum exhibitions and content-based experiences speak to and about pedagogy indirectly through multimedia environments that create, in visitors' and viewers' bodily sensations and movements, "effective resonances" with events and experiences in the world, and even with ideas. The permanent exhibit of the U.S. Holocaust Memorial Museum, for example, seeks to function in ways analogous to the operations of *memory* by staging the lighting and placement of displays in a way that causes artifacts to recede into semidarkness. This requires visitors who desire to view the artifacts to actively pursue what is partly obscured by the exhibit design itself. A design with qualities such as these compels viewers to expend deliberate physical, emotional, and cognitive effort to access the museum's materials in ways that implicate viewers in sensations and movements that are analogous to the efforts required to remember traumatic histories and knowledges. Multimedia environments like this one seem well suited to creating effective resonances between bodily sensations and ideas, especially ideas that attempt to make sense of self in the world. Museum designer Juan Insua, for example, created an interactive museum exhibition that offers to its visitors experiences analogous to the sensory range and cognitive register of the writer Franz Kafka. In *City of K: Franz Kafka and Prague*, Insua uses video, light, and sound to enter into the world of Kafka's imagination as it was shaped by his experiences of Prague. In an exhibition for the Manhattan Children's Museum entitled *Art Inside Out*, designers transformed the work of three artists in four media (painting, photography, video, and sculpture) into three-dimensional spaces that children could enter and, once inside, put various objects and media to creative use in their own unique ways. Designers of *Art Inside Out* thus created an interactive museum space analogous to the aesthetic and imaginative processes of visual artists.

Speaking of Pedagogy Through the Vernacular of Education

When talking about their own work, many of the designers, architects, and artists of the places and events that I consider here use the word "pedagogy." The word also surfaces in reviews and analyses by critics such as Herbert Muschamp and, as we will see in Chapter 5, Leon Wieseltier. As an educator, I find this intriguing, even exciting. Creators and reviewers of some of the most highly acclaimed spaces, events, and environments of the last decade are using this clumsy and obscure word to articulate the intent behind contemporary icons of architecture and design.

For example, in an article for *The New York Times Magazine*, Muschamp critiqued the designs generated by an architectural charrette to reimagine downtown New York City after the attacks on the World Trade Center. Muschamp applauded the charrette for conceiving of the city as a "pedagogical center — the paramount learning device of civilization" (Muschamp, 2002a, p. 49). Muschamp framed his evaluation of the designs with a pedagogical conception of architecture, asserting that architecture "is the relationship of visual and spatial perceptions to conceptual abstractions. Or, as Frank Lloyd Wright once said, 'Architecture is the scientific art of making structure express ideas'" (Muschamp, 2002a, p. 49).

Maya Lin also used the vernacular of education to explain her work in her essays about her role as memorial designer, architect, and artist: "My subject," she says, "is not infrequently an idea of our time, an accounting of history" (Lin, 2000, p. 2:03). And, she goes so far as to say that what she makes of her subjects — in the forms of landscapes, sculptures, and architectural spaces — are *teaching tools*. For example, Lin says the following about her design process for the Southern Poverty Law Center's Civil Rights Memorial (Lin, 2000, p. 3:05):

> As I began to learn more about the civil rights movement, I was surprised at how little I knew about the history surrounding the struggle for racial equality. I decided early on that a memorial to civil rights had to evoke the history of that period.... I felt the goal of the memorial would be to present a brief idea of what that time period had been about (as a teaching tool), so that the struggles and sacrifices would not be forgotten.

Wodiczko writes and speaks frequently about his work in terms of its pedagogy. He has described his work as a form of civic pedagogy that is simultaneously a critical interrogation of pedagogy itself, saying that he does not wish to be considered either a pedagogue (as currently conceived) or a demagogue. Unlike either, he intends his work to function as an "*inter-rupteur*, a 'switch' always ready to open rather than close the communications circuit" (Wodiczko, 1999, p. 25).

Suzanne Lacy, an artist and art critic, creates large-scale public performances on social themes and urban issues in ways that juxtapose performance, installation, and video with education for young people and public policy advocacy. She, too, situates her designs of public events and her discussions of her work explicitly within questions of pedagogy and education. In 1992, for example, she volunteered at a public high school and collaborated with teachers to develop a curriculum on media analysis as a means of strengthening youth self-image. The result was a project called *The Roof Is On Fire*. As part of the production of a related documentary video, the project featured 220 teenagers "talking in 100 cars parked on a rooftop about various aspects of their lives in Oakland's public school system and in the community" (Lacy, 1996). The discussions identified conflicts with police and the news media's portrayals of teens as the students' major concerns. These concerns became the starting point for a six-week series of discussions between youth and Oakland police officers intended to break down mutual distrust, develop a youth policy for the city of Oakland, and contribute to a police training videotape regarding community policing. As part of these efforts, Lacy staged a performance event that consisted of a basketball game between police officers and kids. It included live-action video, prerecorded interviews of players, a half-time dance presentation, a sound track, and sports commentary (Lacy, 1996):

> In the fourth quarter, the audience participated as referee. Graffiti murals surrounded the court, and video monitors interrupted the game during fouls to present short interviews of youth or police talking about each other. At the end of the game, the lights went off and when they came back on the audience saw groups of youth and police sitting in the center of the court talking intensely to each other. The audience was able to listen to these conversations.

Lacy speaks in both the vernacular of design and the vernacular of education when she discusses the pedagogical force of this and similar events that she has initiated (Lacy & Wettrich, 2002):

> There is, for example, a direct connection between education and juvenile justice. In 1993, 708,000 Californians were enrolled full time in college, while 930,000 were held on felonies in prison, on probation, or parole. Schools decline and prisons boom.

> Into this void — with more or less awareness — step artists. In the past thirty years, a substantial practice of professional artists working with youth includes overtly political projects designed to

directly confront the situation described above through mass media and public space. Other artists focus on youth education and services. A range of practices exists between these two approaches.

Lacy's anomalous pedagogical practices indeed span a wide range of approaches, from a public arts project in Charleston, South Carolina, aimed at generating conversations about targeting the hidden discourse between races and the ways that inequities remain unspoken in the public realm, to a "guerilla" installation in downtown Chicago, where she placed on city sidewalks 100 half-ton rock monuments bearing bronze plaques that commemorated the accomplishments of 100 Chicago women (including Jane Addams) in a city that did not have (up to that moment) a single major monument to a woman.

Lacy's anomalous places and times of learning attempt to fill pedagogical voids left by other educational practices and the institutions that house them. Such gestures are not confined to the realm of public art. They also are being made by a city planner's designs for waste management facilities. William Morrish is an architect and community planner who involves community members in educational collaborations that inform designs of new urban spaces. Along with the late Catherine Brown, he championed the idea of city infrastructure as a form of civic pedagogy. Morrish and Brown use the vernacular of city planning to speak of the potential pedagogical force contained within unlikely urban spaces such as sewers, landfills, and transportation systems (Morrish & Brown, 1999, p. 10):

> The whole web of infrastructure — roads, water mains, pumping stations, garbage-transfer facilities and water-treatment plants — needs to be more broadly conceived of as not only service systems, but as armatures for culture … to provide a clear curriculum of civic instruction on how to use and value this investment.

In Phoenix, Morrish and Brown turned the Twenty-Third Avenue Wastewater Treatment Plant into an educational landmark designed explicitly to be "didactic — instructing citizens about the meaning, value and function of the systems which support their community" and offering "key lessons in public responsibility" (Morrish & Brown, 1999, p. 11).

Pedagogy's Hinge

Even as these designers make works as diverse as museum exhibitions, public projections on monuments, performances in rooftop parking lots, and didactic waste treatment plants, they use the vernaculars of design and education to speak in similar terms about and within pedagogy. When commenting upon their spaces, events, objects, and pathways as pedagogies, they share concerns — in one way or another — with the ways that their works *put inside and outside into relation.* They sometimes describe, sometimes imply their efforts to put inner thoughts, memories, ways of knowing and being, fears, and desires in relation to outside others, events, history, culture, and socially constructed ideas. This putting in relation may take the form of designing the threshold of a building so that it exists in a specific relationship to its exterior streetscape — one that creates a physical analog for a concept or idea about history, for example. Or, it may take the form of putting internal fantasies, memories, and desires in relation to external social processes through the arrangements of events in public space. Whatever their medium, each expresses a concern with setting the viewer, learner, or audience in motion across boundaries between inside and outside, not with the intent to define or reinforce those boundaries but to forge participation in the times and spaces of relationality between inside and outside. As we will see in following chapters, these designers design *for* a relationality that is perpetually in the making and laden with the potential to reconfigure established boundaries and meanings we have already given to inside and outside, self and other, personal and social.

Designers and their reviewers state their shared concerns with putting inside and outside in relation in various terms. In James Ingo Freed's design of the entrance to the U.S. Holocaust Memorial Museum, for example, the idea of putting inside and outside in relation takes physical form in the nature of the entry to the museum. One reviewer described the entry as "bulging into the space of the street outside as if unable to contain this museum's excessive history." In Lacy's *The Roof Is On Fire* project, teens were given the opportunity to put internalized senses of both selves and others (the police) in relation to external practices and conventions such as media coverage of youth–police conflicts. Attie's side-by-side projections of various immigrant groups' internalized memories of their shared Lower East Side neighborhood onto its tenement buildings placed radically different inner realities in relation — and gave visual form to the space of relationality created when one group's projected inner realities are staged in a way that shapes another social group's cityscape. By also projecting immigrants' inner dreams and memories onto historic buildings — onto a neighborhood's architectural past and present — Attie invites a visceral sense of how social and cultural forces are both lived and embodied internally in individuals' histories *and* "coagulated" in the exterior forms and aging surfaces of the shared spaces that we build and inhabit. Morrish and Brown's designs that transform landfills, waste treatment plants, and other city infrastructures into "educational landmarks" create civic lessons by externalizing the hidden, internal infrastructure of the city. They reveal the deep relationalities of infrastructure with urban environment and make them available for educational use. The *Art Inside Out* exhibit at the Manhattan Children's Museum externalized the interior space of three artists' imaginations through interactive environments that give figurative and material form to aspects of the artists' inner perceptions, fantasies, and processes. By getting "inside the artist's head" to play, create, and imagine, designers invited young visitors to imaginatively and physically move outward from their own inner realities to encounter the inner realities of outside "others" — in this case, three visual artists.

Muschamp describes assemblages of pedagogy and architecture quite literally as efforts to put inside and outside into relation. He describes architecture, for example, as possessing the ability to materialize pivot points between binaries such as public/private, self/other, personal/political, street/home, politics/psychology, and social/aesthetic. Based on Iris Murdoch's claim that the pivot point between our inner and outer worlds is a fundamental point of moral action (Rothstein *et al.*, 2003, p. 32), Muschamp asserts that the architect's articulation of inside/outside is a performance of a social service. Muschamp was instrumental in organizing an architectural charrette that resulted in a design proposal for reimagining downtown New York after September 11, 2001. The one structure that participants in the charrette deemed most appropriate to be placed closest to the footprints of the Twin Towers was a school, designed by Richard Meier. Meier writes of his design (Muschamp, 2002b, p. 50):

> This school, the Urban Faculty, should offer a place for architects, scholars, and the public to create solutions for city problems — from traffic congestion to air pollution. Adjacent to the twin-tower footprints, the center would have auditoriums, classrooms, offices, and meeting spaces … sheathed in glass, the center would provide a transparent gateway to a plaza.

Muschamp applauds Meier's school design for its aspirations to connect pedagogy and the city, as expressed in Meier's statement that: "The openness of the [school] building says, 'What goes on inside is also what's going on outside'" (Muschamp, 2002b, p. 50).

In a radically different context, Jessica Benjamin enlists Winnicott's notion of transitional space in her discussion of the design of the public events that constituted the reconciliation process in South Africa. Her analysis of that process focuses on its ability to materialize a space of relationality between apartheid's insiders and outsiders — a space that had collapsed under the weight of apartheid's violence and exclusion. She calls the reconciliation process an "historic exemplification of the breakup of exclusion, of the self-enclosed [inside] world of the subject." The self-enclosed inner worlds of both perpetrators and victims of apartheid are broken up, she says, by the way the reconciliation process was designed deliberately and precisely to create the time and space for the "intervention of the [outside] Other as subject" (Benjamin, 1998, p. 98). The reconciliation process creates a means through which the outside others of apartheid can intervene as subjects, not as objects. It allows them to intervene as agents of change both in other subjects' senses of self and other as well as in the collective "outside" of a society in the process of redefining itself. The design of the reconciliation process created potential for the time and space of this pedagogical pivot place. It created the potential, Benjamin implies, for Winnicott's transitional space.

Wodiczko also turns to Winnicott for ways to explain how his "interrogative designs" offer audiences pivotal vehicles of transit across the porous boundaries between self and other, between inner and outer realities, and into a felt reality of relation. Designed to teach about and from the experiences of immigrants, strangers, and aliens, Wodiczko builds his "critical vehicles" for travel within what he calls the often-shaky third zone between the psyche and the social — a psychosocial zone made shaky by the political, demographic, and cultural transformations of our times (Wodiczko, 1999, p. 24). Wodiczko explains:

> Shifts in external boundaries (ethnic and state borders, for example, North–South, East–West) are closely bound up with migrations and the crossing of those boundaries. These in turn impose themselves on shifts in internal boundaries — ideas, beliefs, ideologies, languages, metaphors, slogans — psychological traces, lines, both shortcuts and roadblocks, running across the individual territories of human minds. The migratory movements within each of us necessarily includes crossing one important internal boundary, the line drawn between the person one has been but no longer is and the person one will become....

So, we have designers who are creating environments, events, and experiences that are pedagogical in diverse and anomalous ways. They and their reviewers speak of the pedagogy of their designs in the terms of putting inner realities in relation to outer realities. Whether their primary medium is architecture, multimedia, sculpture, public event, or performance, they incorporate into that medium a *pedagogical* address to their audiences and users. And, in the resulting assemblages, these designers give pedagogy a very specific place — they locate pedagogy at and as a pivot place. Architecture becomes pedagogical and pedagogy becomes architectural when their place of joining creates a membrane where the brain/mind/body and the "outside world" touch and interpenetrate, flow into and interfuse each other. A staged public event becomes pedagogical and pedagogy becomes a public event when, together, they create a space between that reforms both the self and the other, the self and its lived relations with others.

Taking a closer look at several places of learning through the lenses of these ideas, we can see how the designs of particular objects, environments, and social gestures do just that: They actualize, in objects, spaces, and event times, the abstract pedagogical pivot point that sets inner realities in relation to outer realities.

Wodiczko's Pedagogical Hinge

Wodiczko's work addresses issues such as militarism, xenophobia, urban violence, domestic abuse, and homelessness. Between 1981 and 1992, Wodiczko staged more than 70 public projections around the world that used large outdoor laser projectors to cast photographs, film, and video on the surfaces of public architecture. Recently, he has worked in another medium — communicative instruments that assist their wearers, in cyborg fashion, to survive and transform the conditions of their social existence. He has dubbed one of his instruments the *Alien Staff.* The staff resembles a shepherd's rod, but instead of having a hook at the top we find a miniature video monitor, loudspeakers, and field-sensing circuitry. Wodiczko describes the *Alien Staff* as a portable form of public address equipment and cultural network for individuals and groups of immigrants. Chelle Hughes, an interaction design researcher at the Royal College of Art, describes the *Alien Staff* this way on his website (http://www.crd.rca.ac.uk/alumni/98-00/chelle/related.html):

> As the small image on the screen may attract attention and provoke observers to come very close to the monitor and therefore to the operator's face, the usual distance between the stranger and the observer will decrease. Upon closer examination, it will become clear that the image on the face of the screen and the actual face of the person holding it are the same. The double presence in media and life invites a new perception of a stranger as imagined (a character on a screen) or as experienced (an actor offstage, a real life person). This change in distance and perception might provide the ground for greater respect and self-respect and become an inspiration for crossing the boundary between a stranger and a non-stranger.

> The subsequent version of Alien Staff exposes the respective histories of the singular operators. The owner is understood as a separate human being who happened to become an immigrant.

Wodiczko designed a different public speech instrument called *Dis-Armor* for "school refusers" — Japanese high school and middle-school dropouts who have survived neglect, violence, and abuse. *Dis-Armor* is a "prosthetic" aimed at helping school refusers to overcome a false sense of shame and to speak publicly about individual experiences that implicate social and cultural issues and problems but that are considered too shameful to address publicly. Student feedback and input helped with modifications and adaptations of the instrument. Described as a "new kind of cultural armament — whose function is disarmament, the *Dis-Armor* project resembles historical Samurai armament and ornament, including a helmet with horns and flaps and a crescent neck guard and chest guards" (MIT School of Architecture and Planning, 2000). *Dis-Armor* uses the ancient tradition of arms making to conceive of a playful alternative to face-to-face communication that the students would otherwise experience as intimidating. Liquid-crystal display (LCD) screens on the wearer's backpack display live images of the wearer's eyes as they are transmitted from cameras installed in a helmet. The helmet covers the wearer's face. Loudspeakers below the screen amplify the user's voice. Attached to the helmet is a rear-view mirror, a microphone, and a headphone which make it possible for the user to see the face and hear the words of the person behind him. Wireless video equipment installed in the helmet allows two users to work in tandem by showing each the other's eyes and broadcasting to each the other's voice.

Reading Wodiczko's communicative instruments through Winnicott's notion of transitional space, they seem designed for media-powered travel into the often-shaky third zone between the psyche and the social — what Wodiczko called that psychosocial zone made shaky by contemporary global transformations. According to Wodiczko, the goal of such equipment is to enable people to master "critical, honest public speech usually concealed behind the armor of proper social behavior — armor which keeps private experience from becoming a vital contribution to democratic discourse" (MIT School of Architecture and Planning, 2000).

It could be said that Wodiczko's critical vehicles and communicative instruments literally materialize the space of difference between self and other, same and different, inside and outside. They do this by shaping media-based communicative objects in ways that give material substance and weight to the otherwise abstract, hidden, or invisible processes that take place within such spaces between. The *Alien Staff* and *Dis-Armor* instruments give material form, for example, to invisible, elusive processes such as the effort to speak and create a public presence across cultural differences and misunderstandings and across social differences such as gender and age. Wodiczko's homeless vehicle gives material form to invisible economic forces and relations by articulating through industrial design elements the qualities of daily life as the politics, economics, and social relations of homelessness shape them.

By assembling with Wodiczko's instruments and vehicles, the wearers and users render, embody, and enact the volatile spaces between self and stranger in ways that make those spaces palpable, public, and addressable. Sometimes, the user/instrument assemblage literally extends the inside to the outside in a way that transports the space and time of the individual/personal into the space and time of the social/historical. For example, immigrants' prerecorded performances of their multiple and sometimes contradictory inner stories about who they are, where they come from, and what their presence means for nonimmigrants, when replayed on a video screen atop the *Alien Staff* and in the context of its use on a public street, externalize immigrants' inner memories and sensibilities and extend them — through the reach of the staff — into and across the space of difference between immigrant and nonimmigrant knowledges. *Dis-Armor* external-izes school refusers' inner defenses in the form of serious–playful body armor that makes the wearer resemble popular cultural action figures.

Wodiczko's intent in making sometimes painful and difficult inner reali-ties visible and audible in the form of instruments, objects, and perfor-mances is not to mark or celebrate the victim but to reposition and reshape both private experience and social conditions. For example, by allowing young people to address others through their turned backs, the *Dis-Armor* instrument materializes indirectness of communication in a way that reit-erates the social isolation of school refusers but with a critical and some-times humorous difference. That difference displaces the meanings and effects of indirect communication away from a false sense of shame and the misleading placement of blame for dropping out on the young person's "personal problems" and toward a critical interrogation of social taboos that make it dangerous for the young people to tell their stories.

The pedagogical force of Wodiczko's designs consists in the ways they serve as hinges upon which inner realities pivot, extending into and thereby reforming the ways we embody and inhabit spaces of difference between self and other. Simultaneously, they serve as pedagogical hinges upon which outer realities turn and extend into our inner senses of reality, of "us" and of "them" — those spaces of difference between self and other that we inter-nalize and make necessary to our personal senses of self and identity.

The Pedagogical Hinge of the U.S. Holocaust Memorial Museum

In Chapter 5, I offer an extended analysis of how the U.S. Holocaust Memorial Museum in Washington, D.C., uses media and architecture to stage a particularly powerful and compelling scene of pedagogical address. But, this place of learning also serves as an example of how architecture has been used to create a powerful pedagogical pivot place that puts inside and outside in relation. The pedagogical hinge of this memorial museum is a configuration of time and space that invites in its visitors the sensa-tions of "inside" and "outside" (the Holocaust), "insider" and "outsider." Such sensations, this design seems to say, are critical to the paradoxical understanding of the Holocaust as exceeding all attempts to render it understood — as rendering impossible all attempts to access its "inside" and to "know" it — as well as all attempts to exist outside of its continuing unfolding.

Architectural critic Adrian Dannatt describes how the space and time of the building itself put inside and outside in relation in a way that carries a very particular pedagogical force (Dannatt, 1995, p. 14):

> From either entrance one passes through an antechamber, a room for security, baggage, and then on into … what? Into a large, hollow interior that resembles another hall of arrival. It is not clear whether

> one is already in the building or still trying to enter it. One has come in only to go outside again....
>
> In a quest to locate the core of the building, the visitor is obliged to reconsider the notion of any singular center, wandering through a variety of other spaces, spaces which may convey information about the Holocaust without words or photographs.

Upon entry to the museum, Dannatt describes that he is put *in motion* physically and cognitively in ways that make it impossible to ever settle into a position that would place him either inside or outside the Holocaust — as either insider or outsider to its events: "One has come in only to go outside again" (Dannatt, 1995, p. 14). The architecture makes any easy physical distinctions between inside and outside impossible: "The dominant skylight of exposed structural steel is twisted and buckled; wrenched and turned it is like the Hall, neither inside nor outside" (Dannatt, 1995, p. 18).

Dannatt describes being put in motion cognitively as well. The architectural elements and qualities of the building teach what he calls a "grammar of history," but this building offers an anomalous history lesson composed of potential — not actualized — metaphors, associations, and overlapping significations as its details of shape, material, light, and darkness never resolve into the reassuringly symbolic but remain dangerously suggestive. These allusions shimmer, dissolve, disappear, and haunt. The architecture stages historical associations that "never force themselves but linger instead like a suggestive stain" (Dannatt, 1995, p. 18). Instead of ushering visitors into knowledge about the Holocaust from the inside, instead of trying to make visitors think "you are there" by providing realist representations of knowledge already made about the Holocaust, this building deflects visitors' expectations or desires for direct knowledge of the Holocaust and renders cognition indirect, or oblique. Our thoughts cannot enter the Holocaust. They can only pace back and forth and re-encounter themselves and others along the line to which this museum's space gives dimension through its pedagogical force: the severing line of violence that attempted to enforce absolute separation of those who witnessed the inside of the Holocaust from those who were its outside. This museum creates instead a space of radical relationality by putting visitors' selves in relation to history not by collapsing the difference between now and then through realistic representations of the Holocaust "as it was" but by insisting on displaying the *space of difference* between here and there, now and then, insider and outsider to the Holocaust.

The architect of the museum building has configured space but has deliberately refused to direct visitors' movements through it; rather, the pedagogical force of this space's configuration paradoxically "takes control and manipulates the visitor into the position of taking on responsibility" (Marshall, 1992, p. 154) for where she will cut and connect, for why she will turn here and not there, for attending to this but not that, for punctuating the space (this is inside, this is outside) and thereby making the meanings she makes. Such ambiguous, suggestive, irreconcilable architectural configurations of space and time provide visitors with a "map of the Holocaust where all coordinates have been displaced or half erased" (Dannatt, 1995, p. 14).

The pedagogical hinge of this place of learning therefore invites us to enter into "knowledge" of the Holocaust, only to place us outside again. It challenges us to discover a route through which we might read the Holocaust, only to have us discover that any route leads to another directional and interpretational dilemma. We never do reach the "inside" of this building, nor of the Holocaust, but, as we will see in Chapter 5, neither can we leave this place and presume to have reached the "outside" of the Holocaust — and that is the genius (and anomaly) of the way that this place of learning uses pedagogy as a hinge to put inside and outside in relation.

Maya Lin's Pedagogical Hinge

Maya Lin employs landscape, sculpture, and architecture to create pedagogical pivot points between inner and outer realities. By eliciting visitors' physical passages through time and space, Lin's assemblages of landscape architecture and memorial can be read as attempts to extend personal memories into public spaces and events and to extend social histories and events into personal experience. For Lin, the sensation and duration of physical movement into and through the outside of public space are crucial elements in her work (Lin, 2000, pp. 2:07, 3:11).

> I cannot see my architecture as a still moment but rather as a movement through space. I design the architecture more as an experiential path....
>
> The experience of the work is critical to its understanding....

Lin describes her work as giving dimensionality to the line that, in binary ways of thinking, divides inner and outer, personal and social. It is as if by giving the line that divides dimensionality, Lin allows it to take on a sense of place and shape so that it becomes, simultaneously, a line that divides and a path that connects. In her process of designing the Vietnam Veterans Memorial, Lin says that she "had a simple impulse to cut into the earth" (Lin, 2000, p. 4:10). That impulse became the polished mirrored surface of the black granite face of the Vietnam Veterans Memorial — a line that both divides and connects the living and the dead. "It would be an interface," Lin writes, "between our world and the quieter, darker, more peaceful world beyond." As she explains it (Lin, 2000, p. 4:14),

> I always saw the wall as pure surface, an interface between light and dark ... pure and reflective surface that would allow visitors the chance to see themselves with the names ... a shadowed mirrored image of the space, a space we cannot enter and from which the names separate us, an interface between the world of the living and the world of the dead.

To walk this line is to inhabit the reality of relation of self to self, self to others and to history, and consequently to feel the reality of a relationality that is neither inside nor outside, both inside and outside. Lin structures this passage or journey in very particular terms, following a very specific pedagogical desire shared by the other designers I am considering here. She declares: "I create places in which to think, without trying to dictate what to think" (Lin, 2000, p. 2:03).

The Paradox of Designing Pedagogy as a Hinge to an Open Future

With that declaration, Lin names the paradox at the heart of pedagogy. If teaching is about thinking and not about complying; if thinking is, as Gilles Deleuze and D.W. Winnicott suggest, a confrontation or encounter with an outside — an encounter with the unthought; if thinking is that space outside the actual that is filled with things in the making (virtualities, movements, trajectories that need release); if the unthought is a sea of possible desires waiting their chance, their moment of actualization (Grosz & Eisenman, 2001, p. 61), then for pedagogy to put us in relation to that outside — for pedagogy to put us in relation to thinking — it must create places in which to think without already knowing what we should think. It must create for us a relationship to the outside, to others, to the world, to history, and to the already thought in a way that keeps the future of what we make of that relation and what we might think there open and undecided, and this would make it impossible for an artist, designer, architect, or teacher to anticipate what form a learning will take or how it will be used. It would also make it impossible to conjure a learning. You cannot give someone the experience of their learning self; yet, we are capable of designing places that elicit profoundly moving experiences of encountering the "outside" and the power which we attribute to "masterful" teaching and to "pedagogical masterpieces."

Like all paradoxes, the paradox of pedagogy implies "a movement of systems — here systems of reason — beyond their own systematicity, and modes of containment that are unable to quite contain or control that which they draw into their circle of influence" (Grosz & Eisenman, 2001, p. 131). The experience of the learning self is generated by at least two systems that constantly move beyond their own systematicity and draw to them forces that they cannot quite contain. One of those systems is the pedagogical address. Like all systems and structures of address, pedagogy is unable to contain or control where and when its address arrives or how it is taken up (Ellsworth, 1997). The other system is the mind/brain/body. Like all living systems, it is in perpetual self-unfolding in directions that can never be presumed beforehand. When these two moving systems — pedagogy's address and the student's mind/brain/body — meet and mingle, they generate the potential to breach their own modes of constraint. In excessive moments of learning in the making, when bodies and pedagogies reach over and into each other, the pedagogical address and the learning self interfuse to become "more" than either intended or anticipated. In some cases, they become more than they ever hoped for. The instability and fluidity of pedagogy hold the potential for an unknowable and unforeseeable "more," and the actualization of that potential is what springs the experience of the learning self (Grosz & Eisenman, 2001, pp. 162–163).

The places of learning that I have considered here address us in ways that put to powerful use the understanding that learning involves cognition — but never direct, unmediated cognition. Learning never takes place in the absence of bodies, emotions, place, time, sound, image, self-experience, history. It always detours through memory, forgetting, desire, fear, pleasure, surprise, rewriting. And, because learning always takes place in relation, its detours take us up to and sometimes across the boundaries of habit, recognition, and the socially constructed identities within our selves. Learning takes us up to and across the boundaries between our selves and others and through the place of culture and the time of history.

The buildings, objects, mediated environments, and staged events discussed here actually impinge upon, relate to, and assemble with the bodies of their users and viewers in a web of interrelational flows in material ways (Massumi, 2002). *"Something in the world forces us to think"* [italics added] (Grosz & Eisenman, 2001, p. 61, quoting Deleuze). The designers of these anomalous pedagogies recognize that if interaction between inner reality and outer reality allows neither to impose itself on the other, but results instead in both being interrelated, then thought is able to confront us from the only place where it *can* confront us: from outside the concepts we already have, outside the subjectivities we already are, outside the material reality we already know.

The designers we have considered use cityscapes as public screens for the projections of personal memory. They use landscape, performance, media, experience design, and interactivity as ways to extend the human into the material and the material into the human (Grosz & Eisenman, 2001, p. 182). Their designs locate pedagogy at and as the pivot place where "internal imagination meets the external world of reality" (Dunne, 1999, p. 13). In these places of learning, design and pedagogy are strategies for linking these two worlds. Their designers invite us to feel the reality of relation and then "hold" us in that sensation so that we might participate in the relationalities that are there in the making — so that we might participate, that is, in opening the future.

These thoughts about pedagogy inform us about the look we see on the faces of children undergoing their own learning selves in the making. They suggest that we begin to understand that those learning selves are looking into an open future, and that we are witnessing the faces of thinking bodies. We might begin to recognize that the expressions on those faces are giving form to "shocks" from the outside — to the very moments when the outside obliges the inside to think and feel in a new way.

The following three chapters approach pedagogy as an unsettling and always unsettled question of design: the design of learning experiences that set teachers and students in relation to the future as open and to teaching and learning as always in the making, never guaranteed and never achieved. This undecidability creates the opportunity for an ethics of responsibility in the pedagogical relation. It creates the opportunity for a pedagogy in which we come to know the world by acting in it, making something of it, and doing the never-ending work and play of responding to what our actions make occur — both inside and outside.

3

Pedagogy's Time and Space

In this chapter, I want to see what might happen for us as educators when we allow ourselves to think of the pedagogical force of several anomalous places of learning side by side with D.W. Winnicott's idea of transitional space. We will take a closer look at several of the pedagogical designs that we glimpsed in previous chapters, as well as several new ones. I am going to examine the pedagogical pivot points of each of these places — their times and places of putting self in relation to self, others, and the world — through Winnicott's notion of transitional space. We will explore how transitional space, as an ambiguous and paradoxical notion, allows us to grasp pedagogy as an undirected dynamic of interrelation. We will read Winnicott as speaking not only as a child psychologist but also as a teacher. Here and in later chapters we will engage Winnicott as a teacher who realized and described in graphic terms the hazards of addressing students as fixed and static subjects of pedagogy rather than as moving subjects on a continuous passage toward knowings that are always incomplete. We will see that the notion of transitional space invites us to reimagine pedagogy as an economy of moving forms and selves that operates through a logic of open-ended relationality, and this means that it invites us to imagine pedagogy as addressing the learning self as an emergence — as a self and an intelligence that is always in the making.

Let us see what happens, then, when we use the idea of transitional space to look closely at the pedagogical pivot points of the learning environments, experiences, and events that we are considering here. Let us see what ideas about pedagogy and the experience of the learning self become thinkable and intelligible when we use transitional space to ask: What, exactly, is happening at the pedagogical pivot points of these anomalous places of learning? Who or what do we find there that is inviting us into relation? Once there, where are we? And, what might we make of our time there?

We are going to take up these questions by considering Anna Deavere Smith's work side by side with Winnicott's notion of transitional *space*. Her theatrical performances seek to bring antagonistic selves and others into intimate proximity without closing or presuming to know the spaces of difference between them.

We will take a closer look at the pedagogy of Shimon Attie's projections and how they juxtapose images, languages, memories, and histories with urban buildings and streets. We will use Winnicott's understanding of transitional space as *event* to see how these juxtapositions turn urban spaces into event potentials — places in which Attie alters the uses and meanings of public space in ways that hold the potential for education to be contemporaneous with social change and identities in the making.

We will look at what we might learn as educators by reading Frank Gehry's design of the Ray and Maria Stata Center for Computer, Information, and Intelligence Sciences on the MIT campus — an elaborate environment for teaching and learning — as a materialization of the qualities of transitional space that led Winnicott to call this space *potential* space. We will explore how Gehry's design attempts to actualize a space in which learning and teaching about the world are seen as a constant movement of folding, unfolding, and refolding of inside to outside, outside to inside. We will consider the pedagogical value of the design of the Stata building and how it attempts to give material form to cognition's detours when it becomes inventive.

Then, through *Art Inside Out*, a major exhibit of the Manhattan Children's Museum, we will encounter the difficulties that educators and designers face when they try to create exhibits, environments, and events that address a *moving subject* and try to invite the playfulness that Winnicott saw as essential to transitional space. We will see how *Art Inside Out* vacillates between addressing its students as in motion and static, as on the way and finished, as playfully unknowable, and as subject to rigid assessment.

Finally, we will take up Tom Hanks' character's use of a volleyball in the popular Hollywood film *Cast Away*, along with Peter de Bolla's reading of a text-based, aesthetic–pedagogical object — a poem — to explore how and why Winnicott also spoke of transitional space in terms of transitional *objects*. We will see how Chuck uses the volleyball and de Bolla uses the poem as transitional objects that "spring" for them experiences of their learning selves.

I am going to use Winnicott's notion of transitional space, then, to gain us some leverage on the question of where and how pedagogy operates as a pivot place in the designs of several anomalous places of learning — not because I believe the answer to this question can be found in the idea of transitional space. Just the opposite; I am drawn to Winnicott's notion of transitional space because it is an idea designed precisely to keep these questions unanswered in any once and for all way. As an ambiguous, paradoxical idea, transitional space resists any singular definition, taxonomy, or reduction to a model or to a technology. It is an idea designed *not* to be the kind of answer that brings thinking to an end. Transitional space is an "answer" that provokes us to keep thinking.

Reading Places of Learning Through Transitional Space

Winnicott invented the idea of transitional space out of his work as a pediatrician and a child psychologist. That work focused on how children's experiences of their learning selves were related to their active creations of their senses of self. He formulated his ideas out of his direct observations of mothers and infants and of children evacuated to hostels outside of London during World War II. During the war, he served as Psychiatric Consultant to the Government Evacuation Scheme in Great Britain. He and Claire Britton, a social worker, set up evacuation hostels for children and suggested what qualities made for good wardens there. In radio addresses with titles such as "Children in War" and "The Problem of Homeless Children" and in papers co-authored with Britton, he talked to parents and teachers about the effects of homelessness, dislocation, and war on children, and he offered recommendations about the kinds of environments evacuation hostels should provide for them.

Winnicott based his ideas about transitional space on observations of children as they went about the work and play of separating from their mothers while at the same time staying in relationship to them. For him the most important work of growing up — work that he saw as continuing throughout life in ever more complicated and nuanced ways — was the work of developing a sense of aliveness (Phillips, 1988). He believed that to have a sense of aliveness a person needs a capacity to access the world around her and then to use it creatively and responsibly rather than simply to comply with it. This sense of aliveness requires us to be able to do this even in the context of (*especially* in the context of) traumatic experiences, because traumatic experiences are the ones that threaten to sever our capacities to connect as well as our capacities to be separate and to be creatively alone with ourselves.

Adam Phillips says that the ideas and practices that grew out of Winnicott's work show us what can happen "to the scientific pragmatist when he allows himself the idea of an unconscious" (Phillips, 1988, p. 33). One of the things that happened is Winnicott's notion of transitional space. Winnicott used a number of terms to refer to transitional space. He also called it a *transitional phenomenon, potential space, transitional object,* and *good-enough holding environment* (Winnicott, 1989). He talked about it as a time and space of play, creativity, and cultural production. He also saw transitional space as a place of learning about what already is and what cannot be changed in a way that teaches us about what *can* be changed.

The multiple names that Winnicott gave to this potential points to the ways that he found it nearly impossible to talk about its qualities through any kind of direct or linear story of what it "is" or how it comes about. That is because, when it happens, transitional space is a simultaneous convergence of multiple events, sensations, actions, and experiences.

Each of the various names Winnicott gave to this convergence approaches it from one of its different aspects or moments. Winnicott called it *transitional space* because it is a process that moves inner realities into a special relation to outer realties. He saw it as the relation of an unknowable (to itself as well as to others) mind/brain and body "interior" to an unknowable and radically other "exterior," and this transit across the space of difference between inside and outside is transitional because encounters with the "not me" that one finds there and the actions that we take in response to such encounters change both the inside of the self and the outside of the social environment. He saw the convergence of inner and outer events and qualities that inaugurates transitional space as a *transitional phenomenon* because it happens in time, not only in space. The space of difference between is an eventful one of movements and changes that reconfigure it as it happens.

These qualities of transitional space and phenomena can take material form when we use people, things, or events as what Winnicott called *transitional objects*. We use transitional objects to imaginatively put our selves in a transformative relation with the outside. Winnicott enjoyed the fact that some commentators saw Linus' blanket in the *Peanuts* comic strip as a transitional object. Linus' imaginative uses of his blanket, like many children's uses of teddy bears, helped him through the effort and risk of being in relation with things, people, and events that made him feel insecure, and this made it possible for him to actively engage with the outside world.

Winnicott sometimes called transitional space *potential space*. Transitional spaces, phenomena, and objects are potential because nothing makes them inherently or inevitably transitional. Their users must both find transitional space (thanks to, say, an artist's design or performance) and create it (through their own idiosyncratic and imaginative uses of its transitional potential). This makes transitional spaces, objects, and phenomena potential in the additional sense that, while they can be designed for, they cannot be predicted or wished into existence by artists, architects, or teachers.

Yet, the convergence of the qualities and events that creates the potential for transitional space can be invited and supported by what Winnicott called a *good-enough holding environment*. By this, he meant the space and time of an attentive, responsive holding of demands and invitations that carry the potential for transitional experience. Like a good conversation, the good-enough holding environment does not collapse the space of intermingling between self and other. It does not allow either self or other, inside or outside, to do all the talking, but even when it does manage to be good enough to hold the potential for transitional space the good-enough holding environment cannot guarantee the arrival of transitional experience. It can, however, hold the potential for springing the surprise of a transitional experience, and transitional experience always comes as a surprise for both the teachers and the designers who invite it or design for it and for the students and audiences who take up such invitations or use such designs.

What Winnicott's notion of transitional space suggests to us as educators is this: The limits of our knowledge of self, of other, and of the world require us to put ourselves in relation while at the same time keeping ourselves separate. What we cannot know requires us to constantly traverse the porous boundaries between self and other, individual and social, personal and historical. We cannot know self in absence of separate different others. We cannot know others in absence of self. We cannot know only through distinction, difference, and cutting, and we cannot know only through connecting, integrating, and cohering. We think only in relation. We think only in process and in the constant movement across the boundaries between our inner and outer realities, and that movement, in its very crossing, reconfigures those boundaries and what they makes of our selves and of others.

Winnicott's "answer" to the question "What kind of environment (what means and conditions, what pedagogies) best invite and support the constant movement of putting in relation that transforms the person one has been into the person one will become?" is not an answer at all. It is more of a statement of design principles or elements. His answer takes the form of laying out desired qualities for the design of an environment that will not be complete or realized until and unless its users enter it and find their own uses for it.

Unlike spaces that put inside in relation to outside in an attempt to make the inside comply with the outside, transitional space opens up a potential for learning about the outside without obliterating the inside. Transitional space allows for expressing the inside without obliterating the outside, and for desiring the outside without turning it into self, making it self-same, or controlling it. Transitional space allows us to use the environment to get lost in oneself, to make a spontaneous gesture, to get interested in something new, to surprise oneself, to organize bits of experience into a temporarily connected sense of self and then to allow those bits to "un-integrate" so that they can be surprised by themselves and reconfigured in new ways. And, so they can be reconfigured into new thoughts and ways of being with self and others.

For a surprising moment of spontaneous play, creativity, and imaginative putting to use — when we are in transitional space — we are neither ourselves as we have come to know them nor are we our others. We are in transition. We are traversing the boundaries between self and other and reconfiguring those boundaries and the meanings we give them. We are entertaining strangeness and playing in difference. We are crossing that important internal boundary that is the line between the person we have been but no longer are and the person we will become.

The indirectness of the path to transitional space and the simultaneity of the events, experiences, and invitations that inaugurate it lend themselves to being explored and experimented with through nonlinear, three-dimensional, body-full, time-based experiences — such as those offered by media, as well as by architecture, sculpture, performance, and lived experiences of environments. This may be why some contemporary designers, artists, and architects are drawn to Winnicott's idea of transitional space. Especially those whose works engage issues of cultural difference, social responsibility, and violence and who think that linear, purely cognitive approaches to alleviating racisms, sexisms, and other oppressive structures have failed or proven to be woefully inadequate.

A space and time of potential mutual transformation exists in the difference between self/other, inside/outside. This potential experience can be invited and, if both found *and* created by both teacher and student, it can be put to pedagogical use. The qualities of a potential space of learning gesture and suggest. They shimmer and linger — for example, in the indirect analogies that certain museum exhibitions, walkable pathways, or critical vehicles make to the actual lived transitional experiences that users might make of them.

What might it be like to move into potential transitional spaces as educators and to hold school there? How might pedagogy be made analogous to the constant work and play of putting inside in a relation of difference to outside — of creating spaces in which to think without trying to dictate what to think?

Anna Deavere Smith and Transitional Space

Smith began her project *On the Road: A Search for American Character* in 1983. It resulted in a series of highly acclaimed, award-winning theatrical productions that attempt to document the ways that racial identity, sexual politics, and multiculturalism shape American culture and social interaction. She created *Fires in the Mirror: Crown Heights, Brooklyn, and Other Identities* (1992) and *Twilight: Los Angeles, 1992* (1994) in response to riots and uprisings in Crown Heights, Brooklyn, and Los Angeles that pitted ethnic, racial, and socioeconomic groups against each other. *Fires in the Mirror* addresses the Crown Heights riots that erupted in 1991 after a black child was killed by a car that was part of a motorcade of Hassidic Jews, and black youths responded by fatally beating a 19-year-old Hassidic student. *Twilight: Los Angeles* is Smith's response to the uprisings that resulted after the verdict that acquitted police officers charged with beating Rodney King.

In 1996, Smith received a MacArthur Foundation grant. The grant cited her skills "in creating works that help those whose viewpoints are diametrically opposed to see the viewpoints of the other side." Smith's process begins with interviews. For *Fires in the Mirror* and *Twilight: Los Angeles* she interviewed hundreds of people who had lived through extremely diverse relationships to those two events. She interviewed rabbis, rappers, housewives, teachers, police officers, activists, mothers, grocers, teenagers, academics, politicians, clergy, and business owners.

The hallmark of her process is that after listening repeatedly to the recording of an interview, she then performs them by taking onto her own body the words, intonations, affects, gestures, rhythms, and accents of those she listened to. But, she says the purpose of her process is not merely to give impressions of other people; rather, she says she uses her "ability to mimic to sort of get at those moments when people are ... becoming themselves in language" (Smith, 2000, p. 52). Those are the moments that concern her the most as an artist and an educator. She can tell when they occur, she says, because they are the moments when "smooth-sounding words fail us" (Thompson, 2003, p. 7):

> [The American character] lives not in what has been fully articulated but in what is in the process of being articulated, not in the smooth-sounding words but in the very moment that the smooth-sounding words fail us. The act of speech is a physical act. It is powerful enough that it can create, with the rest of the body, a kind of cooperative dance. That dance is a sketch of something that is inside a person and not fully revealed by the words alone.

Smith explains (Smith, 2000, pp. 52–53):

> I believe identity is a process and that we are every moment making an adjustment, and sometimes those moments happen while we are talking....

> They start out singing a familiar song, with a predictable pattern.... It might be a pattern that they learned from their mother or father or friends or on the television ... but what I want to do is get them to break that pattern while they are talking to me, because when they break it, they do things that are so specific to them and only them....

> I think we can learn a lot about a person in the very moment that language fails them. In the very moment that they have to be more creative than they would have imagined in order to communicate.

Something inside, trying to find a way through the body, through speech, into expression on the outside ... into the social and semantic space between interviewee and interviewer, performer and audience — this is where we find the pedagogical pivot place in Smith's work. It occurs at the moment when the smooth-sounding words fail us — that is, at the moment where and when the individual act of speaking comes into relation with the turbulence of social and cultural negotiations and modulations of racial and ethnic identities. At this moment of socially produced identities in the making, something (new, different) is trying to find its way into relation.

Being in relation, as Winnicott points out through his discussions of transitional space, requires a time and place that I am able to experience as neither all inner, as in "all me," nor all outer, as in all "not me." Being in relation opens up a space of difference between self and other, inner and outer realities. It opens up a third zone, a space that I can experience as both me and not me.

Smith's performances inscribe on her body the simultaneity of me and not me. In the space and time of her performance she is both herself and an other. She occupies the space between, the space and time of relationality itself that is both me and not me. She performs selves that are made up not only of their own experiences but also of their fantasies and misconceptions of others. By performing her interviewees' physical acts of stuttering and searching for words, she inscribes on her body the human labor of putting inner realities into relation with outer realities and outer selves. At the moments when smooth-sounding words fail her interviewees, she displays the work that they perform as they negotiate and express identities that are in the process of emergence out of events but that do not yet exist in actuality. She displays the work and process of how her interviewees invent themselves in and through the time and space of the interviews themselves. Her performance materializes the space of difference between self and other that makes negotiation and modulation of identity both necessary and possible.

Transitional space opens up the space and time between an experience and our habitual response to it. It gives us time and space to come up with some other way of being in relation at that moment. It introduces a stutter, a hesitation. It jams the binary logics that keep self/other, inner/outer, individual/social locked in face-to-face opposition. It is a space where the skin-to-skin face-off between self and other has been pried apart so that a reordering of self and other can be set in motion and so that we might go on relating to each other at all.

For Winnicott the *space* that is the ground for this transition, the space in transitional space, refers to the environment that best invites this transition. It refers to the means and conditions, the pedagogies, that support the never-ending work and play of putting self in relation in ways that are not habitual but are creative and contemporaneous. One Winnicott scholar, Robert Young, described his experience of transitional space this way (Young, 1994):

> The very idea of something that is partly internal, partly external, or of a zone or third world between the internal and the external, is to some a sloppy thinking. Yet that sense of intermediateness is exactly what I feel sitting in a theatre, listening to music, reading, watching a sunset. I cannot say where my hopes, dreams and longings end and what I am taking in from the experience begins. I am in the theatre, in my mind and in the cultural experience — all at once.

When viewed through Winnicott's notion of transitional space, Smith's work becomes visible as an attempt to offer to her audiences the experience of the learning self — the experience of being in motion across the porous boundaries between self and other in ways that reconfigure and rewrite their meanings. The pedagogical pivot place of Smith's performances, then, consists in a jamming of received logics of where "she" ends and where "they" (those whom she portrays) begin, and she invites her audiences into the resulting interfused space between.

Who or what do we find there, inviting us into relation? We find Smith's performance of the emotional, intellectual, bodily, and spiritual labor required to negotiate identity in relation to others and to keep similarity and difference in relation, to keep self in relation. But, the terms of her performance there and the design of her pedagogy there also make the center of her performances a non-place. Her performances center on the gaps that are opened up by the failures of words. If and when we accept her invitation to meet her in the spaces of difference between self and other, we find ourselves in empty spaces of hesitation, stuttering, and identities in the making but not quite yet.

The power of Smith's performance as pedagogy lies in the way that it *simultaneously fills and empties its pedagogical pivot place.* Her performance becomes pedagogical at the paradoxical moment when the force (the "teacher") that "springs" transitional space simultaneously appears and disappears. Here, pedagogy takes place as the space and time of pure relationality. Here, the teacher's place is a powerful non-place that a teacher both actualizes and vacates.

Shimon Attie and Transitional Phenomena

Attie's projections stage events that intervene in both public space and public time. His site-specific projections have juxtaposed contemporary and archival photographs, maps, letters, laser texts, newspaper clippings, residents' memories, and dreams onto buildings, street pavements, harbor waters, and the ruins of once-vibrant neighborhoods. We can see Attie's public projections as attempts to teach histories hidden and nearly forgotten in the here and now of contemporary urban space. Attie describes his work on the Creative Time website as "peeling back the wallpaper of today and revealing the histories buried beneath" (http://www.creativetime.org/ between/). His work does so by turning our attention to how, in the here and now, history is in the making. Attie attends to the here and now as it is in the midst of being shaped by the invisible past. His projections witness the here and now as it is unfolding so that its future might remain open to thought rather than being determined already by thoughtless compliance to what is already becoming or thoughtless repetition of what has already been.

For example, in Boston, Attie's work entitled *An Unusually Bad Lot* (1999–2000) projected laser text and slides onto the building that used to serve as a police station and temporary prison but that now houses The Institute of Contemporary Art. He generated the slides and laser text from old police files found in the prison's archives. He put the official language that arresting officers and judges used to represent those whom they imprisoned side by side with the unofficial language that the same inmates and their friends and relatives used in their communications with each other and with prison officials.

In 1993, Attie created *The Writing on the Wall*, which projected historic photographs of Jewish people taken as they went about their daily lives against the backdrop of the buildings and streets of Berlin's Jewish ghetto before the Holocaust, onto the very same streets and buildings of contemporary Berlin where the photographs were originally taken. Young (2002, p. 10) described his response to the projection this way:

> Once projected onto the peeling and mottled building facades of this quarter, these archival images seem less the reflections of light than illuminations of figures emerging from the shadows.... From the doorways, in particular, former Jewish residents seem to be stepping out of a third dimension. Some, like the resident standing in the doorway at Joachimstrasse 2, are caught unaware by both the original photographer and now, it seems, by us. The religious book salesman at the corner of what was formerly the corner of Grenadierstrasse and Schendelgasse seems to have been interrupted by the photographer and has turned his head sideways to gaze impassively back at us.

> Ironically, of course, the "voice" Attie gave these absent Jews was at times also the voice of residents objecting to the project itself. While Attie was installing the Buchhandler slide projection, for example, a 50-year-old man suddenly came running out of the building shouting that his father had bought the building "fair and square" from Mr. Jacobs in 1938. "And what happened to this Mr. Jacobs?" Attie asked the man. "Why, of course, he became a multi-millionaire and moved to New York." Of course. All of which was captured by German television cameras who broadcast the confrontation that night

on national news. Attie couldn't have scripted this particular projection any more powerfully. Another resident called the police to complain angrily that Attie's projections of Jews onto his building would make his neighbors think that he was Jewish. Make him stop, he pleaded. The response is as much a part of these works as the installations themselves, the artist says. The installation thus included both the projections of Attie's inner obsessions, as well as the counter-projections of the neighborhood residents' own obsessions. Without these responses, the installations, like the buildings themselves, remain inert, inanimate, dead.

Reading Attie's works and reviewers' responses to them through Winnicott's notion of transitional space, we could say that the pedagogy of Attie's works consists in the ways that they actualize the eventfulness of transitional space. They materialize what Winnicott called transitional phenomena. They give body to the time of transition itself. The time of transition is neither past nor future. Transition is neither the unthinking extension of the past into the present nor is it the unthinking projection into the future of what we already know to be possible in the present; rather, the time of eventfulness and of transition, according to Brian Massumi (2002, p. 58):

> … belongs to the virtual … whose reality is that of potential — pure relationality, the interval of change, the in-itself of transformation. It is a time that does not pass, that only comes to pass.

The time that is the duration of transition is not simply the present; it is the eventfulness of becoming and of emergence. The time of a transitional phenomenon is the duration of action and participation. Attie's projections hold the potential of activating the felt reality of being in the time of transition — that sensation of being contemporaneous with events as they are in the process of coming to pass.

This time of transition is the pedagogical pivot place of Attie's projections. Audiences come upon these projections and see that these projections are making something (else) of these buildings. What is happening? What is it meaning? What am I supposed to make of this? What is this for? What is it making of me? What was inert has been put in motion. These buildings that have become mere wallpaper no longer hide the past or cover over the present. The familiar street is filled with otherwise hidden, buried, denied, or forbidden memories, dreams, identities, and languages: "The past is always contingent on what the future makes of it" (Grosz & Eisenman, 2001, p. 104). The time of transitional phenomena is the time of the question: What are we making of the past right here and right now … and what is that making of us?

What might we make of the pedagogical time of Attie's projections? Attie's projections turn buildings and public places into events that recall to memory the histories that shaped those public places and continue to shape the present. They make those histories contemporaneous again. By making histories contemporaneous, Attie's projections "reanimate and revivify in another direction" (Grosz & Eisenman, 2001, p. 104) the historical forces that the buildings and their public spaces have congealed:

> Power relations are subject to the laws of iteration or futurity: They function and remain cohesive only to the extent that they repeat themselves and congeal over time, retaining a fundamental identity even amidst ever-changing details. Power relations, like matter and like life, are dissipative structures that also exercise chaotic bursts, upheavals, derangements, reorganization, quantum leaps. Insofar as they retain any identity, they also continually transform themselves, while nonetheless clinging to the goal of freezing, arresting, or containing the future in its own image and according to its own interests.

Attie's work, then, can be seen as an attempt to subject power relations to the law of futurity. He opens congealed ways of making sense of the past to the dissipative forces of the present as in the making. He loosens the future from the arresting grasp of the past. He creates a space in which the past's real difference from now and its potential difference from the future are made visceral.

Who or what will we find in this time of transition, inviting us into relation? We find what conditions the present. We find the projected uncanny shadows of historical others. As they come to pass through us, they are neither alive nor dead. If and when we accept Attie's invitation to meet them there, we find ourselves in a moving present that is uncertain and still in the making. We find ourselves at a temporal hinge where past and future fold into proximity and create the time between past and future: the interval of change. Attie's projections as events open themselves and their participants to the "co-implication of bodies and cities, their relations of mutual production and definition" (Grosz & Eisenman, 2001, p. 100) and to their contingent and unexpected mutation.

Attie's projections give body, then, to the abstract processes that impinge upon power relations: processes such as iteration, change, dissipation, upheaval, derangement, and reorganization. If, as Elizabeth Grosz says, "the present consists in the consciousness I have of my body" (Grosz & Eisenman, 2001, p. 120), then Attie's projections can be seen as prosthetic events for sensing the present and becoming contemporaneous with it. They can be seen as prosthetic events that enable us to sense congealed power relations in the forms of the buildings, public spaces, absences, and habitual public gestures that surround us. They enable us to sense how these materials "already made" impinge upon our bodies and modulate them in ways that attempt to contain the future within the past's own image.

We might use the time of these projections to become contemporaneous with the others around us. We might use them to make a personal and social transition from what has been and what still shapes the present through our collective habitual reactions and compliance — to what no longer has to be as we responsively and creatively put the present (and our stories of the past) to use. And, that is just what the present is for: action and invention. The present, in Grosz's reading of Henri Bergson, "is that which acts and lives.... The present is a form of impending action" (Grosz & Eisenman, 2001, p. 121).

The pedagogical power of Attie's projections lies in the ways that they simultaneously fill and empty transitional time as a pedagogical pivot place between past and present. At the center of their pedagogy a *hinge effect* folds past and present into close proximity, but the events of this enfolding — Attie's projections — are unrepeatable and disappear without leaving a trace. The force that "teaches" in the time of these projections *must* disappear because it is not an answer. By disappearing, it refuses to serve as an answer. Disappearing, it keeps open the space and time between the question and the habitual, complying answer. The pedagogical pivot place at the center of Attie's projections is the time of inventing a response that is up to the moment both in the sense of being contemporaneous with it and in the sense of being capable of mounting a creative response to it. In fact, for Grosz, the intervals between past and future, self and other, are the only spaces/times in which social and cultural transformation can possibly take place (Grosz & Eisenman, 2001, pp. 92–93):

> The space of the in-between is the locus for social, cultural, and natural transformations: It is not simply a convenient space for movements and realignments but in fact is the only place — the place around identities, between identities — where becoming, openness to futurity, outstrips the conservational impetus to retain cohesion and unity....
>
> Instead of conceiving of relations between fixed identities, between entities or things that are only externally bound, the in-between is the only space of movement, of development or becoming: The in-between defines the space of a certain virtuality, a potential that always threatens to disrupt the operations of the identities that constitute it.... The space in between things is the space in which things are undone, the space to the side and around, which is the space of subversion and fraying, the edges of any identity's limits. In short, it is the space of the bounding and undoing of the identities that constitute it.

For Winnicott, the time of transitional phenomena, as the interval of change between the self's past and future, is pedagogy's time.

Frank Gehry and Potential Space

Winnicott used the term *good-enough holding environment* to highlight ways that the interval of change, the duration that is a transitional event, is also inhabitable as an environment, and he considered what qualities might invite and then host the time of the fraying of a learning self's edges and the bounding and undoing of a learning self's identity. We are going to look at architect Gehry's design for the Stata Center for Computer, Information, and Intelligence Sciences on the MIT campus as an attempt to make material some of the qualities and elements of Winnicott's notion of a good-enough holding environment — namely, the space and time of an attentive and responsive holding of the potential of the experience of the learning self.

The good-enough holding environment is a potential pivot place between inner and outer realities, but it cannot guarantee the arrival of learning as the experience of knowledge and self in the making. What the holding environment holds is the potential for innovation and learning, a potential energy that waits to be released by its intermingling with its user. The good-enough holding environment waits to be found by a user when she actualizes it in a way that springs a surprise for both herself and the environment's designer or teacher.

When Gehry was hired to design the Stata Center, his charge was to create a space that would support interdisciplinary projects and encourage audacious innovation — a space, in other words, that would encourage and support continuous learning and hold the capacity to spring the surprise of a new idea; a space, that is, in which architecture incorporates pedagogy.

For Winnicott pedagogy is, in part, about hospitality. As host to the learning self, the good-enough holding environment must offer some measure of continuity and reliability. It must, indeed, hold us, support us, and attend to us. Because only with a backdrop of continuity can we risk the audaciousness of not complying with the environment or with tradition and become bad guests who dare to experiment, break continuity, and consider the difference that such a break inaugurates. But, even as it offers continuity, support, and attentiveness, Winnicott warns that the good-enough holding environment must never be an impinging host. It must never preempt the learner's own half-formed thoughts and feelings. Like a good building, the good-enough holding environment will give form to its guests' desires without erasing those desires or being erased by them. This means that Gehry was presented with the challenge of creating a "Gehry building" that bears the stamp of his vision and unique approach to hospitality without imposing one man's vision on its guests, because these guests are being invited in, after all, precisely to invent their own unprecedented visions.

How might Gehry design a building so that it is capable of presenting both the continuity and reliability of an auteur's vision and voice *and* a third area of experiencing that is neither all Gehry nor all MIT student/

teacher? How might he create a holding environment that speaks in the voice of a knowledgeable "teacher" who shapes the materials to be worked with *and* invites the audacious break with the teacher's voice — the break that creates the experience of the innovative, learning, inventive self?

Through his collaboration with MIT students, professors, and researchers, it seems that Gehry did indeed arrive at an element of architectural design that might prove capable of sustaining such a precarious balance. In that collaboration, he learned that the success of his new building would inevitably be measured against a much older building, MIT's fabled Building 20, known to those who worked there as the "magical incubator" and the "plywood palace." Home of the Rad Lab, where microwave radar was developed as well as underwater cameras, solar vehicles, and Noam Chomsky's linguistic theories, Building 20 was built as a temporary research center during World War II, but it was never torn down and it continued as a scientific hothouse until the late 1990s. It was a shack with asbestos tiles, exposed beams, and plywood walls, but, because it was always considered to be a temporary, transitional building, scientists repeatedly knocked down walls to facilitate collaboration and interdisciplinary exchange, punched holes in the ceiling to wire a laboratory for a new prototype, and did whatever they felt would facilitate their inventiveness. According to a tribute to the building on MIT's website (http://www.eecs.mit.edu/building/20/), complete with personal stories by some who worked there, "its 'temporary nature' permitted its occupants to abuse it in ways that would not be tolerated in a permanent building. If you wanted to run a wire from one lab to another, you didn't ask anybody's permission — you just got out a screwdriver and poked a hole through the wall." A journalist described the building as "the kind of academic melting pot that gives university presidents indigestion. Famed linguist and antiwar activist Noam Chomsky works just a few doors away from MIT's ROTC offices, which have decorated one whole wall with a colorful mural of an F-16 fighter" (Beam, 1988).

Along with its former residents, Gehry realized that the flexibility of Building 20 and its responsiveness to its guests were something that facilitated and even inspired innovation. While the exterior of the new Stata Building displays Gehry's signature curves and folds, Gehry described the inside of the building as "simple, with flexible spaces made of concrete floors, sheetrock and plywood, with moveable walls and flexible classrooms intended to provide space for new teaching formats. It will be a place were people don't have to worry about dirtying the decor so they can feel free to create " (Story, 2002, p. 2).

The pedagogical pivot place of Gehry's design of the Stata building consists of its flexible and unfinished interior. What is happening there? A holding of environmental qualities that strive to keep open the potential for a surprise, for an audacious learning. Inside is an already-shaped environment that invites itself to be changed, meaning that the fluid movements and sensations of teaching have a chance to unfold and actualize pedagogy's time and space; inside is an already-shaped environment where "space is opened up to time" (Grosz & Eisenman, 2001, p. 116) through an invitation to students and teachers to change its very nature as a way of discovering what can be changed. This holding environment invites students into relation with the limits and conditions that call up and shape innovation. Stepping inside, we find ourselves in an unfinished (and, it is hoped, an unfinishable) environment that invites its own temporary, transitional, never-ending completions. Such an environment holds us not as a container would, not as a passive receptacle of what we already are; rather, it holds us in passage and accompanies us from one emergent space to another (Grosz & Eisenman, 2001, p. 120).

This means that the pedagogical pivot place of the Strata building is simultaneously full and empty. It is built and unbuilt at the same time. It is both designed and undesigned. It holds an environment that is simultaneously hospitable and inhospitable, whose attentive host accommodates best by being simultaneously present and absent, available and off on a break. Gehry invites his guests to use this environment to become their own hosts. He invites his guests to shape their own experiences of this building in ways that allow them to both find and create their own learnings.

Art Inside Out, Play, and Transitional Space

The major and widely reviewed exhibition at the Manhattan Children's museum, *Art Inside Out*, incorporated the medium of pedagogy in its hands-on, interactive installation. The museum invited three artists to design the exhibition environment in a way that would teach young people about the creative process. Elizabeth Murray, Fred Wilson, and William Wegman invited children inside their own creative processes. They met with public- and private-school children and asked for their ideas for the installation. Children who met with Murray, for example, were fascinated by a huge abstract painting she had just finished. One of them said, "'What I'd really like to do is jump into the picture.' Another suggested turning the painting into a room to walk through" (Winship, 2002). As a result of such collaborations, Murray's part of the installation invited children to "step inside" a room configured as an over-sized, three-dimensional version of her expressionistic painting of a table setting whose utensils bend and melt like Salvador Dali's timepieces. Once inside the painting as playroom, children could rearrange large cutouts of elements of the painting on the surface of a blank wall, or they could listen to the same music Murray listens to while she paints and explore how mood and sound relate to the process of painting, or they could use computers to make their own digital collages of Murray's designs. By touching computer screens, they could elongate elements of their collage and add their own colorful brushstrokes and shapes while the results of their digital painting appeared overhead, projected on a large screen.

Wilson's art takes existing objects from museum collections and juxtaposes them to reveal meanings and assumptions that underlie the ways in which art is displayed in museums and especially how histories and stories about race and social relations are embedded in museum displays. His part of the installation, *Power Games*, was about bullying. In one Wilson tableau, a white marble bust of Napoleon faced an ebony bust of a Senegalese soldier. In between were small sculptures depicting animals and prey. Children were invited to arrange and rearrange objects to create their own tableaus by mixing and matching heads and bodies on sculptures. They could use computers to compose, record, and play back stories about power and what is fair or unfair in the relationship suggested by Wilson's configuration of a pair of facing busts.

Wegman's installation was a fantasy house inhabited by dogs in the spirit and visual style that has made his videos and photographs of Weimaraners famous. Wegman's art challenges how we see the everyday and the normal. Children were invited into costume and makeup rooms to dress up a dog or their parents *à la* Wegman. In a photography studio, they could arrange objects to invent Wegmanesque scenes and shoot Wegmanesque videos.

In interviews with the curator of the museum, in reviews of the installation, and in the invitation and instructions to visitors at the entrance of the installation, one aspect of its design emerges as its pedagogical pivot place. It is described as a key aspect that takes on responsibility for the pedagogical intent of the installation. It is the invitation to step inside the creative process and to *play* there. In an interview, the curator describes the installations as "very playful." In a review, a critic comments: "These installations are certainly playful ... the results make up a show that the museum says is the first of its kind, combining original contemporary works with an invitation that children (and even some adults) find irresistible: to come in and play" (Graeber, 2002).

Play, it happens, is at the center of Winnicott's discussions of transitional space: "It is through play that the child begins to include in his personal pattern of preoccupation those things that he is ready for, that he finds himself interested in and enjoying" (Phillips, 1988, p.144). Winnicott, Phillips says, saw the capacity to play, not the capacity to know oneself, as integral to the developmental process. "Playing is the process of finding through pleasure what interests you, but it is by definition a state of transitional knowing, creative by virtue of being always inconclusive" (Phillips, 1988, p. 144). If we know exactly where play is leading or how it will end up, it is no longer play. If we know how a game will end, it is no longer a game. Playing breaks down, according to Winnicott, when either inner or outer reality begins to dominate the scene, just as conversation stops when one of the participants takes over or becomes dogmatic. "For Winnicott the opposite of play is not work but coercion" (Phillips, 1988, p. 142).

As a playmate, the *Art Inside Out* installation had an interesting — and disturbing — split personality. Its invitation to play spoke with two distinct voices. One was the shared voice of the three artists, present as text on the walls, telling stories about where their inspiration came from and how they worked and played with their materials. Close by on the same walls appeared the text of a second voice. That one spoke a very different language.

Wegman's installation included a quote from the artist:

> I like things that look ordinary but have something a little bit wrong with them — or a little right with them, or a little unusual — to make you rethink what you see.

Adjacent to this was a block of unattributed text:

> Bill made lots of short videos in the 1970s. Sometimes Bill acted out particular stories and situations. How are these videos different from what you see on TV?

Another Wegman quote appeared:

> One day I walked by three of my dogs nestled together, dozing on the couch, and I noticed how earthlike they appeared. They didn't look like dogs at all. In the studio, I mushed the dogs into a heap, put colored paper in the background and added a piece of masking tape. I brought the camera in close, I was amazed at the results. In my pictures the dogs became all sorts of things.

And, next to this, another block of unattributed text:

> Experiment with putting these images together in different ways to create your own 2-panel or 4-panel picture; which way looks best to you?

In the *Power Games* area was a Wilson quote:

> I don't write a story down; I put the objects together and soon a story comes from having them together. I try to unlock the meaning of objects by setting up conversations between them. I manipulate the space subtly to guide the viewer to see, to think and to feel particular emotions at various moments.

And, next to this:

Fred's work explores how people relate to each other. He's especially interested in how people's backgrounds or histories affect the way they experience the world. Fred's art draws from his feelings about his past to encourage us to think about our attitudes toward ourselves and other people. What do you think about when you look at Fred's artwork? Does it remind you of something that happened to you? Do you think there is a story or feeling behind the way Fred arranged these sculptures? What you see in each piece is called your "interpretation" of the artwork. Share your thoughts with a friend or family member.

In the spirit of the unattributed text, I ask: Whose preoccupations are these questions? Whose desires? In which voice does a good-enough playmate appear? In which voice does an impinging playmate appear? When does playing stop because of someone else's desires? Which text forces the child to see not her own desire but the desire of someone, some institution, and some habitual expectation about … what? Learning? Museums? Adult–child interactions? How children like to be spoken to? Why did the designers of the exhibition feel they had to put the unattributed text there? Why did the designers feel the need for these unattributed questions and exhortations?

A designer of interactive games for children offered a critique of some recent digital products for young people. In that critique, he said (Bruinsma, 1998):

Playfulness, applied to the surface of things, often denies the true sense of the word, which is to explore for the sheer joy of it, and for the experience it can bring. The designer who applies a touch of playfulness to an otherwise purely rational product behaves like a *magister ludi* — a schoolmaster.

As for the idea that the unattributed voice is needed to assist children's comprehension of the myriad concepts at play in contemporary art, Wegman offered the following in comments to an interviewer (Holmes, 2002):

"I think that misunderstanding is as good as understanding at that age," said Wegman, noting that he had already seen children visiting the exhibit using display elements in ways neither intended nor imagined by the curators. "I think there are layers of my work that wouldn't occur to adults," he added.

The figure of the rigid, imposing, preemptive presence haunts Winnicott's work as a negative ideal, the saboteur of personal development, says Phillips. This figure for Winnicott is anyone — mother, father, child psychologist, teacher, warden at an evacuation shelter — who impinges on the infant with his or her own desires. The child, instead of finding out through play what interests her, finds out what interests the teacher, the school administration, the federal government, the parent, the bully, some political party or universal standard. This burdens the child with an imposed sense of what is real, what is important, and what is dangerous. It enforces the attention of the child not on his own needs or interests — but on those of others — requiring him to comply in order to survive. Nothing is learned in complying, not in the sense that I have been speaking of learning here.

Winnicott knew, says Phillips, that as a child psychologist he was always in danger of offering interpretations to his patients that they were not ready or willing to accept. As teachers, we are always in danger of offering lessons and posing lesson-filled questions that our students are not ready or willing to accept or that preempt their own half-formed thoughts or interests. The "unacceptable interpretation" — an interpretation or a lesson that knows too much about the student, or knows too little, or comes too soon, or hides a desire for compliance with the teacher's understanding — "can only be reacted to by the [student], not taken in and used" (Phillips, 1998, p. 143).

Winnicott was quoted in Phillips (1998, p. 143):

> Dogmatic interpretation leaves the child with only two alternatives, an acceptance of what I have said as propaganda, or a rejection of the interpretation and of me and of the whole set up.

Every teacher knows that this fraught situation is not unique to child psychologists. Liberal education is haunted by the ever-present potential and threat that moments of education will tip over into moments of propaganda ... and they do, but the child knows what interests him, Winnicott assures. An interpretation or a lesson cannot be forced: "It is there to be used, not revered, copied, or complied with" (Phillips, 1988, p. 143). When it is revered, copied, or complied with, playing stops, and the potential for the experience of the learning self is contained. The creative, playful activity that is learning requires a playmate who does not dominate and who is not preoccupied with his agenda or with a predetermined outcome. It requires a playmate who does not impinge, is not preemptive, and does not presume to know the best outcome of the play.

The pedagogical pivot place in the *Art Inside Out* exhibition works; it preserves the potential for a transitional experience — when its invitation to the learning self to come out and play does not dictate the play itself or the final correct answer. Its pedagogical pivot place is filled by the playful pedagogical address that is present there, along with the rules of the game. Winnicott did not advocate for silent analysts or, I would add, authority-less teachers. He did not for the reason that a silent analyst or, again I would add, a silent teacher might give the patient or student the impression that the analyst or teacher understands everything. "In other words," Winnicott said, "I retain some outside quality by not being quite on the mark — or even by being wrong" (Phillips, 1998, p. 152). With this, Winnicott suggests that one of the best arguments for filling the pedagogical pivot place, for speaking *as a teacher* and creating pedagogies and curriculums, is that by doing so we teachers reveal how wrong or off the mark we inevitably are. We reveal that we do not and cannot ever know what really interests the student or what the student really needs right now. We reveal that our knowledges are always partial, insufficient, and in the making. We reveal that we teachers are not the students' learning selves; we are forever outsiders to students' learning selves — and that opens up the critical space of difference between student and teacher that allows students to have the experience of their *own* learning selves in the making.

Winnicott strains to articulate, without imposing or prescribing, how to simultaneously fill and empty pedagogy's pivot place. "He aims to be an attentive but unimpinging object," Phillips says (Phillips, 1998, p. 142). He attempts to be nondogmatic and to move according to the patient's time and rhythm. He attempts to welcome and invite surprise through play — especially those surprises that show him that he has been "wrong." When they do, he attempts to unconditionally withdraw what impositional or untimely interpretations he might have made (Phillips, 1988, pp. 142–143).

When it works, when a good-enough holding environment successfully holds the potential for putting inner realities into relation with outer realities, its pedagogical pivot place is also *empty*. The outcome and direction of play are unknowable when there is a release from compliance to everyday rules and habits. It is unknowable even to the good-enough teacher or, rather, *especially* to the good-enough teacher. Pedagogy, as the time and space of the emergence of the experience of the learning self, is never coincident with the position of the teacher. It always takes place elsewhere, in the space of the play of difference between teacher and student.

Wilson, Artworks, and Transitional Objects

Winnicott used the term *transitional object* to describe any number of objects used by infants to alleviate the anxiety of finding out that they cannot determine their mothers' comings and goings and that their mothers have a separate existence outside of their control. Winnicott believed that adults continue to create and use transitional objects to alleviate the anxiety of the ongoing work of putting inner realities in relation to outer realities, learning about the world by negotiating similarity and difference and being in radical difference from others while simultaneously needing to be in relation to others and to the world. Winnicott saw transitional objects as fundamental elements of culture and the way into the worlds of play and creativity, including the arts, religion, and science. An individual's *use* of an object, experience, person, or event is what turns it into a transitional object. Nothing is intrinsically transitional outside of its use. Transitional objects become transitional for us when we use them to creatively put ourselves in relation.

Albert Einstein received a compass from his father at the age of four or five. According to biographers, Einstein tried to imagine the mysterious force that caused the compass needle to move and it was that experience that sparked his lifelong sense of wonder. The world provides the object, and our creative use of it makes it transitional for us. As Winnicott put it, the transitional object must be found in order to be created (Phillips, 1988, p. 146). Einstein's father could give his son the compass, but he could not give it to him as a transitional object. He could only give it to him as something he might consciously or unconsciously choose to turn into a transitional experience.

In the film *Cast Away*, Tom Hanks plays Chuck, a FedEx employee whose plane crashes and leaves him stranded alone on a tropical island. One day, a volleyball washes ashore from the wreckage of the plane. Soon after, when Chuck cuts himself while trying unsuccessfully to make his first fire, he grabs the volleyball in his bloody hand and in a temper tantrum flings it as far as he can, but the volleyball survives Chuck's rage over discovering his own limits, and this gives the volleyball the status of a real — not imagined — external other. Only the outside other can break up the closed energy system of one's inner life, only "the other who can be moved but not coerced by us can take on some of what is too much for the self to bear" (Benjamin, 1998, pp. 91–92). Chuck recovers the volleyball and traces a face out of the bloody smear of his handprint. "Wilson" thus comes into being accidentally and spontaneously. The volleyball itself exists outside of Chuck's internal fantasies and imagination; it is discovered. But, the volleyball *as* Wilson is created through Chuck's imaginative use of its accidental appearance.

Chuck uses Wilson in his transition from seeing himself as separate from the environment of the island and fighting to control it — to working with the island and being in relation to it. He uses Wilson to make the most difficult of transitions: from complying with the harshness and strangeness of this new outside world (giving up and starving to death) or habitually reacting to it (trying to turn it into a version of his lost suburban life) to participating in it, affecting it and being affected by it, and using it to give form to his desires. He recognizes that he cannot destroy or control the place or situation he is in but neither is he powerless. He can use it. He can transform it in ways that allow him to survive in relation to it. His imaginative uses of Wilson as a companion imbue his experience on the island with meaning, and that is how Chuck is able to and eventually does transform himself.

A transitional object becomes pedagogical when we use it to discover and creatively work and play at our own limits as participants in the world. As pedagogical pivot places, transitional objects are both real and imagined. They occupy real space because they are found objects presented from the outside. At the same time, transitional objects operate in an intermediate space of illusion, culture, and imagination. As material objects in the world they occupy physical space, but as they are made transitional in their use they move into the virtual space between inner realities and outer realities, and that space is both filled by the presence of a transitional object and void of it.

Soon after Chuck finds and creates Wilson he resumes his attempts to start a fire by rubbing sticks together. In a series of alternating shots of Chuck and Wilson, it becomes clear that Chuck is imagining that Wilson's presence might be having some positive effect on his efforts. Within moments the kindling catches fire. It is never suggested that Chuck believes Wilson literally caused the fire to start. Chuck "knows" that the volleyball did not do such a thing. Yet, it is clear that Chuck continued to use Wilson imaginatively in ways that allowed him to relieve the anxiety of having to be responsive to and work creatively with the realities of the context for his efforts to survive. He used Wilson creatively to be in relation with the island as well as with the world from which he was now separated. Wilson was both real and not real, both present and absent from Chuck's experiences of self-transformation.

In his series of essays on aesthetic experience and what it is that we do with works of art, de Bolla suggests that all aesthetic experiences can be seen as being, in at least one respect, experiences of the learning self. That is, he suggests that artworks can be seen as being, in at least one sense, pedagogical. In his discussions of the pedagogy of aesthetic experience and of the knowledges that our engagements with artworks make potential, I believe we can see de Bolla's discussions of artworks as discussions of what Winnicott would call transitional objects.

de Bolla describes his experience of artworks as something that originates neither in him nor in the artwork; rather, he sees his aesthetic experience as taking place in the space of difference between himself and the artwork. Art takes place, he says, in his response. The materiality of the "art-ness" of a work consists in that response. Inasmuch as his response is elicited by the artwork, it lies outside of him, but inasmuch as his response (the very materiality of art) is a feature of his own preoccupations, attitudes, and lenses, it lies inside of him. de Bolla (2001, p. 135) strives to find a language for articulating his experience of this space between:

> I have spoken about feeling or sensing something as a way of identifying an aesthetic experience. But I have also taken pains to point out that the vocabulary I have been exploring ... is intended to name not a feeling or emotion in me but a quality in the work.... Or, more precisely, it is intended to name a virtual quality of the work residing in the space between the object and my appreciation of it. As noted, we only sense it to be in the work — this is its distinctively aesthetic character — since it is clearly within us. What I am trying to direct attention to is a peculiar feature of the artwork, its "art-ness" rather than a feature of my response. The difficulty here is that such a feature of the work is only visible to me in my response.

One Winnicott scholar describes Winnicott as grappling with the same difficult task of giving language to the nonlinguistic, prelinguistic experiences of even language-based transitional objects such a poems (Szollosy, 1998):

> One cannot make a text entirely one's own object, to consume the text within one's own internal phantasy world and thus deny the ontological status of the external object. To claim, for example, that another's poem is actually a story of one's own life … would not only be an act of hermeneutic tyranny, but is indicative of a paranoid or narcissistic character. On the other hand, to speak only of the structural, stylistic or historical elements of a work of art, without reference to its subjective emotional impact, is too greatly to objectify and de-ontologise both the text and one's self.

Or, as I quoted Young (1994) as saying earlier:

> I cannot say where my hopes, dreams and longings end and what I am taking in from the experience begins…. I am in the theatre, in my mind and in the cultural experience — all at once….

> What exists between subject and object is in some sense a zone and in some sense a permeable boundary with constant traffic both ways and with objects often multiply represented.

Young, de Bolla, and Chuck in his use of Wilson struggle to articulate what Winnicott called a "third area" that is more than the "commerce between" the inner world and external reality. It does not simply connect two separate entities. Wilson did not simply connect or bridge the island and Chuck, Chuck and his lost home. A poem, for de Bolla, does not simply deliver or bridge his own experiences into those of Wordsworth, or *vice versa*; rather, when found and used as a transitional object, a poem or someone's Wilson is a site of the "constant traffic" of imagination, action, and emergence of newness across the permeable boundary between inner realties and outer realities. In this site, inner realities and outer realities are "often multiply represented … this third area might turn out to be the cultural life of the individual" (Winnicott, 1989, p. 57).

Pedagogy's Time and Space

The time of the learning self is contemporaneous. It is the duration of a learning self's participation in knowledge and in self as simultaneously in the making. It is the transitional time of self in motion toward an open future yet to be decided. It is the time of pure relationality. The space of learning is the space of self in relation. It is simultaneously and paradoxically full and empty, built and incomplete, spoken and unspoken, me and not me, a volleyball and Wilson, mere words on a page and a poetic artwork. Pedagogy's space is a space that the learning self must simultaneously read and write, and this means that pedagogical pivot places must turn around an *empty center* — a center both filled and vacated by a teacher who is present but whose supposed superiority "ceases to be relevant to the matters at hand." Sometimes our experiences of these designs and the uses we make of them can transform the teacher's superiority "into useful, or bearable, or even pleasurable difference" (Phillips, 2002, p. 31).

By inviting us into relation, by holding the potential for our engagement, by requiring our participation in order to be transitionally complete, by authenticating themselves as pedagogy through the surprising uses that our learnings selves make of them, the anomalous places of learning we have looked at here make themselves the product of an exchange. The environments, events, and objects we have looked at here create the potential for a paradoxical exchange between the pedagogical voice that speaks in the vernacular of design and the user/learner/audience of the design. What is exchanged is something that can be neither possessed nor given. It is the exchange of the difference between self and other, self and the world, the self in the here and now and the self that is in emergence.

4

Oblique Pedagogies, Conflict, and Democracy

Brancusi's "Bird" soars higher without wings than it would be able to with them. His "Endless Column" would go nowhere if you stuck an infinity sign on top. And the idea of freedom would be conveyed with far greater conviction by a tower that did not try to dictate the meanings that people might see reflected in it. The point is that with abstraction meanings can expand without limit. In this sense abstraction is democratic. It reinforces the concept of the public realm.

—Herbert Muschamp

Nearly a year after the World Trade Center towers were attacked and destroyed, *The New York Times Magazine* and Herbert Muschamp, architecture critic for *The New York Times*, extended an invitation to a group of architects who had expressed dissatisfaction with the planning process for rebuilding Ground Zero. The invitation was "to organize their frustrations into what might best be described as a study project" (Muschamp, 2002a, p. 49). The result of their response was published in *The New York Times Magazine* one year after the attack. It was an ambitious plan to "reimagine" the entirety of lower Manhattan offered to the public in the spirit of a "material tale" or "genotype" to provide options and widened possibilities for the rebuilding. According to Muschamp, the plan arrived at what amounts to a recasting of the cultural identity of New York for the twenty-first century (Muschamp, 2002a, p. 55). It helped to shape public debate and imagination concerning both the process of arriving at an architectural plan for Lower Manhattan and the plan finally chosen.

In January 2003, on the eve of the Lower Manhattan Development Corporation's announcement of its choice for the final plan, Muschamp wrote about one of the designs under consideration. In an exuberant declaration of his personal choice, Muschamp named the THINK design team's proposal entitled "The World Cultural Center." Muschamp's criteria for his selection: the design that best used space, structure, and visual perception to express an idea — not just any idea, but the idea that public spaces can be designed to function as civic pedagogies. For Muschamp, this meant a design that would function as the "connective tissue that binds stray pieces of memory, experience, and anticipation into a civilization's fabric" (Muschamp, 2003a, p. 1).

Muschamp's choice this time went not merely to a school building honored with the location closest to the footprints of the towers (see Chapter 2). It went to two towering latticework structures — "totemic images of the twin towers" themselves — *as school*. The proposed towers form an infrastructure for a vertical complex of cultural and educational buildings: a conference center, concert hall, library, interpretive museum about the events of 9/11, viewing platforms, and aerial paths. What drives the THINK design and his enthusiasm for it, Muschamp says, is the "elevation of the public realm" (Muschamp, 2003b, p. 1). THINK's design recognizes that we need new forms of social space amid urban density. Part of the design consists of a pathway that climbs ten stories through a garden sky park covering ten blocks. In Muschamp's words, the design says: "Let's go up there and see what [those new forms of social space] might look like" (Muschamp, 2003b, p. 1).

From up there, we can use our view of the spatial texture of the city as inspirational data for inventing new forms of public space. From up there, Muschamp says, we can see "thresholds between public and private space; the transitional areas between transportation systems; the irregularities on the cityscape that occur where, for example, Broadway slices through the Manhattan grid" (Muschamp, 2003b, p. 1). We can see overlapping categories of experience and surprising connection. We can see, in other words, abstract, "poetic" connections, stories, associations, and the possibilities for new associations.

With this, Muschamp seems to concur with Adam Phillips' take on democracy. Democracy, Phillips says, "works through the encouragement and validation of new forms of association and the conflicts they inevitably reveal" (Phillips, 2002, p. 21). New forms of encounters and the conflicts they inevitably entail are the raw materials that democracy needs to keep itself in the making (Phillips, 2002, p. 21):

To have an appetite for association — of a political or psychic kind — is to have an appetite for, if not to actually seek out, fresh forms of conflict; and to see conflict as the way we renew and revise our pleasures. Democracy … extends the repertoire of possible conflict.

> It fosters an unpredictability of feeling and desire. It makes people say, or people find themselves saying, all sorts of things to each other.

From this perspective, the THINK designers seem to be saying: "Let's go up there and see what new forms of social space, designed as potential transitional spaces, might make of us." How might we use a building designed to resemble a vertical matrix (a form analogous to the city as cultural crossroads) to set ourselves in motion across the grids that lock us in place, opening us to fresh forms of association and unpredictable connections, surprising exchanges of energy, appetites, and conflicts? "There is no reason," Muschamp says, "to believe that cities have exhausted their potential to realize new types of public space" (Muschamp, 2002a, p. 1). Muschamp believes that the THINK design offers just that — the potential for a new type of public space.

Let us go up there, then, along the experiential path designed for us by THINK — a path that materializes the simultaneous separation and connection that is being in relation. In the proposed buildings, the sharp lines of either/or, us/them, and insider/outsider, which severed and separated on 9/11, are transformed into a pathway that also connects.

In this chapter, I explore pedagogy as an experiential pathway that simultaneously materializes the space of difference between self and other and offers a mode of transit into relationality within that space. I read Muschamp's take on the THINK design through D.W. Winnicott and through the places of learning we have considered so far. Out of that reading, I suggest that the new type of public space that Muschamp says this design makes potential is a space where a paradoxical and powerful civic pedagogy might take place. It makes potential a civic pedagogy that binds pieces of memory, experience, and anticipation into a cultural fabric and, at the same time, productively frays the edges of the social identities that compose such a fabric.

The Risk of the Experience That Is Learning

Architecture scholar Francesco Careri writes in the book *Walkscapes: Walking as an Aesthetic Practice* (Careri *et al.*, 2002) about the power of pathways to set us in motion along the line that divides and to set us in relation with what exists on either side without collapsing the space of difference between — without enforcing sameness. The power of the experience of such a path is acknowledged, he says, in the indo-European root of the word "experience" which is *per*, meaning "to attempt," "to test," "to risk." These connotations survive in the word "peril." "The oldest connotations of the trial of *per* appear in the Latin terms for experience: *experior*, *experimentum*" (Careri *et al.*, 2002, p. 41). We can take experience, then, to be in a sense an experiment. It is the putting of self in relation to the world and to others in order to test and to see what happens. We could then take learning to be a participation in the world and the self as they are in the making. Careri points out (Careri *et al.*, 2002, p. 41):

> ... many of the secondary meanings of *per* explicitly refer to motion: "to cross a space," "to reach a goal," "to go outside." The implication of risk present in "peril" is evident in the gothic kin of *per* (in which the P becomes F): ferm, fare, fear, ferry ... to go out, to cross or to wander.

Going outside, ferrying back and forth between inner realities and outer realities instead of staying put and staying the same, forces the observer "to participate, to share an experience that ... addresses, like architecture, the entire body, its presence in time and space" (Careri *et al.*, 2002, p. 138). The one who walks captures the "changes in the direction of the winds, in temperature, in sounds" in the shifting landscape and cityscape "*as the measure of the world*" (Careri *et al.*, 2002, p. 148). The space and time of experience measure us. "The path," Careri says, "unwinds amidst snares and dangers, provoking a strong state of apprehension in the person walking," in both senses of apprehension: apprehension as "feeling fear" and apprehension as "grasping" or "learning" (Careri *et al.*, 2002, p. 82).

The places of learning that we have explored so far seem to pose the questions: Are we up to it? Are we up to the trial of experience, to walking the spaces of difference between? Are we up to putting who we think we are at risk by putting ourselves in relation to outside others, the very others who we have used through our fantasies of them to create a sense of ourselves?

I believe that the anomalous places of learning we have considered answer the first question with a resounding "yes!" — and that is part of their attraction for me as an educator. They declare that we *are* up to it. We must be up to it, and we do not have to be up to it alone. In fact, we cannot be up to it alone. Perhaps we can be up to it with others, without collapsing the irritating and productive differences between us that democracy requires. In various and often moving ways, the designs of the environments, experiences, and events that I am taking here to be places of learning acknowledge the perilous nature of the journey to the outside. They acknowledge the meaning of apprehension in both senses: feeling fear and grasping (as in learning).

Here, for example, Lawrence Halprin describes the creative process he brought to his design for the Franklin Delano Roosevelt Memorial in Washington, D.C. (Halprin, 1997, p. 7):

> I decided that only a slow-paced, personal experience, which would take place over sufficient time, could transmit the importance of this era to future generations. I wanted this Memorial to be an experiential history lesson that people could grasp on their own as they walked through it.

Revisiting Halprin's description of the public spaces and monuments that shaped his approach to designing this memorial through the notion of *per*, we can sense Halprin's appreciation for designs that acknowledge both the risk and the taxing nature of such a journey (Halprin, 1997, p. 7):

> They unfolded like voyages, based on movement along prescribed routes; their entrances were welcoming and signified importance; and pathways led onward from the special gateways in linear progressions. At each site, there were also stopping places along the way, which allowed for time to contemplate or mediate on experiences felt along the route.

> The stops on my favorite memorial pathways always came naturally. They were associated with views, events, sculptural objects, places to sit, and magnificent landforms. There was always something with which to interact physically, emotionally, intellectually, or spiritually. These processional paths always offered variations in pace through their design, yet there was always a consistent sense of physical and emotional choreography. Visitors were drawn on through a sequence of experiences … some calm, some intense, and there was a pervasive sense of drama. At the end of such experiences, I felt that in a profound way I emerged deeply changed. I felt that I had come through a focused slice of life that affected me intensely and emotionally.

A pervasive sense of drama … the experience of being drawn on through … profound and deep self-change … intense, emotional, affecting: What is it about the journey to the outside that makes it so perilous? What is tested so dramatically when we put our knowledges and our selves in relation? What is so risky about learning?

Krzysztof Wodiczko's communicative instruments and interrogative designs offer similar gestures of acknowledgment and accommodation aimed at alleviating the peril and protecting the excitement of going outside. He speaks of his designs as articulating the "stranger's pain in survival" and the pain and the triumph of surviving as an other, an immigrant, alien, or refugee in a city that is not one's own. He goes so far as to compare his designs to bandages — the oldest and most common articulation of "pain in survival" (Wodiczko, 1999, p. 10):

> A bandage covers and treats a wound while at the same time exposing its presence. Its presence signifies both the experience of pain and the hope of recovery.… Could we invent a bandage that would communicate, interrogate, and articulate the circumstances and the experience of the injury? Could such a transformed bandage address the ills of the outside world as perceived by the wounded? To see the world as seen by the wound!

Wodiczko designed what he called the mouthpiece or the *Porte-Parole* as a way of addressing such questions. The mouthpiece is an electronic device that fits, ambiguously and even humorously, like a bandage or a gag over the mouth. In the center and in front of the speaker's mouth is a small video monitor and loudspeakers. These "'replace' the immigrant's actual act of speech with the moving image of the immigrant's lips and the sound of the immigrant's voice" (Wodiczko, 1999, p. 118) as the device "speaks" prerecorded stories, statements, questions, and answers. The wearer can quickly cue up and play the prerecordings in response to encounters with others.

The performers' or speakers' process of choosing, recalling, articulating, and editing their speakings in anticipation of their performances for others is, for Wodiczko, as important to the psychological, political, and artistic meanings of the device as are any public appearances with it or the social interactions it might provoke. Wodiczko envisioned "official events and symbolic environments" as the best situations for using the mouthpiece, because (Wodiczko, 1999, p. 120):

…they are the situations where immigrants are least expected….

Exposing their own disintegration and displaced identity, they provoke and inspire the larger process of the disruption of identities among non-immigrants. They may spread the communicable (contagious) process of the exploration of one's own strangeness. They may help create new links and affinities between immigrants and nonimmigrants on the basis of the recognition of their common strangeness.

Wodiczko thus takes the line that divides and separates, such as a stranger's silence, difference, inability to speak the language, or a painful memory unknown to the nonimmigrants around them, and gives it dimensionality. He gives it shape and substance in the form of a metaphorical gag or bandage ... or could it be one of those facemasks intended to stop the spread of contagion? By making the gag speak and the facemask communicable, he transforms the line that severs into a space or place that connects. By allowing the stranger the opportunity to thoughtfully and artistically shape her stories and then call them up at the push of a button, the mouthpiece bandages the wounds of misunderstanding and silencing and alleviates the exhausting effort of having to repeatedly explain oneself. The mouthpiece, in other words, offers itself as an aide to those others who risk the perils of the journey into spaces and places that are not "their own."

The outside, the outside other, the different other, are problems for us because they bring us up against our limits. Going outside and encountering different others means facing over and over, Jessica Benjamin says, the fact of dependency on others, on events, and on a natural environment outside our control. Whether we want to or not, she says, "merely by living in this world, we are exposed to … the *different* others who …. in their mere existence as separate human beings reflect our lack of control" (Benjamin, 1998, p. 95).

Beyond that, going outside we risk finding out that the others are not who we thought they were, are not the image we have constructed of them, are not who we want them to be or hate them to be or need them to be so that we can continue to be who we think *we* are. Going outside to encounter others whose differences survive our attempts to deny, change, assimilate, demean, or control them creates its own possibilities for the self. The different others who refuse to become like us or to be erased by our fantasies of who they are embody the potential for our own self change. That different other is what Benjamin calls a *productive irritation*.

So, going outside is perilous because it threatens my identity. It threatens who I think I am. The "I" who goes outside might get lost, or, as James Baldwin put it in "A Talk to Teachers," in which he spoke about being addressed as a "nigger" (Baldwin, 1963/1988, p. 8):

> If I am not what I've been told I am, then it means you're not who you thought you were either. And that is the crisis.

That crisis is also the crisis of learning. In order to learn something new, as in previously unthought, we must lose that part of ourselves whose identity depends on not thinking that thought. We must lose that part that depends on not being the kind of person who entertains such thoughts or understands such thoughts or who finds pleasure in such thoughts. We must lose that self that is predicated on not being that kind of person who gets caught up with the knowledges of "those other people."

The crisis of learning, then, is that moment of letting go of a former sense of self in order to re-identify with an emerging and different self that is still in transition. It is that moment in which what will emerge from transition is still in the making and as yet unclear. In the crisis that is learning, I am suspended in the space between losing myself and finding myself caught up with different knowledges and other people. In the moment of learning, I am simultaneously me and not me.

Pedagogies That Both Facilitate and Alleviate the Crisis of Learning

Winnicott recognized that the transitional space of learning not only is a source of creativity but can also be the source of a terrifying anxiety. When fear or anxieties are too great to allow us a positive experience of the paradox of being simultaneously in difference and in relation, Winnicott says, we are unable to act creatively. Instead, we often comply with the people or discourses that dominate and threaten to overwhelm. Like pedagogy, as pedagogy, the designed spaces and times that we have been looking at here set out to both facilitate and alleviate the peril of putting self in relation.

Halprin's memorial to Roosevelt provides resting places and places of contemplation, soothing waterfalls, and scenic vistas. Wodiczko's communicative instruments provide aliens, strangers, immigrants, and teenagers with the means to negotiate the terms of "going outside" and being in relation. The *Alien Staff* and the mouthpiece give their users the option of speaking directly to an interlocutor or playing a prerecorded story or presentation of self. The *Dis-Armor* instrument allows the speaker to address others while facing the opposite direction or to navigate through public space in a way that makes being looked at an act of social and cultural critique. Maya Lin's work memorializes traumatic histories but does so through metaphor and abstraction, thus sparing us their literal repetition. The permanent exhibit at the U.S. Holocaust Memorial Museum stages our encounters with its representation of the Holocaust through an emotional and intellectual choreography that never requires us to identify as victim, perpetrator, or bystander. Thus, it refuses to reinscribe and present us yet again with the very positions that made the Holocaust possible and that would perpetrate, in another form, its very dynamics of relationality.

Being in relation and the anxiety it raises, says Benjamin, results in peace (the negotiation of difference) or war (the struggle to triumph over and annihilate that difference). For a negotiation of difference to be possible, according to Benjamin, we must be able to see the other as simultaneously outside of our control and non-threatening. One of the many problems of domination enforced by violence is that it intrinsically prevents us from seeing others who are outside our control as non-threatening.

How, in a time when domination is being enforced by violence, can we embrace a view of pedagogy that equates learning with the breaking up of our identities, the suspension of who we think we are, and an opening up to the outside other — especially those outside others whom we have used as repositories for what we have repudiated about ourselves? Especially those others who are threatening to enforce domination by violence in my name? Or those others who seek to enforce domination in *their* own names by doing violence to *me*? But, this is exactly what these designs, as civic pedagogies, ask of us. They ask us to suspend who we think we are and to open to outside others as a means of converting difference from the threat that leads to violent enforcement of domination to the productive irritation that alters both "us" and "them."

These anomalous places of learning set out to put their visitors, users, and students in relation to history, to the present, and to others in ways that connect "occasionally losing oneself" not with danger but with the opportunity and occasion for inventing new forms of nonviolent (even if conflicted) association with each other. Maya Lin's Vietnam Veterans Memorial and Civil Rights Memorial and the U.S. Holocaust Memorial Museum's permanent exhibit strive to connect learning about traumatic historical events with public spaces that are sources of more life not less life, more association not more separation, more reflection and meetings around tables. They strive to create places that are places to go on from. Wodiczko's communicative instruments seek to connect exclusion and superiority with useful, bearable, even pleasurable difference. His designs invite from their users playful, sometimes humorous responses to serious social and cultural issues. Shimon Attie's and Wodiczko's public projections connect the silence of public monuments and spaces that were at one time sites of violence or silent witnesses to violent events with the contemporary voices of the human witnesses whose lives were shaped by those events and whose speakings and actions now shape the future.

Pedagogy as Productive Conflict

Anna Deavere Smith's theatrical performances invite her audiences into relation with violence and rage but in terms that transform both into potentially productive conflict. As pedagogy, they attempt to put the radical separation that is violence into relation with the simultaneous separation and connection that represent productive irritation. To do that, Smith offers herself as connective tissue. She dares to picture a bringing together, in one body, of the adversaries, victims, eyewitnesses, and observers of the violent events of the Los Angeles uprisings and the riots in Crown Heights. According to the Public Broadcasting System (PBS) website featuring Smith's *Twilight: Los Angeles* (http://www.pbs.org/wnet/stageonscreen/twilight/twilight.html), she figuratively embodies adversaries, victims, eyewitnesses, and observers who "have never stood within the same four walls, let alone spoken to each other."

Doing so, Smith asks her audiences to picture what Benjamin calls a "new ground for a self that would live without identity." Such a new ground is possible, Benjamin argues, because "self does not equal identity" (Benjamin, 1988, p. 104). The self is capable of much more than identity. Smith, we might say, stages her performances on that new ground. She stands in the space between realities that are in conflict without losing any of them (Bromberg, quoted in Benjamin, 1988, p. 106). In that space, she replaces (violent) exclusions of that which her interviewees hate, fear, or desire too much with internal conflict. Her performance gives body to selves with the "growing ability to call all those voices 'I,' to disidentify with any one of them as the whole story" (Rivera, quoted in Benjamin, 1988, p. 106). Grounding one's self in the space between self and others might activate the self's potential to tolerate opposing attitudes toward self and others, to tolerate "ambivalence, being able to feel both love and hate toward the same object" (Benjamin, 1988, p. 105) — not in a synthesis of love and hate so that we can say we have triumphed over hate but, rather, in a way that means that hate can be borne, inside, and not exported as violence to the outside (Benjamin, 1998, p. 105).

In *Twilight: Los Angeles*, one of Smith's interviewees is Mrs. Young-Soon Han, a former liquor-store owner. Her store was one of the 90% of the South Central Korean-owned stores that were destroyed in the riots. Smith says of her interview with Mrs. Han: "I actually think that what she says is the most sophisticated thing I have come across about race in this country." I believe it is possible to read Mrs. Han's interview as one woman's struggle to articulate a self capable of "being able to feel both love and hate toward the same object," capable of the internal conflict that allows her to tolerate opposing attitudes toward self and others. I believe this may be the "sophistication" that Smith senses in Mrs. Han's interview.

That interview begins with Mrs. Han's account of feeling betrayed by the Los Angeles Police Department, after which she continues:

> Koreans are completely left out of this society and we are nothing, nothing.... Is it because we are Korean? Is it because we have no politician? Is it because we don't speak good English?

> We didn't qualify for medical treatment, no food stamps, no GR, no welfare, anything. Many African Americans who never worked get minimum amount of money to survive. We didn't get any. Because we have a car and a house and we are high tech. Where do I find justice, OK?...

> They were having a party ... they celebrated, all of South Central, all churches. Finally justice has done in this society ... they got their rights by destroying innocent Korean merchants, and I wonder if that is really justice for them to get their rights in that way. I was swallowing the ... bitterness. Sitting here alone and watching them. They became all hilarious.

> But I was happy for them, I was glad for them, at least they got something back, OK?... They fought for their rights for over two centuries and maybe because of their sacrifice other minorities, Hispanics, Asian, we won't suffer more in the mainstream. That's why I understand. I have a lot of sympathy and understanding for them. That is why I have mixed feeling about the verdict. But I wish I could be part of their joyment. I wish that I could live together with black people. But after the riot there's too much difference. The fire is still there ... it can burst out any time.

Smith concludes the videotape version of *Twilight: Los Angeles* with her portrayal of a young man identified as "Twilight Bey, activist" and whose name gives the production its title. He says that his homeboys think his ideas are before his time, such as his idea for the gang truce that he proposed in 1988 but which did not get "made realistic" until 1992. Says Bey:

And so sometimes I feel as though I'm stuck in limbo the way the sun is stuck between night and day in the twilight hours. I'm in an area not many people exist ... and then relative to my complexion, I am a dark individual ... and with me being stuck in limbo, I see the darkness as myself and I see the light as the knowledge and wisdom of the world and the understanding of others. And I know that in order for me to be a true human being I cannot dwell in darkness. I cannot forever dwell in the idea of identifying with those like me and understanding only me and mine. And so twilight is that time between day and night. Limbo. I call it limbo.

In an interview on the PBS website about her work, Smith says that she hopes it leads audiences to realize "you think you knew that story but actually you didn't and why didn't you? Because you didn't know *her* and you didn't know *him*.... Did we come out with some answer? No, but we're in the middle of the operation and the least we can do is get some people around the body that is ailing" (http://www.pbs.org/wnet/stageonscreen/twilight/twilight.html).

Reading Phillips side by side with Smith's pedagogical theater, we might say that, through the experience of *Twilight: Los Angeles* or *Fires in the Mirror,* a person might "rediscover an appetite for talking and for listening and for disagreement." Which is, according to Phillips, "an appetite for democracy" (Phillips, 2002, p. 12). This is a self, Phillips says, who would be able to bear to listen to what other people have to say (Phillips, 2002, p. xiii). Inner qualities and capabilities such as these are not needed simply to alleviate individuals' anxieties about transitional space as the space of relation between self and other; they are the "very condition of democracy's existence" (Phillips, 2002, p. 11).

The whole idea of democracy, says Phillips, the whole idea of "extending effective political power to more and more people ... turns the world upside down" because it makes "new kinds of association between people both possible and necessary" (Phillips, 2002, p. 25). Once hierarchy becomes a matter of negotiation rather than divine or other kinds of "natural" rights, people have to put themselves in relation in ways they never had to before. "We," "them," and hierarchies still exist in a democracy, Phillips explains, but instead of being imposed through authoritarian order they are drawn through conflict and disagreement. Democracy is not the absence of oppression and violence. It is the presence of institutions that limit and contest oppression and violence. Democracy, he says, requires wildly inventive practices, experiences, spaces, artifacts, and personal and interpersonal skills and appetites that are capable of moving competing values out of violence and into conflict. It must do that in ways that do not guarantee or presume to know the outcome in advance. Democracy requires forms of public space, social encounters, and civic pedagogies that keep the future of associations, conflicts, inventions, and new forms of self and other open and undecided (Phillips, 2002, pp. 9–14).

This is because democracy is the absence of the superordinate expert. There can be no one in a democracy that is presumed to be "tuned in to the real or true nature of things (as a dictator would claim to be) because there is deemed to be no real, or true, or absolute foundation of society" (Phillips, 2002, p. 22). Authoritarian order loves the one who is supposed to know, because what he knows suppresses conflict. By telling us the "truth" about ourselves, "he can dispel the rival truths" (Phillips, 2002, pp. 13–14). Instead of having to stand between realities, instead of bearing internal conflict, instead of tolerating opposing attitudes within ourselves about others and ourselves, through the super ordinate expert, "we can, simply, attain a superiority of knowledge" (Phillips, 2002, p. 14).

Authoritarian order, the authorized answer, preempts conflict, and a superiority of knowledge preempts pedagogies that are for knowledge in the making. Violence, Phillips says, "can be the attempt to make disagreement disappear" (Phillips, 2002, p. 16). It can also be the attempt to make uncertainty disappear, and, when it is, disagreement itself becomes a solution to violence (Phillips, 2002, p. 16).

Pedagogy's Hinge as an Armature for Democracy

Lin's and the THINK team's walkable pathways along the line that divides and severs, Smith's performances that "confer some version of equal status on the conflictual voices that compose and decompose" (Phillips, 2002, p. 17) herself as performer and her audiences as Americans, Wodiczko's instruments that give dimension and materiality to the space of difference between, Attie's projections that put past and present in intimate relation, and the U.S. Holocaust Memorial Museum's permanent exhibit, which refuses to magically transcend the limits of teaching and knowing — these are what pedagogy looks like in practice when it refuses to suppress conflict or uncertainty by imposing a superiority of knowledge or an authoritarian order.

We might see each of these learning experiences, environments, and events as a kind of armature. In sculpture, armature is the framework that serves as a core for clay as it is being shaped. In biology, armature is the name given to a covering or structure like the shell of a turtle that protects the softer, vulnerable tissues inside. In various ways, the designs we have looked at act as the armature for social and cultural change. They act as a framework that protects as their users "go outside," and they provide supports for standing between realities and for being in transition during the time that the old self is lost and the new self is in the making.

This brings us back to the paradox at the heart of pedagogy. If teaching is about thinking and not about complying with the one who holds the superordinate knowledge, if thinking is an encounter with the unthought, then for pedagogy to put us in relation with each other in ways we have never been before, for pedagogy to be a democratic civic pedagogy, it must create places in which to think about "we" without knowing already who "we" are. It must keep the future of what our engagements with those places make of us open and undecided.

The beauty of the THINK design for Lower Manhattan is that it dares to respond to a past, a present, and a future that we still do not know how to think about. It dares to propose a place to go on from without knowing already where we are going and without presuming to know in advance where we should go. It dares to imagine a building plan capable of holding the paradox of democracy and making the power of that paradox available to us. For Muschamp, the beauty of THINK's proposed building as matrix is that it keeps open the future of the building's program and its uses. "The building's program," he says, "is not locked into a particular set of uses, so it can evolve" (Muschamp, 2003a, p. 1). The plan proposes to hold within its framework a changing juxtaposition of buildings and spaces designed by different architects and responding contemporaneously to economic, social, cultural, and urban forces in the making. According to Muschamp (2003a, p. 1), this makes it sufficiently flexible to:

> ...include, in institutional form, the educational process that has been unfolding globally for the last 17 months, namely, a complex pattern of actions undertaken by individuals and groups around the world who seek to comprehend the deeper historical meanings of 9/11. This pattern has become a phenomenon in itself.... It recalls an idea that in the 20th century was called the open university or the museum without walls: a network of learning, a free-floating space open 24/7 and accessible to all. The price of admission is curiosity, periodically boosted by the desire to survive.

This global network of learning was marked by an ongoing exchange of intellectual, emotional, aesthetic, political, educational, military, and ritual-based efforts to respond to the events surrounding 9/11. Efforts to both interpret and construct the broader contexts, histories, and meanings of 9/11, Muschamp implies, have constituted an adventure in global public education. The design process for rebuilding Lower Manhattan has become an adventure in public education, as well. "Last year," Muschamp recalls, "many New Yorkers learned what a building program is. People learned to recognize retrograde architectural aesthetics as a byproduct of cultural isolationism. They learned how to derail an official design process that was headed toward disgrace" (Muschamp, 2003a, p. 1). In the process, "the public has, in effect, created the program for Ground Zero. It has created a school." Also, he continues, "THINK has created a schoolhouse: an open, flexible framework to support the pursuit of ideas. The framework itself ... is an eloquent statement of the values that should guide that pursuit." Part of what this design says so eloquently, Muschamp concludes, is "that we can do even better than retaliate against attack by enemies." We can, Muschamp implies, use this building as a pedagogical matrix in the making — a vehicle for moving us into new associations with our selves and with our others.

What might we, as educators, make of Muschamp's reading of the THINK design? What does such a reading make of pedagogy? If the soaring, lattice-like structures that form the heart of this design are indeed frameworks to support the pursuit of ideas, what constitutes its pedagogical pivot place? What, or who, teaches there? What do such structures "know?"

If this design states values that should guide the pursuit of ideas, we might then say that this design formulates its pedagogical pivot place as a *guide* — a guide for the pursuit of the unthought. But, as guides go, this one is certainly surprising and maybe even a bit troubling, because this guide admits that it does not know where it is taking us. It admits (indeed, it celebrates) that it cannot know beforehand what forms this city's public spaces should take. It does not even desire such knowledge. Yet, this building guides us. It takes responsibility for "filling" its pedagogical pivot place, for stepping into that place of the teacher and offering guidance, but simultaneously and paradoxically it also empties the pivotal place of the guide who would have a superiority of knowledge. As designers, teachers, citizens of New York City, American or global citizens, no one of us, no group of us, possesses superordinate knowledge about who we are and therefore what we will want and what we will need. This guide cannot, and wills not to, direct us to a place it has already decided for us and which therefore already decides "us."

Yet, the pedagogical pivot-place-as-guide of this design points out a direction by seeming to say:

> Come up here and make something of this space. This armature will hold open a space for you to be in the making. It will hold open the possibility of unfolding time through innovation rather than through prediction. This armature will push back on physical forces — such as gravity and wind — and keep this vertical space open for your use. But, there are other forces, both inside ourselves and outside, that seek to yet again collapse this space between and turn it into a line that divides and severs, foreclosing the future in the name of a superordinate knowledge about what that future should be or already is. In the face of those forces, this armature will also hold open the future by inviting you into the kind of conflict that redraws the boundaries of who you think you are and who you think they are, leading to associations and exchanges that we cannot even imagine from here.

This, then, would be the genius of this building's pedagogical design as civic pedagogy — namely, that it envisions a cultural fabric woven out of the most resilient (as in most flexible and most responsive) material: the frayed edges of the social identities that compose it.

Pedagogy, Democracy, and Teachers' Free Associations

The anomalous pedagogical designs we have looked at so far have invited us into spaces between education and architecture, education and performance, education and sculpture, education and public exhibitions and events, education and media. We have freely associated there with architects, artists, performers, media producers, industrial designers, inventors, and sculptors. In these spaces between, the questions of how to teach and what to teach are not already legislated. Here, cognition is merely one among many ways of learning. Here, we are outside of the range of the voice of the superordinate educational expert and its preemptive speech about what teaching and learning really, finally, scientifically, are. The nonrational, nonlinguistic, prelinguistic spaces and times at the frontiers of the cognitive are not empty, meaningless, irrational, irrelevant, or dangerous to teaching and learning. They are, rather, filled with other knowledges and practices that make all sorts of anomalous pedagogies thinkable and intelligible.

We could now step back inside education to ask: What might our encounters with the pedagogical pivot points in the places of learning we have looked at mean to us inside the places of public education? Can we step back inside without leaving the spaces between that these designs have opened up? Can we step back inside without leaving these spaces where we do not know, already, what is going to happen here — spaces where there is a chance that I might learn something?

I wonder if the political, economic, ideological, and logistical difficulties of freely associating with all sorts of anomalous places of learning outside of education's borders might be deskilling (us) educators as democrats. I wonder what might happen to how we teach if we allowed ourselves, if we demanded the resources and the democratic right, to associate freely as educators and in the name of educational research and practice, with the pedagogical pivot places now being created by architects, documentary filmmakers, performers, artists, user experience researchers, museum exhibition designers, and industrial engineers. I wonder what might happen to how we teach if we designed pedagogies for ourselves that put us, as educators, in relation to education's outside — if we broke up closed circuits of exchange of ideas, identities, and practices inside education. What might happen, for example, if we held public design charrettes that invited the future of our practice to unfold through innovation rather than through prediction, that invited the Anna Deavere Smiths, Krzysztof Wodiczkos, Maya Lins, Herbert Muschamps, Shimon Atties, and many others to reimagine pedagogy in and as public space? What might happen to public schooling if we held school and teacher education inside those public charrettes? I wonder what new social, political, and professional identities we might construct for ourselves as teachers out of so freely associating.

5

The U.S. Holocaust Memorial Museum as a Scene of Pedagogical Address

Soon after it opened to the public in 1993, the U.S. Holocaust Memorial Museum was hailed as "one of the late twentieth century's most profound architectural statements." It houses a permanent exhibit that Leon Wieseltier has called a "pedagogical masterpiece"; he declared that "the building itself teaches" (Wieseltier, 1995, p. 20). Under any circumstances, the making of profound architectural statements and the achievement of pedagogical masterpieces are no small feats, but the accomplishments of the architect and exhibit designers of the U.S. Holocaust Memorial Museum seem all the more profound given the philosophical and pedagogical problems that challenge any attempt to teach or memorialize the Holocaust.

In a recent analysis of the museum, Adrian Dannatt, an architectural critic, listed some of those challenges. How might exhibit designers "elucidate without lapsing into entertainment?" How might they "give form to the act of memory?" How might their designs hold the lack, the absence, of millions of European Jewry even as the museum is filled by artifacts, text, photographs, and films (Dannatt, 1995, p. 6)?

The challenges for teachers and students of "traumatic historical events" are similar to those faced by the museum's designers. Teaching and representing traumatic histories such as the Holocaust or the Middle Passage brings educators up against the limits of our theories and practices concerning pedagogy, curriculum, and the roles of dialogue, empathy, and understanding in teaching about and across social and cultural difference.

If, as Michael Berenbaum asserts, "children have to learn about the untrust-worthiness of the world as they learn to trust the world," how might teach-ers teach distrust (Goldberg, 1997, p. 319)? Such questions have become more urgent in the wake of recent anniversaries of events connected with the Holocaust, the wars in Bosnia and Kosovo, the events of September 11, 2001, the Iraq war, and hate crimes in the United States. Just how should teacher educators respond to mandates such as the Wisconsin Department of Public Instruction's requirement that student teachers learn about sla-very, genocides, and the Holocaust?

As a concrete materialization of a particular pedagogical approach, the permanent exhibit of the U.S. Holocaust Memorial Museum provides a rich context for studying key challenges and opportunities involved in teaching the Holocaust in particular, and in teaching about and across social and cultural difference in general. An analysis of specific moments and scenes of pedagogical address in the museum's permanent exhibit pro-vides strong support for the following assertion: The power of the address of the pedagogy of this museum lies in its indeterminacy. This museum, with its primary objective of education, paradoxically embraces the ways that histories of the Holocaust throw the pedagogical relation between teacher and student into crisis. I suspect that the usefulness of the pedagogy of the Holocaust museum to teachers lies in the ways that it embraces the dilemmas and impossibilities that confront teachers and witnesses of the Holocaust. Far from leading to paralysis or despair, an analysis of the peda-gogical address of this museum reveals concrete instances of how the para-doxes of teaching and learning can be productive and can assist teachers and students in accessing moral imperatives without absolutes.

The Pedagogical Problem

In cultural studies, literary criticism, and philosophy, scholars have debated theoretical aspects of the seemingly insurmountable dilemmas faced by designers of the permanent exhibit. Some argue that the Holo-caust exceeds representation and is unrepresentable (Linenthal, 1995). Others argue that the Holocaust exceeds understanding and is unteachable (Felman & Laub, 1992; Copjec, 1996). According to some teachers of the Holocaust, such as Claude Lanzmann, director of the film *Shoah*, any attempt to "understand" the Holocaust is "obscene" (Lanzmann, 1990). Writing about the production of *Shoah*, Lanzmann declares that the ques-tion "Why have the Jews been killed?" reveals right away its obscenity. He writes: "…not to understand was my iron law during all the eleven years of the production of *Shoah*. … [It was] the only way to not turn away from a reality which is literally blinding" (Lanzmann, 1990, p. 279).

A teacher of literary responses to the Holocaust, Shoshana Felman argues that the paradox of knowledge is that there are only misunder-standings. The testimonies contained within the museum do not consist of "understandings" of the Holocaust; rather, they are "bits and pieces of a memory that has been overwhelmed by occurrences that have not settled into understanding or remembrance, acts that cannot be construed as knowledge nor assimilated into full cognition, events in excess of our frames of reference" (Felman, 1995, p. 16). Yet, representations, memorials, museums, websites, and videotaped testimonies of the Holocaust proliferate. No longer rare, Holocaust memorials and museums "form a specific genre of architecture … indeed there may even be a certain world-weary resistance to their proliferation" (Dannatt, 1995, p. 5). As Wieseltier observed, the Holocaust is the "subject of astonishing mass curiosity; it doesn't seem to diminish with the years, it gets larger" (Wieseltier, 1993, p. 19):

> This is affecting, and this is revolting. It certainly makes the fear that the Holocaust will be forgotten seem faintly ridiculous. And worse, it ensures that if the Holocaust is forgotten, or if it is pushed to the peripheries of consciousness and culture, then it will be partly owing to the memorials themselves, which will have made the horror familiar and thereby robbed it of its power to shock and to disrupt…. Too little memory dishonors the catastrophe, but so does too much memory. In the contemplation of the death camps, we must be strangers, and if we are not strangers, if the names of the killers and the places of the killing and the numbers of the killed fall easily from our tongues, then we are not remembering to remember, but remembering to forget.

The proliferation of efforts to represent the unrepresentable and to understand that which exceeds all frames of cognition threatens to trivialize.

The debates over Roberto Benigni's film *Life Is Beautiful* put such tensions in stark relief. The film has been criticized for offering up "Holocaust lite," or *Holokitch*. Art Speigelman, creator of *MAUS*, commented in a National Public Radio (NPR) interview that *Life Is Beautiful* contributes to the Zeitgeist shift toward using the Holocaust with impunity as a metaphor. Speigelman concedes that he, too, used metaphors in *MAUS*, his Pulitzer Prize winning "comic book" about the Holocaust, but he used the metaphors to try to approach the actualities that can never be met directly or finally: "I see that as a rather different project than taking the Holocaust and using it as a metaphor for a bummer" (Speigelman, 1999).

Arguments, debates, and analyses about the politics of representation, the social construction of knowledge, the space of difference between history and memory, or the uses of metaphor to gesture toward the unspeakable could hardly remain abstract or academic during the design of the museum exhibits. In fact, these issues and dilemmas were integral to the design of the museum (Linenthal, 1995) which is what, for me as an educator, makes my own encounter with the U.S. Holocaust Memorial Museum so productive. In its architecture and in the design of the permanent exhibit, this museum materializes the ongoing social and cultural struggle about if, how, and why to represent the Holocaust: "It is from these very issues that the architecture of the museum stems" (Dannatt, 1995, p. 5).

The Permanent Exhibit

How, then, have the architects and exhibit designers addressed these pedagogical issues? The permanent exhibit of the museum has a potential of five hours of reading material and an additional five hours of audiovisual material. It presents artifacts, documents, poetry, letters, drawings, narrational text, film, photographs, and video. The visitors' routes through the permanent exhibit follow a corkscrew pattern from the fourth floor to the third and then to the second floor using both wings of the building. Visitors cross from one wing to the other through steel-framed glass bridges suggestive of both camp observation systems and ghetto walkways. The visitor's experience of the exhibit is made up not only of artifacts and documents but also of space, time, and a sequential montage of elements.

With characteristics such as these one could almost call the permanent exhibit a multimedia exhibit, but that would be like calling Speigelman's *MAUS* simply a comic book. The brilliant cultural achievement of *MAUS* lies in the ways Speigelman explodes conventions and banalities of representation by exploding the received form, style, and structure of the comic book itself. Similarly, designers of the permanent exhibit set out to shatter conventions of pedagogy by refusing the obscenity of presuming to know or to understand the Holocaust.

As reported in the official description of the museum, it was the view of the designers of the museum that the educational work of this museum must take place in the *spaces of difference* between history and memory, the concrete and the abstract, the unique and the universal. Only by locating its pedagogical address in such spaces between could the museum's educational mission be realized. Michael Sorkin writes (Sorkin, 1993, p. 74):

> Perhaps the only way to approach the unrepresentable is to represent the impossibility of representing it, turning representation inside out to confront this horrific sublime.

In his architectural critique, Dannatt describes the museum's design as forming a "grammar of history," but, as we saw in Chapter 3, it is a peculiar grammar with deliberate ambiguity, confused and oblique metaphors, and overlapping levels of signification (Dannatt, 1995, p. 6). If, as Herbert Muschamp writes in his review of the museum, "a place is a form of knowledge" (Muschamp, 1993, p. 22), what does such a place know? If, as Wieseltier writes, the building itself teaches, if the museum is a pedagogical masterpiece, then what is the genius of its pedagogy?

Refusing Narrative Closure

The terms of the permanent exhibit's pedagogical address to its student invite her not only into the activity of knowledge construction but also into the construction of knowledge from a particular social and political point of view. This makes "learning" not simply voluntary and idiosyncratic but relational. It makes learning an assumption of particular relations of self to self and between self, others, knowledge, and power. According to this perspective, not only do visitors experience the style and story of the exhibit but they also experience and respond to how the structure of address solicits a certain reading from them. The narrative structure and visual design of the exhibit, for example, construct and "speak from" a particular position within a constellation of meanings surrounding the Holocaust and Holocaust pedagogy. Not unlike the postal system, elements of the exhibit construct an address to or for the visitor. This address offers the visitor a "*structure*, a linguistic structure by which to relate himself to other human beings; a structure, therefore, in which meaning … can later be articulated (Felman, 1987, p. 114).

The pedagogical address of the permanent exhibit, therefore, invites its visitors into a relation. It articulates the relations of the objects in the museum among themselves and includes the visitor as one of the objects in the system. What makes the address of the exhibit "pedagogical," what a visitor "learns" from the terms of the exhibit's address, is to assume herself in relation to the symbolic constellation surrounding Holocaust history and memory. In other words, the visitor "learns" a relationship to Holocaust history and memory — a relationship into which meanings can later be articulated. The museum's pedagogy addresses students and teachers in ways that invite them into a highly particular symbolic constellation and, as a result, into the social relations articulated and inscribed in that constellation.

This reveals the analytical importance of the notion of pedagogical address. The terms of the exhibit's address to its visitors and the terms of its invitation into a relationship with Holocaust history and memory render certain meanings and relations possible and impossible, intelligible and unintelligible, within the symbolic constellation that it offers. The question "Who does this exhibit think you are?" underscores the assertion that to learn about the Holocaust in the terms set forth by the exhibit is to assume a relation within a system of meanings. Assuming a relation within a system of meanings is what permits the "learner" to relate symbolically to other humans.

Of course, no system of meanings can exhaust or contain all human relations, histories, and memories. Human experience and desire exceed any single system of meanings. All modes of address misfire one way or another. A student and a teacher never "are" the "who" that a pedagogical address thinks they are, and that brings us to the troubling scene of pedagogical address. How might a pedagogy address its students in ways that acknowledge and put into play the fact that the structure of relations being offered by any curriculum necessarily represses, denies, or ignores the very identities, ideas and events that would undo it?

The pedagogy of the U.S. Holocaust Memorial Museum acknowledges and makes that question pivotal to the design and educational approach of the permanent exhibit, and this is what saves its pedagogy from being a closed system of exchange. By embracing the impossibility and undesirability of offering its visitors a fixed or knowable address within the constellation of meanings surrounding the Holocaust, the pedagogy of the exhibit opens the door onto the possibility for something else. It opens the door to the possibility, the paradoxical possibility, of a narrative without closure. It opens the door, in other words, to what Felman calls an "interminable learning" (Felman, 1987, p. 88).

The pedagogy of the exhibit refuses narrative closure in at least two ways. First, it interrupts the logic of narrative structure throughout the exhibit, and, especially, it refuses to provide an "ending." Second, meta-communicative layers imposed upon the narrative structure break any illusions of narrative completeness or adequacy; in other words, the very narrative frame of the story being told is shattered by continual references to its own limits. It is shattered, that is, by self-referential gestures at the impossibility of its own project — the impossibility of narrating the Holocaust.

According to the exhibit catalog, the museum is a "narrative museum, because its display is organized along a story line" (Weinberg & Elieli, 1995, p. 17); yet, the official description of the exhibit takes pains to explain that this is not a "traditional history museum" — it is a "museum of a different kind." Part of that difference lies in the way it addresses visitors (Weinberg & Elieli, 1995, p. 19):

> In the process of becoming exposed to the Museum's exhibitions and activities, visitors … find themselves positioned between two poles: between the concrete and the abstract, the historical and the metaphoric, the unique and the universal. The tension and discourse between these poles is inherent in the essence of the Museum and its educational work. One can say that, at any single moment, the educational process is taking place in the space between one pole and the other. To preserve the overwhelming power of the concrete event and, at the same time, the symbolic, universal implications inherent in it, there should never be an attempt at resolving the tension between the poles.

In other words, the "story line" of the permanent exhibit is the line inscribed by visitors as they traverse the space *between* binaries, and how could it be otherwise? To address visitors in ways that invite them to take up positions at either one binary pole or the other would be to invite them to assume positions within the very configuration of relations that perpetrated the Holocaust: insider/outsider, us/them, human/inhuman, victim/perpetrator, Aryan/non-Aryan. On the other hand, to promote a story that resolves the tensions between the poles would be to promote what Adam Phillips calls the "misleading idea that we are all in search of completion" (Phillips, 1994, p. 122). Phillips continues:

> Bewitched by the notion of being complete, we become obsessed by notions of sameness and difference, by thoughts of what to include and what to reject in order to keep ourselves [and our stories] whole.

Phillips argues, however, that "there is no cure for multiple plots" (Phillips, 1994, p. 75).

As visitors walk through the "story" of this narrative museum, they are literally positioned in the spaces between video monitors, life-size photographs, displayed artifacts, text, and audio recordings. Even though the texts presented are arranged in roughly chronological order along a corkscrew path we do not read or hear or view a linear story line; rather, we are placed physically in the spaces between elements of the story. We are entwined with the story elements. From the spaces between there is no story line — only a three-dimensional competition for our attention. Every visitor to the exhibit will "traverse [their] own path, crossing previous lines of locomotion" (Dannatt, 1995, p. 14). No two paths or lines of attention compose the same story; indeed, the story of the narrative exhibit is never stated. Instead, there is a constant deferral of the story, a continual opening up of the space between resolved binary terms or resolved endings, knowings, or understandings. This is accomplished, in part, by repeated interruption of any single line of attention or of any single sequential development of a story line out of separate elements of the exhibit.

For example, while elements are grouped into themes and events such as "Nazi Propaganda" or "Resistance," no linear cause-and-effect explanations link these groups. Within each grouping, elements can be encountered in any order, as when visitors come upon groupings of elements labeled "Nazi Propaganda," "Nazi Society," and "Search for Refuge" simultaneously. Even within the groupings, relations between elements are seldom linear. On any given display panel, video testimonies or archival footage are not offered as direct illustrations of printed text, nor does the text explain the video. Their association is not one of illustration or explanation; rather, their association is topographical. Each element provides another facet, another perspective, another relation to the theme or event.

The display area labeled "To Safety" is one instance of this refusal of a single story line. The area addresses the events in which some Holocaust survivors were brought to "safety" in the United States. The video, photographs, narrational text, and artifacts each offer different perspectives from within the ambiguous space between the binary safety/danger. Despite the title of the display ("To Safety"), the various accounts of individuals' or groups' movements in the space between the poles of "safety" and "danger" are never unproblematically resolved in favor of "safety." A heroic narrative of escape or rescue is not allowed to manage the complicated relations between the elements of this grouping. For example, the first block of text reports that the U.S. Emergency Visitors' Visa Program was established to save "persons of exceptional merit" and "those of superior intellectual attainment." This is juxtaposed with text containing a quotation from Bertold Brecht: "I know, of course, it's simply luck that I've survived so many friends. But last night in a dream I heard those friends say of me: 'Survival of the fittest,' and I hated myself."

In another instance of interrupted narrative structure, visitors cross from one wing of the exhibit to another by passing along glass bridges. The present interrupts the exhibit's narration of the past: Daylight, the weather, the Washington Monument, the here and now of the nation's capitol break the exhibit's narrative, but not heroically and not even reassuringly as, simultaneously, the past interrupts the present. Inscribed on the glass walls of one bridge are the names of thousands of villages destroyed in the Holocaust. The names of obliterated villages interfere with the view of the Washington monument. They superimpose themselves onto the monument. History interrupts the present and any attempts to use contemporary narratives to resolve the lost stories of these villages.

Ironically, the narrative structure of the permanent exhibit is further interrupted by the narrational text itself. If the narrational text of the exhibit were spoken, it would have the vocal qualities of a very poor storyteller. The voice of the written text is deadpan, devoid of inflection, drama, or embellishment. It lacks any but the most colorless adjectives. For example: "These children's books were intended to indoctrinate young Germans in nationalism, love for Hitler, and obedience to his will. They include *The Poison Mushroom*, a collection of anti-Semitic stories, and *Read Along!*, an illustrated book of Nazi slogans." Or, for example: "Roma (gypsies) were subjected to official discrimination well before 1933. After Hitler took power, long held prejudices were fueled by Nazi racism, although no comprehensive anti-Roma law was ever passed." Or, "Before the war, Warsaw was the center of Jewish life in Poland and contained the greatest concentration of Jews in Europe. Soon after the German conquest on September 39, 1933, Warsaw's 375,000 Jews were required to wear white armbands with a blue Star of David. Jewish Council was appointed. The German authorities closed Jewish schools, confiscated Jewish owned property, and conscripted Jewish men...."

These are not stories nor are they explanations. The voice of the written text of the exhibit refuses to narrate and does not explain what it tells. The text fragments its telling of the Holocaust into roughly chronological bits. By disrupting and dislocating the "apparent but misleading unities" of a story line unified and made coherent and understandable by cause/effect, question/answer relations, the "breakage of [the text] enacts the breakage of the world" (Felman, 1995, p. 32).

Paraphrasing Phillips, it is the conscious intention not to produce an exemplary story that frees the conversation. The story lines that students of the exhibit traverse have multiple beginnings and middles and no knowable ends. It is this refusal of traditional forms of closure that distinguishes this exhibit's pedagogy from moral pedagogy (Phillips, 1988, p. 144).

Constant interruption of narrative structure is one way that the exhibit becomes a narrative without closure. Another way in which the exhibit refuses closure is that it repeatedly shatters its own narrative frame by making reference to its own limits. The exhibit gestures self-referentially at the impossibility of its own project of narrating the Holocaust.

For example, a three-story tower displays photographs taken between 1890 and 1941 in Eishishok, a small town in what is now Lithuania. The photographs describe a vibrant Jewish community that existed for 900 years. In two days in 1941, a *Schutzstaffel* (SS) mobile killing squad massacred the Jewish population. The design of this tower materializes the limits of teaching and knowing. Its construction makes it is physically impossible for visitors to view all of the photographs. The pedagogy of the tower's design, in other words, is one that actually withholds much of the "content material" of its curriculum. The staging of these photographs enacts a pedagogy confronted by a loss of knowability — a loss of mastery of the subject, a loss of closure. Just as it is physically impossible to see all of the photographs, it is impossible to recover and to know the obliterated history of this town.

Perhaps the most profound moment of metacommunication by this museum about the limits of its own pedagogy occurs at the "end" of the exhibition. Wieseltier (1993, p. 20) describes the last element encountered by visitors:

> Its exhibition ends in a Hall of remembrance, a six-sided classically proportioned chamber of limestone … seventy feet high, unencumbered by iconography….

> One of the achievements of the Holocaust Memorial Museum is that it leads its visitors directly from history to silence … the least that you can do, after seeing what you have just seen, is sit down and be still…. This, then, is the plot, the historical and spiritual sequence got right, of the infernal display on the Mall: memory, stiffened by history, then struck dumb.

> The museum is a pedagogical masterpiece.

What are we educators to make of this declaration that it is a pedagogical achievement, it is the historical plot got right, that visitors are struck dumb? What are we to make of Wieseltier's suggestion that the masterful pedagogical pivot place of this exhibition is a place of silence?

The profound pedagogical achievement of the refusals of narrative closure that lead up to this silence is that this final gesture of silence cannot be taken as, simply, silence. All that comes before the silence at the "end" of the permanent exhibit frames it in a way that makes of it a very particular silence. It is a silence that teaches what pedagogy can never speak. In the structuring of all that comes before this last element of the exhibit, it would be a willful "ignore-ance" to call this silence a form of nihilism. It cannot be read as a form of forgetting, nor can it be taken as a melodramatic moment of overwhelming sentimentalism, nor is it the silence of the overwhelmed witness or the patient good listener, and it is not the silence of self-reflection. Like the exhibit's refusals of narrative continuity and closure, the silence with which the visitor is met at the end of the exhibit, a silence that asks to be met in turn by silence, is a communicative act after all. It is an act of metacommunication. This silence is a metacommunicative refusal of the rules of narrative closure. It is a self-referential refusal to offer an ending.

This silence that metacommunicates marks the limits of pedagogy. It marks the limits of knowledge. It is the silence of "passing through our own answerlessness" (Felman, 1995, p. 53). It is the silence of the pedagogue who accepts that she or he does not, cannot, have the last word and who embraces the pedagogical power of not providing the last word.

The Permanent Exhibit as a Scene of Pedagogical Address

The narrative of this museum is a narrative without closure. It is an interrupted narrative that metacommunicates about its own limits and explodes conventions of pedagogy by falling silent at the very moment a conclusion is expected. If such a narrative is at the heart of this pedagogical masterpiece, then what does its refusal of closure through interruption and silence teach? To answer this question, though, would be to have the last word. To provide an answer for this question would be to provide closure, an ending to the exhibit's narrative, a meaning to the exhibit's ending. Such an answer would put an end to the educational project of the exhibit — a project that teaches only to the extent that a conclusion is never reached. To answer the question "What does the exhibit's final gesture of silence teach?" would be to participate in the obscenity of understanding.

This exhibit's pedagogy breaks from the address offered by many other Holocaust "curriculums." It does not create for us the virtual positions of victim, perpetrator, or bystander and then invite us to occupy those positions as a way of accessing understanding of the Holocaust, nor does it address us as witnesses to the Holocaust (after all, as students of the exhibit, we do not witness the Holocaust — we witness representations of the Holocaust). Rather, the pedagogy of the permanent exhibit addresses us as *implicated* — implicated not in the guilt of perpetrators, bystanders, or victims but rather implicated in an ongoing narrative in the making, implicated not as "responsible for" or "guilty of" but implicated as entangled, intertwined, twisted together, wrapped up with, involved in (Felman, 1995, p. 30):

> The witness is pursued, that is, at once compelled and bound by what, in the unexpected impact of the accident, is both incomprehensible and unforgettable. The accident does not let go: it is an accident from which the witness can no longer free himself.

The design of the exhibit materializes the dynamic in which knowledge of a traumatic event pursues the witness and the witness, in turn, pursues the traumatic event (Felman, 1995, p. 30). For example, one dominant structural motif throughout the exhibit positions video, artifacts, and photographs as reaching out toward the visitor, meeting the visitor, pressing toward the visitor, closing in as if in pursuit of the visitor. Yet, at another point in the sequential montage of the exhibit, a second structural motif causes text, video, and artifacts to recede from view. It is the visitor who must pursue the exhibit. The lighting throughout the exhibit contributes to this alternating invitation to pursue and to flee. Areas of palpable darkness interrupt areas illuminated by grainy light. Often, artifacts and text are displayed in near darkness, causing visitors to draw in very close, to lean in and make a deliberate decision to pursue, uncover, and recover what threatens to recede from view.

What the visitor must do with his experience of the museum cannot be prescribed. It cannot be written beforehand. That would be to take visitors out of the tense, volatile space of ongoing cultural production that exists *between* moral, political, or philosophical absolutes. It would be to position visitors instead in the very structure of relations that perpetrated the Holocaust — as occupying one or another moral, political, or philosophical absolute. Addressing visitors in the space between absolutes makes impossible any specification of how visitors should apply the metaphoric meaning of the Holocaust to their lives. At the same time, it is addressing visitors in the space between absolutes that opens up a mode of access to that imperative (Felman, 1995, p. 24). In these ways, the permanent exhibit constructs a pedagogical space that invites the visitor, as Felman puts it (Felman, 1995, p. 31), to...

> ...pursue the accident, to actively pursue its path and its direction through obscurity, through darkness, and through fragmentation, without quite grasping the full scope and meaning of its implications, without entirely foreseeing where the journey leads and what is the precise nature of its final destination.

Indeed, according to the museum's official description, the educational goal of the exhibit is to make it possible for the visitor to pursue the accident without knowing where it will lead, without knowing the precise nature of its final destination (Weinberg & Elieli, 1995, p. 19):

> The museum's educational responsibility is to help visitors apply the metaphoric meaning embedded in Holocaust history to their contemporary experience as individuals and as members of society.... This is indeed what the Museum is all about: creating an encounter between the visitor and this moral imperative.

Paradoxically, of course, the nature of the encounter between the visitor and this moral imperative cannot be specified.

If upon hearing the "news" of the Holocaust, as teachers and students, we cannot ground our responses in what we "know," then what might be the ground for responsibility? If the actions we might take in response to encountering the Holocaust are not to be articulated to *cognition*, then to what? When we read the museum's pedagogy as a scene of address rather than as an offering of security or of cognitive certainty, it becomes possible to imagine what Ernesto Laclau calls a "hero of a new type who has still not been entirely created by our culture" (Laclau, 1996, p. 123). That non-heroic hero is...

> ...a figure who is at the same time profoundly heroic and tragic, someone who, when confronted with Auschwitz, has the moral strength to admit the contingency of her own beliefs, instead of seeking refuge in religious or rationalistic myths.

Teaching Moral Imperatives without Absolutes: The Ringelblum Milk Can

Just how does the museum's pedagogical address open up access to the moral imperative that visitors apply their experience of the museum to their contemporary lives without specifying what the visitors *should* do? I am going to explore one more moment in the museum's mobilization of narrative, visual design, and point of view into its construction of a pedagogical address. It is a moment that inaugurates the psychic split between the self who is held hostage to the moral imperative of the museum and the self who walks away into the daylight. It is the moment of coming upon a particular artifact: the Ringelblum milk can.

Designers of the permanent exhibit write (Weinberg & Elieli, 1995, pp. 17, 108):

> The Ringelblum milk can is perhaps the Museum's most important historic artifact. Under the leadership of Emmanuel Ringelblum, a

university trained historian, several dozen writers, teachers, rabbis, and historians compiled an archive documenting life in the Warsaw ghetto.... On the eve of the final annihilation of the ghetto, Ringelblum buried all records and documents in metal containers and milk cans so they would be found after the war, after his death and the death of all other members of his historical society. So they would let the world know.... Ringelblum was shot by the Nazis in 1944; this can, one of those buried by Ringelblum and his colleagues, was discovered in 1950.

Perhaps this milk can is the museum's most important artifact because the scene of address that it stages also constitutes its pedagogical pivot place.

When I come upon the rusted milk can, I enter a scene of address that is a scene of relationality. Unlike the pile of shoes and broken eyeglasses, unlike the railroad car, unlike the clothing and bunk beds, the Ringelblum milk can exceeds the representational, and it performs an address. It is not simply an artifact that represents something elsewhere at some other time. It exists in the moment as an ongoing call. It is this call that inaugurates the "psychic split" that Muschamp claims this museum recreates with "excruciating fidelity." It is the psychic split that Muschamp says he experienced while visiting Dachau when he stood inside a gas chamber and then walked out again. Muschamp (1993, p. 32) writes:

> It is when you cross the threshold of that door that you grasp the reason for visiting Dachau. You walk out into daylight, but part of you does not leave. The doorway divides you. You feel lightheaded, as though you have broken the law, as indeed you have. Your passage through that door has violated the design. The room was not meant to be exited alive. This is a privileged moment. Not because you are free to walk out of the gas chamber, but because you are not. Because part of us remains behind, wondering how, since no one deserved to die here, we deserve to leave. A moral universe could arise from the imperative to answer the self we left behind.

According to Muschamp, the architecture of the museum avoids any literal representation of Dachau or any of the other death camps; nevertheless, he argues, it recreates with excruciating fidelity the psychic split that he experienced as he exited the gas chamber. In the description of his visit, Muschamp renders this split as a scene of address. The self that is left behind in the gas chamber addresses the self that is free to walk out: "No one deserved to die here. Why do you deserve to leave?" This question can be avoided, denied, repressed, or ignored, but it cannot be answered. It cannot, in other words, be escaped.

The museum is not the gas chamber at Dachau. We do not violate its design by exiting its doors. Nevertheless, its pedagogical address is designed to hold us hostage in another sense. It is designed to hold us hostage to the call, the moral imperative, the address from the other, which we cannot escape. This position of hostage is neither a paralyzing position of despair nor a heroic position of empowerment that enables me to assume the role of rescuer, and this address from the other that holds me hostage does not teach me prescribed responsibility; rather, it stages responsibility as an indeterminate and interminable labor of response. This labor of response can only take place in the space of difference between the self who is held hostage to an imperative and the self who is free to step out into the daylight.

The scene of address staged by this coming upon the milk can sets the stage for grasping how responsibility does not follow from understanding or knowledge. Instead, responsibility, Thomas Keenan argues, is the condition of a structure of address (Keenan, 1997, pp. 19–23). Paraphrasing Keenan, I come upon the milk can, and I become hostage to a structure of address for which there is no escape, no end. The contents of this artifact are addressed ... to me. I am the posterity for whom its contents were assembled and buried. And, yet, as Keenan declares, "there is nothing special about me, no preordained election nominates me for responsibility — no matter how irreplaceable, I could be (I am) anyone" (Keenan, 1997, p. 21). He continues: "There is a cry for help, addressed not to me in particular, not to anyone in particular, but to me as anyone — anyone can help" (Keenan, 1997, p. 22).

I, walking alongside others in the exhibit, turn a corner and enter this scene of address staged by the Ringelblum milk can. Suddenly, no matter how crowded this public space might be, I am alone. The address to me is a "public address with a strangely singular destination" (Keenan, 1997, p. 57). Alone, singular, and yet replaceable — alone because I am replaceable, a substitute for anyone and the one for whom anyone can substitute. Quoting Blanchot, Keenan continues: "I am the one whom anyone at all can replace ... but one for whom nonetheless there is no dispensation: I must answer to and for what I am not" (Keenan, 1997, p. 58). Keenan argues that, if I fail to identify or to acknowledge the address of the messages inside the milk can, this "in no way disqualifies me or indemnifies me — the cry ... insures that I remain in place, even if it is not 'my' place" (Keenan, 1997, p. 23). It is the call and not anything special or "heroic" about me that becomes the condition of my response.

Paraphrasing Keenan, I have not been preordained by the writers of this artifact's contents as the one for whom the messages are intended, nor do I assume responsibility by virtue of my virtues, much less my knowledge, my wisdom, or my experience. My responsibility is not constituted by anything in me, such as my interests, desires, compulsions, ideology, or educated ability to reference rules of ethics or democracy. I simply happen to be there, without deserving it (Keenan, 1997, p. 23).

How will I respond within the structure of the Ringelblum milk can's address? It is impossible to know or to understand the Holocaust fully or finally, so I cannot construct a response to the address of this "call" by successfully articulating what I know to what I do. Its address stages an impasse. I am the singular one addressed, yet I am the replaceable no one in particular who is addressed. Who, then, "takes" responsibility in response to the address? The moment of meeting the address of the call is not a moment of responsible decision making by one who "takes responsibility." There is no "taking" of responsibility. Keenan (1997, p. 32) argues:

> I do not respond or find myself obligated because some self precedes mine and addresses me, but because I am always already involved and entangled with others, always caught up in answering, from the start: We begin by responding.

Coming upon the Ringelblum milk can I reach an impasse. I cannot pass by without inaugurating the psychic split that Muschamp described. Part of me does not leave. It is hostage to a structure of address for which there is no escape, no end. No final and responsible "answer" exists that I might give that would release me from this scene as if I were being rewarded for learning the lessons of this museum.

The U.S. Holocaust Memorial Museum as a Scene of Address

Who does the pedagogy of this museum think I am? If this museum is a pedagogical masterpiece, it is because it does not address me as a victim, perpetrator, bystander, rescuer, or liberator of the Holocaust. It does not reinscribe the very positions and structures of address that were the condition of the Holocaust in the name of preventing another. Rather, this museum is a pedagogical masterpiece because it stages a scene of address that is the very condition of responsibility. In that scene of address, the pedagogy of the museum does not presume to know who I am or who I should become; rather, this museum addresses me as the no one who is always already hostage to its ongoing scene of address. By refusing to suggest or to teach me how I could or should respond, its pedagogy does not leave me "free" to make my own (informed) decisions. Instead, by refusing to teach me my response it *refuses to release me from an ongoing predicament*. It is the predicament of not being able to leave this scene of address. There is no responsible act that I could perform that would put an end to the Holocaust.

If the pedagogy of this museum is a masterpiece, in other words, it is because it knows the limits of pedagogy and puts them to productive use. The pedagogy of the permanent exhibit — the pedagogical pivot place into which it invites its students through its structure of address — not only refuses to seek refuge in religious or rationalistic myths but it also refuses to seek refuge in educationalistic myths — myths such as "Responsibility can be taught," "The Holocaust can be taught," "The needs of the student of the permanent exhibit can be known and met," "Understanding can lead to responsibility."

The terms of the address of the Ringelblum milk can to those who encounter it are not accidental, given, or arbitrary. They are staged. All elements of the museum's exhibit work together to make it happen and to set it in place. They are not inspired by any particular educational theory or practice; rather, they are a social and cultural achievement aimed precisely at staging responsibility as an indeterminate, interminable labor of response.

Refusing the "Last Word"

The silence that meets the visitor at the end of the exhibit and that in turn invites the visitor's own silence is not simply the silence of a narrative without closure or a story without an ending; rather, it is the silence at the end of a story that will never end — a story that is always in the making. Designers of the museum use this silence to structure a pedagogical address that implicates visitors in a knowing that is never complete and that they can never master. It implicates us in a knowing that contains within it an inescapable and profound not knowing.

Far from being the not knowing of willful "ignore-ance" or unconscious denial, the position of not knowing offered to the visitors of this museum is a refusal to give the last word or to presume to know the last word. It is a refusal of the heroic position of mastery. Far from being a refusal of responsibility, it instead marks the struggle to construct a new subject position in relation to the Holocaust — namely, the position of one who is implicated in the task of the museum itself to produce an ongoing social and cultural response to the Holocaust that never bewitches itself with the desire for or illusion of completeness.

The U.S. Holocaust Memorial Museum has begun the cultural and pedagogical labor of creating this new type of hero. The structure of its pedagogical address is designed to implicate visitors in the contingency of knowledge and belief even in the face of Auschwitz — especially in the face of Auschwitz. Its structure of address implicates visitors in the inescapable task of producing an interminable response. By structuring its pedagogy through a silence that marks the limits of teaching and knowing, by refusing to be either master or mastered, this museum, paradoxically, gives access to an interminable teaching and learning.

As a genre of academic writing, research and criticism about pedagogical practice often drives toward concluding statements that offer "best practices," "effective teaching strategies," or prescriptions for "educational interventions." Such an ending would contradict this chapter's own pedagogy and the pedagogical volition of the museum itself. Rather than offering an end to an interminable process through pedagogical prescriptions designed to cure "ignore-ance" or forgetting, the reading I offer of this place of learning attempts to provide questions and perspectives that can be carried over into other sites, opportunities, and problems. Carried over, that is, with the clear imperative not to imitate but to return a difference. Pedagogies inspired or informed by the U.S. Holocaust Memorial Museum must necessarily depart from it if they are to address the unique possibilities and problems of new and other social and historical challenges. The imperative is to work the questions and perspectives offered here or in any pedagogical text in and through new sites so that the new sites teach and transform our settled assumptions about teaching.

I believe that the value of readings like the ones I offer here is their ability to provide "inspirational data" — data that can stimulate educational imaginations and pedagogical design rather than simply define a set of presumably replicable pedagogical strategies. Readings that trace the structures of address that this museum's "pedagogical masterpiece" crystallizes in image, text, sequence, duration, space, and juxtaposition might apprentice us to the exquisite contextual responsiveness required if we are to shape pedagogical designs to their subjects and sites.

6

Media, Architecture, and the Moving Subject of Pedagogy

At this point in our experiment in thinking the experience of the learning self, we are like jugglers on a stage, making every effort to keep a number of plates spinning on top of waving poles. Our experiment is challenging us to keep multiple concepts simultaneously in mind. They include the concept of the learning self as the sensation of coming into relation with the outside world and to the other selves who inhabit and create that world with us. They also include emergent concepts from fields of contemporary philosophy and cultural theory regarding what the fact of embodiment means for thought and for social change. Alongside these we have D.W. Winnicott's concept of transitional space. And, finally, we have up and spinning interpretations of anomalous places of learning and how they create topologies of relationality between self and other, inside and outside, inviting us to inhabit those topologies in ways that release potentialities for thoughts, feelings, and (inter)action that in other old configurations are "captured" and not free to emerge.

We have used these concepts and interpretations to consider how the designs of "anomalous" places of learning construct pedagogical pivot points that attempt to insinuate the outside into thought. They do so by "drawing knowledge outside of itself, outside of what is expected, producing a hollow which it can then inhabit — an outside within or as the inside" (Grosz & Eisenman, 2001, p. 68).

We have let certain plates fall to the stage. We have stopped interacting with those concepts that regard relationship as something immobile — conceived as face-offs of sameness, difference, opposition, or reflexive reaction occurring between fixed subjects (learners) and fixed objects (knowledge made). Such concepts of relationship are of little help to us as we experiment with learning as qualitative transformation.

When watching from the audience, it is difficult to say whether the juggler's plates continue to spin because of the will of the juggler, who rushes from one plate to another to accelerate their motion, or whether it is the plates that keep the juggler in a state of motion, compelling him to dash from pole to pole each time a plate threatens to drop. The entertainment hinges, in part, on this ambiguity.

The pleasures and challenges of teaching and learning hinge on a similar ambiguity. Does pedagogy put the learning self in motion by drawing it outside of itself, outside of what it knows of itself? Or does the learning self put pedagogy in motion through the movements/sensations of its mind/brain/body assemblage as it inhabits and actualizes the time and space of a pedagogical topology? The ambiguity is the productively irritating answer to our question.

In this chapter, I explore that ambiguity further as we now focus on several places of learning in which architecture, media, and pedagogy converge to address the learning self as a self in qualitative transformation — a self in motion. We will see, in other words, how media and architecture create sensational places of learning.

Movement, Sensation, and Pedagogy

> When I think of my body and ask what it does to earn that name, two things stand out. It moves. It feels. In fact, it does both at the same time. It moves as it feels, and it feels itself moving. Can we think a body without this...?
>
> —Brian Massumi

Brian Massumi's work offers extended explorations of embodiment, its meanings for thought, and its potential for generating inventive as opposed to critical engagements with processes of social change (Massumi, 2002, p. 2):

> "The Body." What is it to The Subject? Not the qualities of its moving experience. But rather ... its positioning.... The grid [of cultural codings] was conceived as an oppositional framework of culturally constructed significations: male versus female, black versus white, gay versus straight, and so on. A body corresponded to a "site" on the grid defined by an overlapping of one term from each pair. The body came to be defined by its pinning to the grid.

This grid of cultural codings and its mapping of relative positions in power dynamics has allowed for ways of thinking about resistance as positional change, but it has foreclosed ways of thinking about qualitative change (Massumi, 2002, pp. 3–4):

> How does a body perform its way out of a definitional framework that is not only responsible for its very "construction" but seems to prescript every possible signifying and countersignifying move…? How can the grid itself change…?

> Of course, a body occupying one position on the grid might succeed in making a move to occupy another position…. But this doesn't change the fact that what defines the body is not the movement itself, only its beginning and endpoints. Movement is entirely subordinated to the positions it connects. These are predefined.

When we codify bodies in terms of the coordinates of their start- or endpoints of movement and verbalize an understanding of change only in terms of the positions that have been modified, we eliminate the possibility for grasping the realities and meanings of bodies in the making and knowledge in the making (Massumi, 2002, pp. 3–4):

> The very notion of movement as qualitative transformation is lacking. There is "displacement" but no transformation; it is as if the body simply leaps from one definition to the next….

> The space of the crossing, the gaps between positions on the grid, falls into a theoretical no-body's land.

As a result, cultural theory offers educators and educational media producers few conceptual tools for exploring pedagogy as it relates to the embodied experience of change. If pedagogy consists of the practices and processes that qualitatively transform the ways in which we think and act in the world, then it also qualitatively transforms our embodiments in and of the world. This means that, for those who study pedagogy, the object of attention and curiosity must be change as embodied in the experience of the learning self.

When I think of my mind/brain/body in the midst of an experience of learning and ask what it does to qualify that experience as a learning experience, one thing stands out. It feels itself thinking. In terms Massumi employs to describe philosophical thinking, but which I appropriate here in relation to pedagogy: It feels thought itself becoming sensible. My mind/brain/body in the midst of learning senses the inner movement that is a "conceptual groping of potential-to-be" (Massumi, 2002, p. 242). Along with a sense of expectancy, my mind/brain/body senses the grid coordinates of what "I already know" shift, fringe, and draw outside of themselves as a potential learning — something as yet undetermined by the grid — addresses my learning self. In its effort to meet this address, my learning self is set in motion to an equally undetermined destination.

But, when I think of this experience as an educator who is interested in the question of pedagogy, I feel my body/mind/brain falling into education's theoretical "no-body's land." Education has long been dominated by the same theories of ideology and subject positioning that have dominated cultural theory, rendering both fields unable to think the very notion of movement as qualitative change. Educational sociology and the cognitive sciences, derived as they are in part from the natural sciences, are both dominated by thought processes that produce grids, identities, positions, categories, linear progressions, and causalities. These, in turn, have spawned pedagogical practices such as scaffolding, in which pedagogy functions as a ladder for moving students' cognitions up a hierarchical grid of scripted schemas and concepts. Alternatively, educators have used theories of social positioning to generate constructivist approaches to pedagogy, where teachers facilitate students' idiosyncratic and culturally situated (re)discoveries of the grids of knowledge already in place even as they generate novel rearrangements of familiar expressions of that knowledge. When they define pedagogy as a signifying gesture that participates in the social construction of meaning and knowledge, educators approach teaching and learning as the making and unmaking of sense. Massumi says this renders sensation "disruptive to [the description of signifying gestures] because it appeals to an unmediated experience, which begins to sound dangerously like 'naïve subjectivism'" (Massumi, 2002, p. 2).

Smudging the Learning Self

Assumptions that frame the study of pedagogy as the study of signifying gestures that make and unmake sense relegate that which is sensational about pedagogy to a theoretical "no-body's land." There, the proper object of attention of those who would theorize pedagogy is made invisible by cultural theory's grid of knowledge already known. The grid has no ability to "see" knowledge as it is in the making. It has no faculty to sense the movement/sensation out of which knowledge itself emerges: the experience of the learning self in the making. The qualitative change that is learning goes undetected by curriculums, outcomes, and scripted teaching strategies when they are used to "track" movements from one grid position to the next along fixed routes such as memorization, ventriloquism, citation, and repetition. Pedagogy practiced for the sake of the grid functions as a mere connector between predetermined meanings and identities. It does nothing to address the learning self in motion as it moves between the grid's binary poles and is no longer identifiable with or addressable through socially constructed positions. The learning self when it is in the making no longer coincides with whatever previously constructed knowledge about the learner we might hold.

Because the very possibility for learning depends upon the existence of selves in motion, it is paramount for educators and educational media producers to consider learning selves as being in motion. A body in motion is not limited to any given moment or position in its movement and is thus open to a range of variations, directions, and destinations. The possibility of qualitative transformation — of thinking and being something unprecedented — is dependent upon this "potential to vary." Our embodiment puts us into a moving relation with forces, processes, and connections to others in ways that are unforeseen by consciousness and unconnected to identity (Massumi, 2002, p. 231). If a living, moving, sensing body can be said to "be" anything, it is "an immediate, lived and unfolding relation to its own present potential to vary" (Massumi, 2002, p. 4).

Certain pedagogies do address a student's body in terms of the qualities of its movements and sensations. Various arts-based pedagogies and programs for teaching literature and literacy are informed at least in part by aesthetic theories or psychoanalysis in attempts to address the moving, sensing learning self, but, for all intents and purposes, David Lusted's widely quoted declaration of 1986 remains true: Pedagogy, in all of its dynamic complexities, is "desperately under-theorized" and the lack of this crucial concept's development "has had material effects" (Lusted, 1986).

In 1998, Bill Green gestured toward what he hoped might develop into a "radical" or "progressive" pedagogy. By this he meant a pedagogy that engaged students and teachers in the critique and production of culture and knowledge and not only in their reproduction and transmission (Green, 1998). Starting with Lusted's declaration, he addressed the potential meanings of pedagogy in the postmodern Age of Information by showing that the concept of pedagogy itself is "arguably the most inadequately theorized issue in the whole debate" regarding an educational praxis that might engage teachers and students in the making of "critical" knowledge (Green, 1998, p. 177).

In order to accommodate the "new forms of cognition and learning" associated with media and with the digital–electronic apparatus, Green argued, educators should seek out less "logocentric and print-bound" ideas about learning (Green, 1998, p. 194). He then used Gregory Ulmer to point out that "something 'happens' ... that alters the whole ecology of learning" when we teach and learn through media and within a media-saturated culture increasingly dominated by digital technologies and by "semiosis" (Ulmer, 1989, quoted in Green, 1998, p. 194). A new order of learning is emerging out of a convergence of "oral, literate and video conduct in our society." This convergence, Green says, exceeds text-based learning and understandings and requires us to embrace and engage the "semiotic possibilities of electronic media and the (postmodern body)" (Green, 1998, p. 193). In this new learning order, the school room's or educational researcher's "hothouse versions of meaning are undercut by electronic space and the embodied practices of an expansive popular culture" (Morgan, 1993, quoted in Green, 1998, p. 193).

In order to establish ways in which we might rethink pedagogy in this "new learning order," Green calls for an investigation into the body's association in and with media, digital technology, and the times and places of the creation and consumption of popular culture. But, he is never fully able to escape the boundaries of assumptions and preoccupations that have subjugated pedagogy to the realm of cognitive and language-based processes of meaning making. While cognition is, of course, valuable as a component of the learning process, we must, to paraphrase Massumi, recognize that the sphere of applicability of theories of cognition is limited to a particular dimension of the reality of learning — namely, the degree to which learning coincides with conscious, rational thought (Massumi, 2002, p. 7).

Taking up Green's challenge, we might usefully and inventively breech cognition's sphere of applicability and domination by delving deeper into emerging concepts about embodiment, mediated experience, and the lived spaces and times of self and knowledge in the making. Massumi suggests that cultural theorists look to the life sciences for help in meeting such a challenge. In order to think about the body's movements and sensations in relation to thinking, Massumi has repurposed concepts from the life sciences that he says are better suited for grasping the realities and meanings of emergence than those that are currently available in cultural studies. Unlike cultural studies, biology and neuroscience have been unable to escape the necessity of creating a lexicon adequate for the task of describing the "smudging" of identities, objects, and processes by and within living things that are in constant motion and emergence. And, as we have seen, the movement and moment of self-breeching — the "smudging" of the self one has been into the self one has yet to become — is precisely where the experience of the learning self takes place and time. That is why self-breeching movement/sensation is the proper object of study by those concerned with pedagogy. A body in the process of learning is a body blurred by its own indeterminacy and by its openness to an elsewhere and to an otherwise. This implicates pedagogy in the promise of an indeterminate, unspecifiable future and an unlimited open-endedness (Grosz & Eisenman, 2001, pp. 89–90). The reality of a body's continuous indeterminacy points to the fact that our lives are always verging on the future; they are "virtual" in that they are always breeching into "potentialities other than those now actualized" (Grosz & Eisenman, 2001, p. 89). For these reasons, it is crucial that educators become curious about the qualities of subjects in motion and in emergence and champion their importance in defiance of the positional grid's inability or unwillingness to acknowledge them.

It would be valuable for educators and educational media producers to elaborate on Massumi's gestures in this direction because he has generated analytical terms that articulate the qualities of subjects in self-breeching movement and emergence. I am going to attempt such an elaboration now by exploring how media and architecture contribute to efforts to address the subject of pedagogy as a moving subject. I will turn to three scenes of pedagogical address, each of which uses media and architecture to restore to learning — out of more and more microscopically understood knowledge things — the continuity of learning bodies' movements and sensations and, therefore, the potential for participating in knowledge in the making.

Architecture and Media: Restoring the Body in Motion to Pedagogy

Consider a body in the midst of crossing the gap between positions on the grid of knowledge, meanings, and relations of power that Massumi describes. It has not entered "the niceness of a framed neat closed experience." Rather, it has fallen into life as open and unfinished. Life's potentialities, Elizabeth Grosz goes so far as to say, can be released only through movement into and within the messy intervals of space and time between the "things" we already know and between the "beings" we have already made of ourselves and others.

The space of the in-between is the locus for social, cultural, and natural transformations; it is not simply a convenient space for movements and realignments but in fact is the only place — the place around identities, between identities — where becoming, an openness to futurity, outstrips the conservational impetus to retain cohesion and unity (Grosz & Eisenman, 2001, pp. 92–93):

> … the in-between defines the space of a certain virtuality, a potential that always threatens to disrupt the operations of the identities that constitute it …. The space in between things is the space in which things are undone, the space to the side and around, which is the space of subversion and fraying, the edges of any identity's limits. In short, it is the space of the bounding and undoing of the identities which constitute it.

Grosz, like Massumi, Rajchman, Kennedy, Wodizcko, and de Bolla, is a contemporary philosopher whose preoccupation with the in-between has prompted her to look to architecture and media to inform her thoughts about movement, sensation, and experience. Both architecture and media are implicated in broader social and political issues involving embodiment, inhabitation, space, creating and constructing, desire, sexuality, and economies of exchange. Both "modulate" or inflect bodies as they move in space and time. Both provide material correlates of ideas. Both allow us to think and experience the intrinsic connection between our bodies' movements/sensations and their makings of sense. Media and architecture both provoke theorists and philosophers to talk about phenomena we associate with the learning self, such as "becoming," "emergence," and "change."

The theorists I draw from may not speak explicitly of pedagogy when they explore media and architecture, but they do speak about the ways that both media and architecture fold embodied experiences of space and time into and out of sense making. More and more, designers are employing media and architecture in concert to shape and amend the raw possibilities of movement, sensation, and thought, prompting us to ask what might media and architecture, when inflected with pedagogical intent, make of thinking?

Grosz considers architecture, like shelter or clothing, to be a "measure of reality's incompleteness." To compensate for its own incompleteness, reality demands our participation in various forms of making and doing, including the conception and creation of architecture. By involving us in the design of interfaces between inside and outside, architecture involves us in ways of knowing inside and outside that are available to us only through our embodied experiences of living through or inhabiting architectural space (Grosz & Eisenman, 2001, pp. 178–179).

Because architectural space unfolds and actualizes only as we move, live through, and thereby embody it, architecture has the capacity to generate encounters and events. Our inhabitations and embodiments of architectural space and time facilitate events of movement and use them to open up envelopes of passage across and between inside and outside, self and other. Our participation in architecture as event and encounter offers potential ways out of the subject/object and inside/outside binaries by facilitating flows of movement, use, and inhabitation in the spaces between subject and object, inside and outside. Most importantly, the potential of architecture for shaping the raw possibilities of movement and sensation makes it possible for different corporealities to be expressed.

Grosz explains that, because space is open to different forms of habitation and because bodies are pliable, they are capable of infinite variations on experience (Grosz & Eisenman, 2001, p. 33). Grosz points to the ways in which people are appropriating media and cyberspace as evidence of their "intense desire for refigured embodment" and of their capacity for imagining themselves as inhabiting different corporealities (Grosz & Eisenman, 2001, p. 85). Much attention has been given to the ability of media and cyberspace to allow for imagined and/or real relief not only from the limitations of embodiment itself but also from the limitations placed upon bodies when they are positioned on the grids of (raced, sexed, normalized) cultural meaning in limiting or oppressive ways. Different enfoldings of sensations, movements, times, and spaces by new social practices, new media, architectures, or new pedagogies may lead us "to organize, inhabit, and structure our living arrangements differently" (Grosz & Eisenman, 2001, p. xix).

This prompts Grosz to ask what possibilities bodies have "of living differently in the built and natural world" (Grosz & Eisenman, 2001, p. xxi) so that we might construct different ways of being bodies and selves and different ways of being with others? Indeed, how might different configurations of space and time create different corporealities? Might space be designed and inhabited as, for example, "an envelope, which permits the passage from one space and position to another, rather than the containment of objects and functions in which each thing finds its rightful place" (Grosz & Eisenman, 2001, p. 165)? Might building and architecture — and pedagogy — function less as finished object and more as "spatial process, open to whatever use it may be put to in an indeterminate future, not as a container of solids but as a facilitator of flows: 'volume without contour', as Irigaray describes it in *Speculum*" (Grosz & Eisenman, 2001, p. 165)?

Architecture, like all making, Grosz says, produces objects as the correlate of the intellect. As the facilitator and actualizer of envelopes of passage into and through spaces between, architecture holds the potential for providing educators with material correlates of the moving, sensational experience of the learning self. To the extent that architecture deals in movement, sensation, and the progression of time toward an unpredictable future, it holds the potential to produce spaces and times that are catalysts for rethinking pedagogy.

Grosz's discussion of architecture implies ways in which we might bring media into a conversation with architecture and pedagogy. If we conceive of architecture as the housing or clothing of bodies, matter, and spaces, "then perhaps all technologies are modeled on architecture and thus implicated in architecture" (Grosz & Eisenman, 2001, p. 83). What might it mean to consider media as a technology modeled on and implicated in architecture as the housing of bodies? Could we begin to see media as membranes — as interfacings of inside to outside, outside to inside — as interfacings of self and other?

Like architecture, we might consider media as facilitators and regulators of flows but with their own distinctive modes and potentials for setting learning selves in motion. We might begin to see media as technologies of transitivity, mobilizing fixed points on the grid — culturally encoded images, meanings, discourses, stories — by delivering them to widely disbursed and qualitatively different times, places, and contexts (Massumi, 2002, p. 83). If we define architecture as the shaping and amending of raw possibilities of bodies' movements and sensations, and therefore of thought, we might then consider media to be the shaping and amending of raw possibilities of address and therefore of difference. Media do not simply deliver messages as objects (things made) to identifiable, locatable receivers at fixed addresses on a culture's grids of identities and social positions. By shaping the raw possibilities of address, media strip the addresses from culturally gridlocked images, stories, representations, and meanings and facilitate movement, without a predetermined destination, across and between cultures. Media open and deliver to the "no-body's land" between identifiable coordinates on the grid. What they deliver are not merely meanings made different by their arrival in unforeseen, incongruous contexts. Media deliver difference itself. That is, they create upon delivery what Massumi calls "event potentials."

For example, a soccer game consists of the perspectives and experiences of its participants and fans when it is in the process of being played in a stadium, but when the soccer match "passes from the stadium to the home, piggybacked on televisual images, it changes in nature" (Massumi, 2002, p. 84). Upon its "arrival" on a television set in a home, it has been encoded, "reduced to fit sound speaker and screen," but this is not the only way it is changed. The encoded event has also been "delivered to a more or less open milieu" and now becomes only one part of its new context "which includes the content of the home, as well as the screen and its content" (Massumi, 2002, pp. 85–85). In other words, it is no longer the same event. The soccer game has "fold[ed] out of its own event space and into another" (Massumi, 2002, p. 80). Transmission into its new context has converted it into an event potential. As "event transmitters," media draw events from their spaces of expression and deliver them into new contexts, ready for unpredictable recodings and available to be put to unforeseen uses. What people will make of the "transmitted event" in its new space and time is indeterminate, highly variable, and charged with as yet unrealized potential.

The power of the media thus lies not only in their encodings of meanings and representations of reality, but also in their abilities to "move events" and create "event potentials" in new spaces and unanticipated contexts. As technologies that assist event-transitivity, media give body to relationality as they keep potentiality and difference in circulation and motion. They put diverse and occasionally warring ideas, identities, sensibilities, traditions — and people — into relation with each other, actually or imaginatively. Media thus are imbued with the potential for catalyzing new forms of corporeality, new embodiments, new ways of knowing and being human.

By rethinking media as cultural membranes, it is possible to understand why political and economic forces interested in containing difference have been thrown into crisis. Collectively, media — as technological global interlinkings — have the potential to deliver open-ended and indeterminate sensations, movements, affects, thoughts, actions, and interactions in and across societies with pedagogical consequence. Through their ability to penetrate infinitely variable sociohistorical spaces, media are able to deliver either containment (already created and encoded meanings, knowledges, clichéd images, oppressive stereotypes) or the opposite — the unimaginably diverse things that can be made of already contained meanings in the more or less open event spaces of their arrival (Massumi, 2002, pp. 82–86).

Media thus become the shapers and amenders of the raw possibilities of social and cultural difference. They simultaneously repeat conventions of language, storytelling, identity, and ways of knowing, for example, *and* activate the passages between positions by delivering cultural significations not to codified identities or positions, but to the spaces and times of inhabitation that remain uncodifiable because they are still in the process of emerging as events.

While the specificity and power of architecture lie in its ability to provide an embodied experience of the future as it unfolds in time and space, the specificity and power of media lie in their simultaneous activations of grid coordinates *and* the spaces between them. Media simultaneously activate what is knowable and addressable in and through language, image, and signification, as well as what is knowable and through an entirely different mode: the lived experience of the continuity of the passage into difference and newness.

Such is the ability of media to clothe bodies — both individual bodies and social bodies — in membranes of transitivity. By setting representations into motion across emergent contexts and into event potentials, media bring about new alignments, unexpected intensities, and new connections. These, in turn, generate affective and conceptual transformations that "problematize, challenge, and move beyond existing intellectual and pragmatic frameworks" (Grosz & Eisenman, 2001, p. 58). By delivering difference to addresses not already known or knowable, media, in other words, generate thought.

To paraphrase Grosz's discussion of architecture as making: The task before educators may not be simply to make knowledge or to resolve the moving flux of relations into knowledge things that are "more and more minutely framed and microscopically understood; rather, it may be to liberate matter from the constraint, the practicality, the utility of [knowledge], to orient [pedagogy] not so much to knowing and mediating as to experience and the rich indeterminacy of duration" (Grosz & Eisenman, 2001, p. 183).

At the Limits of the Social Body

While it may appear that Grosz and Massumi leave behind conventional theories that address power in oppositional terms — that is, in terms of fixed grids of identities and social positionings and the static, hierarchical relationalities between them — this is not the case. Although they discuss historical and social change through concepts such as "becoming" and "emergence" and consider the "world as self-augmenting," it is possible to see the workings of power in such concepts, traceable as they are to Michel Foucault's notion of power as productive. For example, rather than resisting through critique, the theorists I have worked with here claim to engage in political practice as they "augment" through invention. For Massumi, the choice of augmentation over critique is strategic, because, at the moment critical conversations within the humanities and social sciences about power and change that emphasize and rely on critique and methods of negation over and above affirmative methods of construction or invention have become counterproductive. Massumi (2002, p. 13) puts it this way:

> It is not that critique is wrong. As usual, it is not a question of right or wrong — nothing important ever is. Rather, it is a question of dosage. It is simply that when you are busy critiquing you are less busy augmenting. You are that much less fostering. There are times when debunking [something that critical thinking desires to subtract from the world] is necessary. But, if applied in a blanket manner, adopted as a general operating principle, [debunking] is counterproductive.

Laurel Richardson made a similar strategic choice from within a Neo-Marxist perspective at the moment when her work as a sociologist and ethnographer led her to question what she calls "resistance narratives." She wonders if the genres and representational structures of the stories that social and cultural theorists and critics tell about power do not sometimes become themselves the problem and "undermine [cultural theory's] own agenda" (Richardson, 1997, pp. 78–80):

> If we think of the narratives we construct as "resistance" narratives, we have dialogically tied ourselves to that which we oppose.... Resistance narratives are tied to that which already has legitimacy, to that which they are resisting.... Conceived and written as responses to dominant discourses, they reinscribe rather than circumvent....
>
> Problems of communication, then, or the kinds of stories we can write, the kinds of lives we can thereby live, are thus most strongly linked to the kinds of communion we can create, not to the hegemonies we can resist ... one way to begin the representing of lives, including our own sociological ones, is to create new forms of telling, new rituals for sharing....
>
> Such understanding shows. It does not "resist." Social science, dance, sculpture, painting, literature. An exemplary text comes to life and creates life....
>
> Let's do it!

The spaces between oppositional positions on the grids of culturally constructed significations are always available to foster and augment the world's "constant qualitative growth ... the fact that with every move, with every change, there is something new to the world, an added reality"

(Massumi, 2002, p. 12). In human processes that are continuous across artificial categorical divides, such as the learning self in the making, all aspects of the process are available, including those that fall into the gaps between or circumscribe known meanings and identities. Power, for Massumi (1995), thus becomes a question of constraining and directing the continuous self-augmentation, qualitative growth, and variation of the world:

> Constraint and creativity are not in contradiction, but in cohabitation. One does not ground or contradict the other. Rather, they relay one another. Constraint is no longer a threat from the outside, or in response to that threat the willful imposition of a self-same form onto that outside. Instead, constraint is the programming of interactions between forces; from those interactions, differentiations unfold....

> ...forces of stasis manage to rein in open continuation of the world's self-augmentation. The space of human life and action is an active space composed of "forces of interaction between dynamic elements" such as bodies and events "whose characteristics shift" in "reciprocal variation" as bodies and events "move about, combine, and inflect."

Or, as Dell Upton puts it in a discussion of architecture and everyday life (Upton, 2002, p. 717):

> Our "sensorimotor" space and perceptual "receptive field," the areas within our immediate grasp and within reach of our perception, respectively, extend our selves into a space much larger than our bodies proper, but they also make us vulnerable to the influence of the architectural and human spaces beyond our bodily boundaries.

If we are convinced by Massumi and Upton that our bodies are porous envelopes in constant exchange with their outside and that bodies and events "move about, combine, and inflect," then we can begin to understand why some cultural critics and philosophers of everyday life are so interested in how relations of power structure space and time. At the same time, we can also see with Grosz that, to the same degree that the heterogeneous mix of everyday life's cohesions, congealed identities, and symbolic structures is possible at all, its same stabilized and congealed forces can be "reanimated and revivified in another direction" (Grosz & Eisenman, 2001, p. 104).

In this sense, power can be seen as operating in and by forces and practices (chaotic bursts, upheavals, and quantum leaps) that are always at hand yet not visible to or expressible by the sociostructural parameters of the grid. Power can be understood as the actions and conditions that limit potentialities, directions, and movements. In this view, power becomes the "usurpation of variation" (Massumi, 2002, p. 72). It is the usurpation of the "very expression of potential. The movement of relationality" (Massumi, 2002, p. 88). The *social* body reaches the limits of the very expression of its potential and variation when the reciprocal variations and shifting characteristics of *individual* bodies are constrained from moving about, combining, and inflecting. The limits of the social body's expression and variation within a given context or event, then, can be said to constitute the limits of relationality.

Media representations and cultural encodings operate as "containers" for people, and their actions "capture," "usurp," and "program" difference and variation. They do this by channeling and regularizing the flow of potentialities and relationalities of bodies within and across cultures (Massumi, 2002, p. 88). By "capturing the elements of expression" within preconstructed cultural frameworks, media participate in power as usurpation, but media also operate as facilitators of potentialities and relationality when, as technologies of "transitivity," as cultural membranes, they circulate potentialities and differences back and forth across the threshold of inside/self and outside/other and "give body to relationality as such and as set in motion — as the passing on of the event" (Massumi, 2002, p. 86). As shapers and amenders of the movements, combinations, and inflections of relationality, media and architecture have the capacity to both usurp variation and express potential. We can see how, with their abilities to circulate event potentials within and across cultures, media in particular become key players in power. We saw how Wodiczko's communicative instruments, for example, use media to locate pedagogy at the limits of relationality. They attempt to modulate the social body's variation by facilitating encounters between bodies and thereby potentializing new combinations and interactions with forces that are in the making outside the known parameters of relationality. Wodiczko thus uses media as a membrane to clothe the individual body in a social space of relationality, and, conversely, to clothe the social body (the collective body of social groups) with a mediatized membrane capable of augmenting the exchange and flow of individual bodies' social and cultural differences within and across collective social bodies.

If I were to enter the space of this exchange, I might find myself in the midst of an intrusion from outside my sense of my social body. I might find myself in participation with, in witness of, and encompassed by that which resists "capture" — the stranger. I might find myself, in other words, in "reciprocal variation" with what I cannot know but what is in emergence — the social body in the making.

The anomalous places of learning that I now take up use media and architecture to send the mind/brain/body into motion within the gaps between fixed positions on the grids of knowledge as a thing made. Doing so, they restore to learning the sensation of being in relation; that is, they restore to the learning self the experience and rich indeterminacy of the social (political) body.

Putting Learning Selves into Relation Through Movement

In a detailed account of his experience of viewing a work of visual art, Peter de Bolla discusses those concerns that Massumi described as existing within a theoretical "no-body's land": concerns for the movements and sensations that arise from the qualitative transformations of self and of self in relation to other. As an educator, I find it provocative that de Bolla's account of his aesthetic experience emphasizes the movement/sensation of passage between one way of knowing and another; it emphasizes the sensation of coming to a knowing.

At the moment when the boundary between his aesthetic experience and his experience of his learning self becomes blurred, de Bolla describes what he calls "states of thinking–feeling" and "states of 'in-between-ness'" that are "part physical and part mental, in the orbit of the emotive yet also clearly articulated or potentially articulatable within the higher orders of mental activity" (de Bolla, 2001, p. 3). In his descriptions of his experience of viewing Barnett Newman's painting *Vir Heroicus Sublimis*, de Bolla delivers a first-hand account of the movement/sensation I associate with learning itself. de Bolla's account is particularly relevant because it traces the connections he senses between a felt qualitative transformation, a learning, and the conditions of that learning's emergence: a pedagogy. His is the chronicle of a person in between, a person in the midst of the transitional space of a learning, a learning self in the continuity of passage between positions on the grid of social and cultural codings. de Bolla's account portrays a transitional space in which pedagogy involves architecture and architecture involves pedagogy. *Vir Heroicus Sublimis* modulates its address to the viewer and the viewer's address to it in a way that reconfigures the architectural space surrounding both itself and its viewer, and it does so with pedagogical consequence. de Bolla suggests that the painting stages a reconfiguration of its own viewing space in order to prevent a learning experience in which knowledge is a thing made and predicated upon a fixed divide between subject and object. By undermining the viewer's knowledge of self/other in terms of static identities and positions (knowledge that makes it virtually impossible to experience our selves as in relation), the painting is able to actualize an experience of self/other as moving/sensing bodies and interactions in the making and, thus, of knowledge in the making.

For de Bolla, experiencing a knowledge of self as both separate from and in relation to others and the world is precisely the project of *Vir Heroicus Sublimis*. This painting sees de Bolla's attempt to view it as a subject views an object, to master it as a sight presented to be seen, and thwarts that attempt. In its presence, de Bolla finds himself in an encounter with an "object" that "looks back." He determines that this aesthetic experience has been staged to give him an "indirect" awareness of self that forms only as it passes through a sense of the "competing presences" of other selves. In this situation, the competing statements of presence made by viewer/subject and artwork/object — a potential standoff — are qualitatively transformed, through movement, into an experience of the learning self.

Here is how: *Vir Heroicus Sublimis* is over 7 feet tall and over 17 feet wide. "If the average person's stride is around three feet, it takes five full strides to traverse the image" (de Bolla, 2001, p. 32). According to de Bolla (2001, pp. 39–40), the canvas...

> ... is so large that it throws into crisis the notion of "proper distance" and, thereby, renders the practice of viewing uncomfortable — as we have to move across it, away from it, up close, far away. The resulting *mobility* [emphasis added] in relation to the distance we gain [threatens a particular version of the viewing subject] ... one in which the desire for mastery determines how the viewer enters into the optical circuits of looking.

As if to thwart the viewer's desire to occupy the "correct viewing position" (static, immobile, and providing a repetitive optical circuit), the painting puts the viewer in motion and actively engages him in a self-conscious viewing process, making him intensely aware of his own looking. It does this, in de Bolla's experience, in part through its scale (de Bolla, 2001, pp. 40–41), which takes...

> ... the single point of viewing, the pinhole that is the viewing subject for unilinear perspectival representations, and elongate[s] it, effectively transforming the pupil from a hole into surface, as if the eye were elongated to include the cutaneous surface of the body so that this somatic envelope becomes sensitized to the visual.... Hence, the presentation of the body to vision — and not just my body, but the somatic in general, the social body constructed in the practice of viewing in public.

de Bolla suggests that the scale of *Vir Heroicus Sublimis* sets the viewer in motion in a way that undermines the subject/object, self/other dichotomy. As he stated above, this produces two distinct consequences. First, it is no longer merely the eye that sees the painting through its pupil, but the somatic envelop of the body that "sees" through its movement. And, second, such "seeing movement" releases multiple cognitive, non-cognitive, and pre-cognitive "knowings," none of which is inherently superior and all of which are implicated in his "final knowing" of the painting. But, de Bolla insists, he is not simply seeing the painting from multiple perspectives (de Bolla, 2001, p. 41):

> While it may first appear as if the viewing subject needs to occupy a series of points in front of the canvas — as if walking across it or tracing an arc from one side to the other were to plot the positions from which a series or views might be taken — this sense is dissolved once one notices the fuller somatic presencing to vision. The singularity of one point perspective has been maintained by troping the organ of sight into the entire cutaneous envelope of the body ... hence the presentation of the body to vision — and not just my body, but the somatic in general, the social body constructed in the practice of viewing in public.

In other words, he is not only viewing the painting from between the various points of view he himself takes up, he is also viewing it in and through the spaces between the viewing perspectives (physical as well as social/cultural) of the others gathered with him in the public space of the gallery (de Bolla, 2001, pp. 38–39), because the size of the painting...

> ... says something about the space in which [it] can be seen, which is much more likely to be a public museum.... We may reasonably conclude, therefore, that this image imagines its site of viewing, location for being seen, as a public and social space. Consequently, the painting raises questions concerned with the social practice of viewing: How does one share a public space in the act of viewing art? To what extent is the viewer allowed to find or construct private spaces in front of the canvas? What degree of permeability divides the public from the private? How far or how easily may one negotiate the boundary between the two? How might this image encourage a sense of community, of belonging to a shared space, inhabiting a communal experience?

The abstract nature of this painting removes the human form from the picture plane. But, de Bolla says, the human form resurfaces "on the other side, as it were, in the space in front of the canvas" (de Bolla, 2001, p. 39). de Bolla rediscovers the presence of the human form "in" this painting upon redefining the painting as an event occurring in the space and time of the viewer's lived response. In this painting as event, the human form is manifest in the motion of de Bolla's body through the space between himself and other viewers. His movements and sensations become modulated by the painting's manipulation of its surrounding viewing space.

And so de Bolla's viewing body undergoes an intense sense of self-presence that arises from both his personal response to the painting and from his sense of the smudging of his own individual body into the collective viewing body. *Vir Heroicus Sublimis* thus represents the "human form" as a social practice — namely, the collective "movement" required to view this artwork in public. This allows de Bolla to conclude that this "abstract image" represents the human as or more powerfully "than any figurative painting might or can" (de Bolla, 2001, p. 39). It does not allow him to project himself into a world predetermined by the painter, as if to say: "I am in that world, the world of this image is mine" (de Bolla, 2001, p. 36); rather, this artwork "presents to vision" the human body as a collective body, as "the somatic in general, the social body constructed in the practice of viewing in public" (de Bolla, 2001, pp. 40–41):

> For me, *Vir Heroicus Sublimis* demands that the viewer ... enter a shared space in which the nakedness of presentation asks one to face up to being here, in the visibility of a communally constructed presence. Here in the hushed sublimity of a shared world. And this, perhaps, provides me with the first glimpse of what this painting might know, or rather what its knowing might be.

Paraphrasing its painter, de Bolla states the intention behind *Vir Heroicus Sublimis*: to make it possible for the viewer to have a sense of her or his own scale in relation to both the presence of the artwork and the presence of others — the "communally constructed presence." Newman said he tried to make it possible for the viewer to have a sense that she or he is there (de Bolla, 2001, p. 48). This sense, de Bolla insists, is not "captured" by the image nor is it the "content" of the image; rather, "it emerges from an encounter between the viewer and the work" (de Bolla, 2001, p. 48). This encounter is shaped and amended by the presence of others and the self as presented to others in the social space of viewing.

This painting's social space of viewing in turn modulates the terms in which de Bolla presents himself to it. It shifts those terms, he says, from *looking* at the work to *witnessing* the work. His sense of being called to witness dawns in his awareness that he is in the "competing" presence of another will to presence, one that asks the viewer to "scale him- or herself as an act of witnessing the work" (de Bolla, 2001, p. 51). In other words, the painting reconfigures the dichotomies of subject/object, self/other into relationalities in which two subjects, two self-presences, stand, as it were, side by side rather than face to face. Painting and viewer each "face up" to being seen, to being made visible to others, in their "communally constructed presence." Each becomes a participant in the unfolding of this scene as a scene of a knowing in the making (de Bolla, 2001, pp. 48–49):

> I become highly conscious of the activity of looking ... the feeling I am trying to get in focus, [is] more like an act of witnessing than an act of seeing. In fact I need to witness that I am looking before I can begin to see this image: in this sense looking is not like a visual

activity at all — it is more like a recognition of presence, or a feeling of or for presence.

This particular recognition of presence can only result from de Bolla's awareness of his self in relation to others. This intense self-in-relation awareness, which stems from his knowledge of his own presence in relation to *Vir Heroicus Sublimis*, is different in nature from the awareness of "being there" that emerges when he simply observes his surroundings. This way of knowing self in relation emerges for de Bolla as an "interleaving of affective and cognitive responses" (de Bolla, 2001, p. 48) — as an embodied thinking–feeling.

The Felt Reality of the Experience of Learning

There is a difference, de Bolla insists, between the "evidence of the ocular senses" in which one notices "that the sensorium has been stimulated" and this other way of knowing, which he describes as an interleaving of affect and cognition. Recognizing the difference, he says, requires the ability to recognize "what it might feel like to be knowing something, to feel the interleaving of the affective and the cognitive" (de Bolla, 2001, p. 49). In this way, he stresses that "feeling" is not the only "material" he encounters in his aesthetic-response-as-knowing. "Indeed, my affective or aesthetic experience is held in a more rarified atmosphere than feeling, between emotive sensation and cognition" (de Bolla, 2001, p. 55).

What is it, then, to sense one's self in the midst of learning as experience, in the moment of learning, in the presence of a coming knowing, in this interleaving of cognition and sensation/movement? As he responsively scales himself in relation to the painting, de Bolla becomes aware of his own presence among others and of his contemporaneousness with them. He discovers that "what this painting knows" and thus what it brings to awareness in him is the "sublimity of a shared world." He becomes aware that his body, the body that is now sensing itself as "being there," is a radically social body. What this painting knows and teaches is that the viewing subject always comprises more than one agent.

de Bolla takes great pains to point out that his highly conscious act of looking at *Vir Heroicus Sublimis* is not merely "seeing" but rather becomes the participatory act of witnessing. When "knowing" itself is in question and "that which we can or cannot know" is in doubt, we are called upon to witness. In response to this painting, de Bolla is compelled to witness the limits of his knowledge regarding his own scale in the sublimity of a shared world. This painting implicates him in a scene of social "response-ability": the act of acknowledging the competing presences of other subjects.

The capacity of pedagogy to access and acknowledge our sensations of being in relation is crucial to efforts to teach about and across social and cultural difference. Such a capacity carries potential for as yet unexplored approaches to "teaching difference," because, as Massumi says, relationality is "open-endedly social." Our awareness of relationality itself allows us an awareness of what it is to be social "'prior to' the separating out of individuals and the identifiable groupings that they end up boxing themselves into (positions in gridlock)" (Masumi, 2002, p. 9). de Bolla's negotiation of the competitions for presence and for subjecthood between *Vir Heroicus Sublimis* and its viewers, and among its viewers, can be seen as analogous to other scenes of competing statements of presence: the teacher/student relation, for example, or relations between members of antagonistic social groups.

What de Bolla describes in his encounter with *Vir Heroicus Sublimis* is a transformation of competing statements of presence into useful, bearable, even pleasant difference. He describes a mutual encompassing that disconnects object/subject from fixed positions on the grid of social significations and sets each into motion in the spaces between fixed meanings and identities, where identities become smudged by the space and time of pure relationality. These smudged identities interleave and emerge as social bodies composed of viewing subjects who are present in ways that cannot be reduced to "selves and their others." Rather, a social body is composed of competing presences made present to each other by virtue of the fact that their claims on "being there" are mutually witnessed.

What happens when we try to take de Bolla's persuasive description of the potential for aesthetic experience and architectural space to set subjects into moving relation with each other — out of the gallery? Does the potential for movement and sensation to shape the experience of the learning self pertain only to *aesthetic* experience? Although de Bolla's knowings as aesthetic experiences take the form of various senses and awarenesses, pedagogy is obligated to make something of the senses and awarenesses it generates. We turn now to a scene of pedagogical address that invites us to put de Bolla's discussion in relation to the collective body of the knowing self and to a collective pedagogical volition. It displays the difficulties of inflecting awareness and sensation toward knowledge and learning without limiting the future of learning selves in the making or prescribing what must remain open-endedly social about knowledge in the making.

Children as the Limit of the Social Body

Edwin Schlossberg has been credited with inventing the children's museum. In 1970, he designed a series of hands-on interactive activities for the Brooklyn Children's Museum, the first of its kind. In his words, he designed the museum to be a place where adults and children "learn about the world and their culture through play" (Schlossberg, 1998, p. 58). It invited children to explore earth, wind, and fire and physically generate the power that runs the exhibits. Recently, Steven Heller described Schlossberg as a "social designer ... someone who considers how people respond and interact and are affected by how an event or environment is designed" (Heller, 1998, p. 240).

Since 1970, Schlossberg has designed numerous interactive environments and experiences, including Macomber Farm, a 46-acre educational farm dedicated to eliminating cruelty to animals by creating empathy for them. At the farm, adults and children could look through devices that allowed them to see the world as various animals see it or could find their way through a maze using only their sense of smell. Other projects include the American Family Immigration History Center on Ellis Island, the Chicago Symphony Orchestra's Education Center (ECHO), and a live interactive television program designed to teach children geography by allowing them to manipulate a televised story using the keys on their touchtone phones.

In 1998, Schlossberg discussed the relation between media, built environments, education, and culture in his book *Interactive Excellence: Defining and Developing New Standards for the 21st Century*. Schlossberg speaks of the need for pedagogy to address its "audience" as a moving, embodied audience in relation. He argues that new media communication technologies have, in effect, made everyone a potential if not actual producer of culture. In response, audiences "have had to take on the role of arbiters of their own culture" (Schlossberg, 1998, p. 50). "The new Mozarts," or bearers of what is valued and excellent in contemporary liberal societies, he says, "may not be the ones simply composing music. They may be those people who create a dynamic compositional experience that enables people to comprehend how music is made, played, and understood" (Schlossberg, 1998, pp. 90–91).

On this issue, Schlossberg shares Leon Wieseltier's view (Wieseltier, you will remember, declared the U.S. Holocaust Memorial Museum to be a pedagogical masterpiece) that the desire to create potential times and places for experiences of the learning self can inspire the design of "masterful" compositions and assemblages of spaces, activities, objects, and interactions crucial to the experience of the learning self. Schlossberg proposes that we measure the excellence of attempts to do so "by the degree of conversation and transformation that occurs in the environment and the degree to which there is a shared sense that everyone is part of the process" (Schlossberg, 1998, pp. 90–91).

Schlossberg's practice, however, rests largely upon social–constructivist and communicational approaches to education, and as a result it frames the conversations and "transformations" that his places of learning invite in terms quite different than the ones we have been working with here. While Schlossberg advocates placing the experience of users and visitors at the center of pedagogy, his means provide a useful contrast to the places of learning discussed so far. He designs opportunities to participate cooperatively in "meaningful activities," and he defines "meaningful" as participation whose outcome depends in part on the visitor's choices and actions. He provides participants with opportunities to take action that makes a difference to their own and others' experiences in a shared environment, and he sees these designed opportunities as material correlates of the challenges that new media technologies present to citizens to act as arbiters of cultural excellence. His designs provide opportunities for the public arbitration of cultural excellence, he says, because they require many people, preferably of many different backgrounds, levels of expertise, and ages, to talk with each other and work together to figure out what his designs "do," how to bring them to life, and how to make them "work" (Schlossberg, 1998).

Rather than emphasizing movements and sensations of learning selves toward an undetermined destination, Schlossberg's designs frame their audience's discursive interaction by what he dubs the "script." By equipping the pedagogical pivot points of his designs with an implied script designed to elicit a desired "conversation" along lines he has already imagined, Schlossberg constrains the potential for open-ended and unanticipated conversations to occur. Heller explains Schlossberg's approach to designing places of learning (Heller, 2002, p. 1):

> For Schlossberg design is not about rearranging the aesthetics of the physical world but making fundamental philosophical changes with existing structures that would have the greatest benefit for the most people.

> "The idea that you make an experience that requires a conversation in a public place is training for the fact that culture is collective," Schlossberg says. Indeed, his design cannot function without proactive participants. His practice is rooted in the idea that people's experiences of things are enhanced through the contributions of others to the same experience. Direct engagement is Schlossberg's métier, and the signature high-tech gadgetry that makes his projects come alive is not an end but a means to draw audiences out of their complacency. "The history of the world is alive only in the nervous system of every body alive right now," he says. "Culture only exists dynamically."

Schlossberg invites an audience to take on roles within the stories, activities, and representations that he offers as material correlates of the conversation about "who, how, why, where, and when we are" (Schlossberg, 1998, p. 32). The activities he designs attempt to give physical, spatial, and temporal form to the processes of invention and democratic social interaction. For example, Heller (2002, p. 2) describes Schlossberg's designs for the Hansen Dam site of the new Children's Museum of Los Angeles this way:

Upon entering the Hansen Dam branch, kids will look up to find a stream of water running through a transparent gutter next to a serpentine pneumatic tube with pictures, drawings, and messages shooting by. This is adjacent to a long LED displaying digital messages. Near that is a movable rack like in a dry-cleaning store, with more things clipped to it, and finally a circuitous conveyor belt that spreads even more information throughout the hall. The attached material allows children to explain, communicate, and exchange their ideas, which then become the centerpiece of the museum for that day or week....

In the center of the space a 30-foot computer-driven tree is a wellspring of activity; visitors can take the water off the tree to feed the roots (the more water you feed it, the greener the leaves get at the top). Next to the kitchen is a place where kids can make food for the tree. The point is to have things in the museum that require kids' intervention to survive.

For the Chicago Symphony Orchestra's Education Center, Schlossberg's design took its cues from the "structural center points of classical music's appeal" — teamwork, sound, ritual, celebration, and mapping and notation. These five concepts became the pedagogical pivot points of ECHO as he transformed them into "something physical" which "actually works." Schlossberg's design incorporates four instrument-shaped boxes. "Each of the five ideas ... is presented at a separate enclosed console," and visitors "use their box at each console to explore one of the concepts" and record what they do there. The box is then put on a shelf on the Orchestra Wall where visitors hear a composition of which their creative efforts have become one part (Schlossberg, 1998, p. 68).

This materialization of shared experience out of the creative efforts of many individuals shows us the broad outlines of the desired and imagined "script" that shapes and informs the pedagogy of Schlossberg's designs. At a time when new media technologies and other sociocultural forces foster intense competition among individuals, Schlossberg finds it crucial for a democratic society to create conversations that spawn the sense of being part of a larger social body. Because he does not believe in the existence or appropriateness of one consensual standard for cultural excellence, he feels that these conversations must include as many viewpoints as possible (Schlossberg, 1998, pp. 18–19):

If the experience at a public event does not enable members of the audience to learn from one another, and if each member of society is increasingly isolated because he or she is getting most cultural events at home, there are no opportunities for the audience members to improve their ability to appreciate one another as well as the works presented…. There is a hunger for community, and if it is not encouraged to grow, some demonic leader could capitalize on the sense of anomie and alienation that isolation causes.

Consequently, he designs his places of learning as "tools that would enable one hundred or even five hundred people to have an interesting, exciting time communicating with each other and being engaged in trying to find more ways to do that" (Heller, 1998, p. 240). Schlossberg intends his designs to act, like art, as a great irritation: "A movie like *The Graduate* or a book like *The Grapes of Wrath* stimulates us — irritates us, in a way — to become part of a new conversation, with others and within ourselves, about who, how, why, where, and when we are" (Schlossberg, 1998, p. 32). The impetus behind his designs lies in his desire for people turn to each other and ask, "What does this mean?" Otherwise, he says, "it's useless to have it in a communal environment" (Schlossberg, 1998, p. 9). Schlossberg (1998, p. 80) describes a successful interactive design as one that …

> … involves a group of visitors in a comprehensible experience that enables them to clearly perceive the value of the other visitors' contributions…. Proper interaction means that each person in the process is affecting the outcome. They are communicating their needs, which are being integrated into the whole experience. And that experience is comprehensible and accessible to everyone.

Schlossberg configures time and space to offer visitors embodied experiences not of knowledges in the making but of *understandings* in the making — that is, he offers experiences of arriving at understandings of ideas and concepts *already made*. Thus, his designs do not address a visitor's learning self as being in the making. Rather than creating the opportunity to participate in an experience of knowledge in the making, he invites visitors to role play within stories about and representations of knowledge already made. Conversations about who we are, what we might become, and what we value are staged in terms of "making fundamental philosophical changes within *existing structures* [italics added]" — which means grounding such changes in what has already been imagined to be the "greatest benefit for the most people" (Heller, 2002, p. 1).

For example, invitations to participate in assembling a "concert" by using the scripted instruments we find at ECHO or to participate in watering a tree in order to turn its top green at Hansen Dam are invitations predicated on the already drawn conclusion that audience complacency is a threat to democratic cultures and that the solution is to open a conversation in which audience members cooperate and participate in creating a pleasing and entertaining shared experience that makes individual contributions to the collective outcome visible and able to be appreciated.

While we can role play within the parameters established by Schlossberg's places of learning, we are not invited to lose our selves in them or to lose them in order to follow an unscripted path. These are not places for us to experience our selves, or the social body, in dissolution. They present a benign irritation, a provocation to conversation, by creating the need for an audience to figure out what an activity or installation (already) "does" so that they might work together in order to make it happen (again). The irritation that confronts the learning self, not with scripted parameters for a conversation but with its own movement into dissolution or into passage between knowledges already made, confronts us with what we cannot know. It is the productive irritation of, say, the aesthetic experience described by de Bolla which dissolves the illusion that we are the authors of our actions and knowledge and replaces it with the irritating reality that we both make ourselves and are made by what we collectively and individually have made to be our other. The difference between places of learning designed to provide experiences of "collective success — with communal roles and responsibilities" (Schlossberg, 1998, p. 72) and those designed to provoke the (individual and collective) experience of the learning self in the making is the difference between a conversation and a metaphor. Or, to put it another way, it is the difference between an explanation and the time and space of play.

The pedagogical pivot point of one place of learning designed by Schlossberg hinges on metaphor rather than on scripted conversation: Schlossberg describes the Brooklyn Children's Museum as offering a "laboratory" or an "eccentric aunt's garage into which people could go and, looking over the shoulder of their aunt, use the available tools to understand the world" and "learn about their world and culture through play" (Schlossberg, 1998, p. 58). In a passage that could pass for a description of Winnicott's transitional space, Schlossberg (1998, pp. 58–59) says:

> I wanted [the Children's Museum] to be a model of how one could learn from the world by experimenting with it. The idea was for it to be a set of tools with which people could experiment — interacting with one another as well as with the museum itself — rather than artifacts that were perceived as being more valuable than children experimenting. The aim was to eliminate any intermediary between the children and their process of exploration....
>
> Lighting and structures are used for tools of understanding ... the physical museum should be responsive to the interests of the children as the children become interested in the museum. Each gesture toward exploration is met with a response and a transformation. I think of the museum as a learning environment, but that environment changes according to the activities of the children.

The Brooklyn Children's Museum's activities were thus framed not by scripts (which, of course, would undermine Schlossberg's desire to "eliminate any intermediary between the children and their process of exploration") but rather by a desire to create a "responsive" pedagogical holding environment with the capacity to meet gestures of exploration with a "transformation" of its own pedagogy "according to the activities of the children."

In this way, the invitation of the Brooklyn Children's Museum to "learn through play" is similar to that of the Manhattan Children's Museum's exhibition *Art Inside Out*. By inviting children to play "inside artists' imaginations," *Art Inside Out* addresses children through a metaphor that breeches identities, roles, and meanings that limit the learning self and sends them into an eccentric dip into the spaces between knowledges already made. Schlossberg's design for the Brooklyn Children's Museum invites children to play in an "eccentric aunt's garage." Its pedagogical pivot place is "filled" by the presence of the imaginary eccentric aunt over whose shoulder children are invited to peer, but the aunt's pedagogical address is an indirect one: Her back is toward the children as she is engrossed in the project before her. She both fills and empties a space of play that children can enter and where they can eccentrically make something of the tools and objects they find there. Here, play is the experience of the learning self in its incompleteness. Here, pedagogy remains sensational. As metaphors and times and places of play, these two children's museums offer roles to play, but not to fill. In play, we find ourselves at the limits of the social body's potential to vary, entwined with other participants in acts of play the rules of which are not determined in advance. Here, participation means participating in the emergence of what the rules and who the players are along with the new concepts created and the new problems posed (Rajchman, 2000a, p. 38).

In contrast, the scripted designs that Schlossberg has since developed for older children, youth, and adults employ an "experiential base" as a pretext for getting to somewhere else already known. In places of scripted play, the experience of learning is the experience of a shared, consensual understanding in the making. In an interview with Heller, Schlossberg voiced his intention to focus future work on addressing the "resistance" some people have had to his designs. "The response has been enthusiastic among those people for whom growth and discovery and other people are attractive, and it has been resistant among those who feel otherwise. In my naïve enthusiasm for making the world better, I expected everyone to embrace the idea, and of course they did not" (Heller, 1998, p. 241). Although he attempts to stage an inclusive democratic conversation, "those who feel otherwise" or those who would not participate or embrace the idea as it is already made are excluded or exclude themselves from the conversation — and that, of course, means the conversation is no longer democratic.

The presence of "those who feel otherwise" brings Schlossberg to the limits of relationality and therefore to the limits of the social body's potential to vary. There, he finds his designs facing the paradox of liberal education. Looking back at them are the faces of children, and on those faces is the look that I have associated with the experience of the learning self in the making. Perhaps we associate that look most readily with children, because in Schlossberg's practice, as in many other pedagogies, the invitation to learn through play, metaphor, and the eccentric dip into the spaces between knowledges already made is one that often seems to be reserved for children or for those deemed to be childlike. It is as if the sociostructural grid allows the social body's potential to vary to be at its greatest in the minds/brains/and bodies of children at play. It is as if the risk presented to the sociostructural grid by an open, undetermined future of thought and relationality is at its least when the thoughts and sensations involved are merely those of children. It is as if children's minds/brains and bodies mark the limits of the social body; yet, while in school, children's bodies also fall outside of the private sphere as delineated by the sociostructural grid. Perhaps one of the most potent challenges that educators could mount against knowledge as a thing already made and the interests it supports and perpetuates would be this: to make schools places where the force of children's passages into and within the spaces between what we already think we know about the world and its relationalities is augmented and assembled in ways that inflect the social body's ways of knowing with children's ways of knowing.

Bravehearts: Men in Skirts as the Limit of the Social Body's Potential

While completing the draft of this book, I attended a conference on museums and difference. One of the participants had just been to see *Bravehearts: Men in Skirts*, an exhibition at the Metropolitan Museum of Art in New York City. He said that the conversations in the galleries among exhibit goers were some of the most "truly useful" he had heard in any museum. He attributed this, in part, to the exhibition's "lack of closure." A few days later, I spent the better part of a day viewing the exhibition, intent on eavesdropping.

Andrew Bolton and Harold Koda of the Metropolitan Museum's Costume Institute organized the exhibition. It explored how groups and individuals (for example, "hippies" and "visionary designers") have promoted the skirt for men as the "future of menswear." The exhibition consisted of manikins arranged in a manner that recalled store-window fashion displays and placed skirts of old and current skirts for men in a number of historical and cross-cultural contexts. The wall text clearly stated the lack of a "natural link" between an item of clothing and masculinity and femininity. In fact, it pointed out that the kilt is "one of the most potent, versatile, and enduring skirt forms often looked upon by fashion designers as a symbol of a natural, uninhibited masculinity." Additional text at the exhibition explained that contemporary designers and male skirt-wearers have appropriated the skirt for at least three purposes: to inject novelty into male fashion, to transgress moral and social codes, and to redefine an ideal masculinity. The website documentation of the exhibition (http://www.metmuseum.org/special/se_event.asp?OccurrenceId=%7B823731F9-6846-4D66-AFF5-AB57B724C97A%7D) reads in part:

> Men who have wished to characterize themselves as resistant, rebellious, or simply contrarian have adopted skirted garments as a sign of their refusal to meet societal expectations. The exhibition concludes with the ways in which various youth and countercultural movements such as punk, grunge, and glam rock have adopted the skirt as a means of transgression and self-expression. Skirts worn by musical icons such as Boy George and Adrian Young of *No Doubt* are among the highlights of the exhibition.

Bolton, one of the organizers of the exhibition, commented in the wall text: "Whether the acceptance of the skirt for men is viewed as a threat or a promise, *Bravehearts: Men in Skirts* will intrigue and provoke."

People who attended the exhibition were perhaps even more self-selected than those who were visiting concurrent exhibitions that day at the Met. *Bravehearts: Men in Skirts* was housed in a lower-level, self-contained space accessed via the stairway or elevator that could be found in a far corner of the museum's first floor. The price of admission seemed to be the effort it took to seek out the exhibition and the willingness to be "intrigued and provoked" enough to consider alternatives to and options presented by skirt-wearing as a particular habit and convention.

While eavesdropping on a number of visitors who were there in pairs or small groups, I overhead various conversations revolving around whether or not the conversations' participants would ever consider wearing skirts of any kind, whether they would wear a particular skirt featured in the exhibit, and under what specific circumstances they might consider wearing a skirt. One man said to his companion: "A caftan — after a shower or in the gym — can you imagine? 'Excuse me, coming through.' Can you imagine?" A number of women viewing the exhibition with men asked their male companions (sometimes seriously, sometimes teasingly) versions of the question: "Would you ever wear that one?" A number of men replied or volunteered without being asked: "Yeah, I could wear that." … "It's cool. I would buy something like that and wear it to the beach. I wonder where you could buy it." … "I could get away with wearing that one to [a particular party or venue]." … "I like the red one, but I wouldn't wear it … but that [pointing to a different skirt] I'd wear."

An adolescent girl refused in disgust to consider the suggestion offered by the wall text that a similarity exists between skirts and the wide pants worn by hip-hop artists. Two older women said to each other: "I can imagine our sons, our grandsons. It's ridiculous, utterly ridiculous." One couple considered whether "S" would ever wear a skirt: "See, that's what I'm telling you, he could do it … next year…. He'd look really cool." One woman said to the man she was with: "It's like the one you had on yesterday [naughty laughter]." Another woman said enthusiastically: "*Metrosexuals*, my favorite new word." When a woman asked a man "Would you wear a caftan?" he answered, flatly, "No." Referring to one of the male manikin's outfits, a woman wondered: "The suit I wear all the time, doesn't it look like that?" Two men talked about how, when men tie their sweaters around their waists and let them hang like a skirt, they get the "skirt effect" without having to actually wear one. One man, reading the wall text about the widespread wearing of skirts by men in "other cultures," said: "God. Three quarters of the world's population [wear skirts]!" A young man and young woman dressed in Goth style had the following exchange:

Young man: "I would be afraid the first time, but after that …"
Young woman: "Are you going to come to school in a skirt?"
His reply: "A denim one."
Her reply: "I'll get a denim skirt and you can borrow it."
He says: "What if I get a lip ring?"
She says: "Get an eyebrow ring."

Several couples or small groups speculated about whether specific people they knew would wear "one like that" or "could get away with it" or "would look good in it." Among a number of people, stories were told about instances in which a man they knew wore a skirt. Other stories were told that had nothing to do with skirts but recounted transgressions of gender or sexual norms or were about people who presumed someone they knew was gay when he was not. In one group, a "dirty joke" was being told. One young woman said to another: "That's so cool [contemplating one of the skirted manikins]. Did you see *Love Actually*? Did you cry? My dad cried." Some of the visitors spoke very little and wore expressions of unease bordering on apprehension. Their engagements with the displays were almost furtive.

This exhibition's explicit invitation to its visitors was to be intrigued and/or provoked enough to question how and why things got this way and to consider whether a trend toward skirts for men in the future really does exist. Less explicitly, it invited its visitors to imaginatively transgress conventions and norms by "window shopping" for alternative forms of inhabitation of public and private spaces through clothing and the new forms of corporeality it makes conceivable and/or possible. The exhibition invited visitors to consider how such a simple act of wearing a simple piece of clothing can have such huge ramifications in meanings, behaviors, everyday life, senses of self and others, and configurations of insider and outsider. It invited us to consider what it might mean to "get away with" wearing some forms of clothing — forms outside the socially sanctioned ways of demarcating and configuring the intimate and the social spaces around us. It asked: How does each of us every day try to "get away with" desires for new forms of embodiment through the use of fashion to regulate the passage of materialities, fantasies, images, and meanings from inside to outside, from outside to inside our individual bodies and the social body. Who (which of the bodies among us) can get away with such movements/sensations? And who cannot?

This prompts me to ask who can get away with "wearing," as students and teachers, the sensations/movements of the anomalous, sensational places of learning that we have been looking at throughout this book?

By inviting us to imagine putting on a skirt and being transformed, *Bravehearts: Men in Skirts* stages the skirt as a transitional object. Who am I if and when and where I wear skirts? Who am I with that skirt on? Who am I if I do not ever wear skirts? In the scene of pedagogical address staged by this exhibition, I am a self in dissolution. The skirted manikins become material analogs, concretizations of the (different) selves that I might imagine.

The power of the skirt as staged in the exhibition (the power of a transitional object) lies in the fact that what it invites me to imagine can never be merely a self. It must always be a self in relation. It is impossible to imagine stepping into one of those skirts without simultaneously conjuring images and scenarios of potentialities for acting and being acted upon. Such is the power of the skirt as a mode of inhabitation of personal and social space. The simple act of wearing it qualitatively transforms personal space into a social act. It does so by reconfiguring the terms in which one "may" act and be acted upon, and it qualitatively transforms social space into something intimately personal by putting the body into intimate and open contact with the outside world. One man, looking incredulously at the "construction worker" manikin, which wore a tool-belted kilt, worried out loud about what kind of "protection" this skirt would afford to men working on ladders and scaffolds.

As a place of learning, *Bravehearts: Men in Skirts* offers itself as a "conceptual model of embodiment." Its skirted manikins encourage critical reflection on the socializing effect of our encounters with everyday fashion products. By doing so in an ambiguous and indirect way, the pedagogy of this exhibition stages complex interactions between reality and imagination. "By imagining the object in use, we become lost in a space between desire and determinism" (Dunne, 1999, p. 57). A pedagogy that invites such imaginings generates a "conceptual space where interactivity can challenge and enlarge the scheme through which we interpret our experiences of using everyday objects and the social experiences they mediate" (Dunne, 1999, p. 66). By imagining living with(in) these simple but forbidden (to some of us) objects, the viewer explores boundaries between himself or herself and the currently "captured" potentialities for corporeality and embodiment that are coalesced in the skirt. As a material analog to critical conceptual models of embodiment and corporeality, the pedagogical scene staged by the skirted manikins has the potential to challenge "how we think about extensions to our 'selves' in ways that do not simply magnify, but, rather, transform our perception and consciousness of our relation to our environment" (Dunne, 1999, p. 56).

This exhibition sustains ambiguity and potentiality at the limits of the social body's potential to vary. It does so in part by deferring an all too easy answer to the question of men in skirts. It must defer that answer because as the answer to the question of men in skirts it is designed to capture and contain the potential for new forms of embodiment and corporeality that men release when they wear skirts. That answer, of course, is that men in skirts must be either gay or queerly effeminate. Instead of entertaining this answer, the exhibition attempts to "prolong the thought-path of movement" of minds/brains and bodies into and through the spaces between gay and straight, masculine and feminine, in and out, male and female. It does so by deflecting the questions of "Who does wearing a skirt mean you are or make you to be in the social body?" or "Might there be not simply a skirt but also a queer moment in your future?" to a less threatening question: "Might there be a skirt in your fashion future?" It deflects the thought-path of movement along the direction of this third question by posing the question of men in skirts as a question of the "visionary" practices and prototypes offered by fashion designers; that is, it poses the question of men in skirts as a question of progress and freedom and not as a question of stigma and oppression.

In the exhibition's online documentation (http://www.metmuseum. org/special/se_event.asp?OccurrenceId=%7B823731F9-6846-4D66-AFF5-AB57B724C97A%7D), Bolton says: "From the 1960s, with the rise of countercultures and an increase in informality, men have enjoyed more sartorial freedom, but they still lack access to the full repertoire of clothing worn by women." The fact that most men in the United States do not wear skirts today is thus framed as an issue of whether or not men will gain progressively more freedom from a restricted code for appearance that has been in place since the "'great masculine renunciation' of the late eighteenth and early nineteenth century." It is framed as an issue of and for the future and an issue of and for "more freedom" and variation: Is the vision of men in skirts a vision of the future? And, in that future, will men be freer? Of course, "being freer with one's self" presents us with a double entendre. It opens the individual body to the social body in ways that, as we have already seen Patricia Williams point out, "complicate definition and give room for the possibility of creatively mated taxonomies and their wildly unpredictable offspring" (Williams, 1991, p. 11). As Grosz observed (Grosz & Eisenman, 2001, p. 92):

> An openness to futurity is the challenge facing all of the arts, sciences, and humanities; the degree of openness is an index of one's political alignments and orientations, of the readiness to transform. Unless we put into question ... the identities of women and women, of different races and classes, and of different religious, sexual, and political affiliations, as well as the identities of cities, urban regions, buildings, and houses — this openness to the future, the promise of time unfolding through innovation rather than production, is muted rather than welcome.

The pedagogical power of this exhibition is that by deferring the question of sexuality to the question of fashion the exhibition activates the limits of the potentials of both the social body and the individual human body to vary. It places the voice of its "teacher" at the limit from which things can be "gotten away with" — which here also means it speaks to and from the limits of how we treat each other as "human." As it does this, it also finds itself — in fact, it *must* find itself — activating the limits of what counts as the human body. The limits of the social body are deeply implicated with what we take to be the limits of the human body's potential to vary. The limits that mark the boundaries where the forces of sexuality, gender, and the social body meet have been turbulent places and often sites of violent acts. As long as the question of men in skirts can be collapsed into the question of whether or not one "is gay" — and as long as the question of whether or not one "is gay" is collapsed into the question of whether or not one "is human" — we will find ourselves at the place where the limits of the social body and the limits of the human body intersect and do so with serious material effects. If it is a male and it wears a skirt, is it gay? If it is gay, is it human? If it is not human, does it deserve to live? If it does not deserve to live, we can get away with making it a target of violence. Killing it ends its future and closes what has opened the social body to an undecided future and to the potential to vary from what here and now is already known to be.

By refusing to state its curriculum in anything close to these terms, by refusing to gesture directly to these points on the grid of social and cultural significations and identities currently associated with skirts, this exhibition skirts these points. In doing so, it attempts to prolong thought-paths that might invent other ways of answering the question of men in skirts. The fixed and encoded points that stake out the limits of what is human and what we can get away with in the social body are gestured toward indirectly at every turn in the exhibit. It is the indirectness of that gesture toward fixed points of identity that makes it possible for knowledge as a thing already made to cohabit with the learning self's "processual continuity across categorical divides." The indirection of this exhibition allows for bodies and identities to move about in an exhibition space that has become, by design, palpably public and private, intimate and anonymous, charged with transgression and playful and to combine and inflect there in reciprocal variation with what is in the making between such categorical divides. By refusing to directly address the congealed forms and cohesions of identities that limit the social body and make it possible to get away with violence against bodies deemed not human, those limiting relationalities and identities are not made present. They are not contemporaneous with the here and now of the exhibition. They are relegated to being after-thoughts (or "ignore-ances"). They are relegated to a (uninteresting? irrele-vant? unfashionably restrictive?) time that is already somewhere in this exhibition's past. By staging the time of this exhibition somewhere in its own imagined future and addressing us as already able to go there in our imaginations if not in our desires, it clears space for the future as that "over which the past and present have no control: the future [as] that openness of becoming that enables divergence from what exists" (Grosz & Eisenman, 2001, p. 142).

Pedagogy's Future

The experience of the learning self in the making is what Irigaray called a category of the future anterior. In that tense, the experience of the learning self is simultaneously the experience of what I shall have become by what I am in the process of learning and the experience of what I shall have learned by the process of what I am becoming. The time of the learning self takes place in the future anterior tense because it is the "only tense that openly addresses the question of the future without, like the utopian vision, preempting it" (Grosz & Eisenman, 2001, p. 147). This is the correct tense for a pedagogical address, because despite many discourses to the contrary, education is not utopic; it is bound to the present by the necessity to tear half-living knowledges out of their histories, to declare what of them is still of use and what of them we must now deem to be dead. Education is, para-phrasing Grosz, "one of the present's ways of conceptualizing its current problems" (Grosz & Eisenman, 2001, p. 147). Because pedagogy is a way of conceptualizing the present's problems, all the work of education, all of its labor of producing alternative knowledges, methods, and criteria, has yet to begin. Learning is beyond the utopian, because no vision, narrative, or plan can anticipate or perform the work of remaking knowledge in the moment. It is entirely of the order of the surprise, of the encounter with the new (Grosz & Eisenman, 2001, p. 147).

We are all brave hearts in skirts when we are teaching. Skirts open bod-ies to being acted upon and to acting upon the outside. They open bodies to relationality, to movement/sensations of exchange with others and with the outside. When we are teaching, we are the impetus for the future ante-rior (Grosz & Eisenman, 2001, p. 150). We are surrounded by our own birth.

Conclusion
Pedagogy in the Making

Does the notion of "things in the making" in and around us then suppose a zone of historical indetermination allowing for such experimentation?

—John Rajchman

If any of the anomalous places of learning that we have considered here can be considered masterpieces, it is because they encompass a peculiar knowledge and skill. By structuring pedagogy through a silence that demarcates the limits of what we can teach and know, they have understood and put to use the very limits of knowledge and pedagogy. As a result, they paradoxically give access to an interminable experience of the learning self — to the experience of the learning self as in the making.

We find no literal acknowledgments of the limits of knowledge and pedagogy in these places of learning, nor do they offer dissertations about their implied theories of pedagogy or explanations of their implicit "lessons" about teaching and learning. Like Peter de Bolla's hypothesis regarding *where* the content or aesthetic material (that is, the art) of an artwork can be found, the pedagogical component of the places of learning we have considered can only be found in the response of one's learning self to a place's assemblage of texts, images, media, documents, objects, address, space, and time. At the same time, a learning self's response is *to a particular pedagogy in its singularity*, which means that the content or material of a pedagogy must also to be found in the place of learning itself.

de Bolla agrees with D.W. Winnicott: We both find and create our aesthetic experiences as we live through them. Painters, sculptors, or writers do not give them to us. Nor do we possess our aesthetic experiences as intellectual or affective properties of our selves. In this sense, the "lesson" regarding the limits of knowledge and pedagogy that I experienced (and described in Chapter 5) in the U.S. Holocaust Memorial Museum's permanent exhibit, for example, is an artifact of my response. It is my response in excess of my self, and it is the exhibit exceeding itself — in the form of my response. My response takes place in and because of the transitional space that I experience between my self and the exhibit, the materiality of which is very real. The space and time of relationality create the content of my "internal" response as both found and created. The pedagogical component of the U.S. Holocaust Memorial Museum exhibit, and each of the places of learning that we have considered, is thus a "virtual quality of the work residing in the space between the object and my appreciation of it" (de Bolla, 2001, p. 135); however, de Bolla asserts, it is the peculiar quality of aesthetic experience that his "own" experience of an artwork seems as if it *must* be shareable. It "takes on the illusory quality of objectivity" (de Bolla, 2001, p. 15) by appearing to reside not in him, but elsewhere: in the artwork.

Because his response to an artwork is both "his" *and* dependent on the presence of the artwork in its uniqueness, what he knows about the artwork and how he knows it easily appears to be a quality of the work itself (de Bolla, 2001, p. 55). This leads him to ask: Does his response to artworks give him knowledge and, if so, of what? In other words, does a particular artwork consist of a way of knowing? de Bolla answers in the affirmative but suggests that to articulate what an artwork knows requires a peculiar sort of knowledge that is neither propositional knowledge nor knowledge by acquaintance; rather, to grasp what artworks know "requires a different conception of knowledge itself. This kind of knowledge would not be exclusively the property of an agent, not something I can own or could be said to be familiar with. It would also be within the artwork, something, as it were, known to it" (de Bolla, 2001, p. 134). Neither the artwork nor de Bolla is the agent of this knowledge. de Bolla calls this knowledge "a knowing rather than knowledge" and describes it as more of a state of mind than an object owned (de Bolla, 2001, p. 135). He concludes that an artwork creates the potential for a knowing that takes place in the rarified atmosphere between sensation and cognition.

Wieseltier's designation of the U.S. Holocaust Memorial Museum as a "pedagogical masterpiece" asserts the right and the possibility to locate the aesthetic in the realm of the educational and to locate the educational in the realm of the aesthetic. By his refusal to separate emotion from cognition in his attempts to articulate the qualities of aesthetic experience, de Bolla asserts the same right and responsibility. He contends that the content of his affective response in the midst of an aesthetic experience is not merely one of feeling. "Indeed, my affective or *aesthetic* experience is held in a more rarified atmosphere than feeling, between emotive sensation and cognition" (de Bolla, 2001, p. 55). As such, his aesthetic experience exceeds feeling and involves cognition.

If we are to agree, we must ask, as I do in this conclusion, what knowing is possible in such transitional spaces between artworks and viewers, pedagogies and learners? What can we "know" from the felt reality of relation out of which categories and identities emerge but within which they remain unnamed? What is the *pedagogical component* of the experience of the learning self?

What the Learning Self Knows of Pedagogy

de Bolla's discussions of his experiences of William Wordsworth's poem *We Are Seven*, Barnett Newman's *Vir Heroicus Sublimis*, and Glenn Gould's *Goldberg* (1981) emphasize his aesthetic experience, but his discussion of Wordsworth's poem also invites us to read his encounter with it as a *scene of pedagogical address.* He invites us to ask, not as literary critics but as educators, what the experience of the learning self might know of *pedagogy*?

The two protagonists in *We Are Seven* are an adult and a "simple child," a "little cottage girl." The adult narrates the story of his encounter with the girl to his brother Jim. He prefaces his story by asking Jim what a simple child should know of death. He then says that he met an eight-year-old girl while he was out walking one day and asked her how many sisters and brothers "may you be?" The girl replied: "How many? Seven in all." He asks where they are. She replies that two live in Conway, two are "gone to sea," and "two of us in the church-yard lie": a sister and a brother.

The adult does the math. He counters: two in Conway, two at sea, "Yet you are seven; I pray you tell Sweet Maid, how this may be?" The girl replies by repeating: "two of us in the church-yard lie." The adult corrects her, saying that if that is so, "Then ye are only five." The girl then tells him that their "green" graves can be seen only twelve steps from her mother's door. She often goes there to knit or hem and to "sing to them." In the evening she often takes her porringer and eats her supper there. Her sister died first, in the summer. Her brother died in the winter. They lay side by side in the graveyard. The adult repeats his question: "How many are you then … if they two are in Heaven?" and the girl replies: "O Master! We are seven." The adult insists: "But they are dead, those two are dead!" The poem concludes with the poet again addressing his brother. He says his insistence that "those two are dead" "'twas throwing words away; for still the little maid would have her will, and said, 'Nay, we are seven!'"

de Bolla locates what he calls the drama of this poem in the distance between its two voices and what this difference puts at stake. He describes that distance as the difference between knowledge and acknowledgment — and by that he means the difference between what we "know" by making sense and what we "know" through sensation and being sensate.

The two voices caught up in this drama are, of course, the adult and the "simple child." To de Bolla (2001, p. 106), the adult appears...

> ...almost like an inquisitor whose voice conforms with and confirms a theory of meaning based within the needs and demands of the social, a kind of contractarian theory of meaning in which the descriptive phrase "we are seven" can only, or must only, refer to beings present or alive, inhabiting the same continuum as the point of speech. The child, by contrast, is portrayed as naïve or uneducated; her voice sounds out the demand that language be subordinated to lived experience. Consequently, for her the meaning of the phrase "we are seven" is to be found outside the present social context of speech, its voicing in the here of the now.

The confrontation of these two voices takes place, de Bolla implies, across the distance and difference between adulthood and childhood, individual and social, present and future. Because most educational practices are motivated by attempts to resolve or negate these very differences, the question de Bolla asks (2001, p. 107) lies at the heart of theories of education: What is at stake when these differences are resolved in favor of the knowledge invoked by the adult voice? What difference, that is, does education make when it usurps the girl's voicing of the world?

> I would like to approach [the knowingness of the poem] by asking what difference it might make if the child were to accept the correction of the adult: what would the difference be if the child were to accede to the demands of the social, that is, to put away childish things and take on ... the adult description of how the world is, of being in the world, and thereby capitulate, acquiesce in the belief that the adult's voicing of the world is more accurate (sustainable, finally, believable?) than her own? What would it mean for the child to speak with the voice of the adult? What fear do we articulate in the demand that children "grow up," that is, put on an adult's voice, thereby negating or erasing the immediacy, which here is co-instantaneity, of speech and world, meaning the experience that seems to be characterized by the girl's insistence that "we are seven"?

Through these questions, de Bolla centers his discussion of his aesthetic experience of this poem on problems of knowledge, knowing, and what is knowable: What "should" be taught to children about death? What do children (already) know but cannot or will not articulate about death? What are adults able and unable to know of death? What kind of "teachers" do the limits of their knowledge make of adults?

As a scene of pedagogical address, an implicit question raised by this poem is how the girl *knows* that "we are seven." In effect, the adult's interrogation is a demand that she "show her work." If she were to explain how she arrived at this answer, it would mean that she had grasped the adult description of how the world *is*. As de Bolla points out, in order to know the knowledge that the adult asks for she would have to employ an adult's sense making, a knowledge predicated on naming and numbering. It is a knowledge that requires that "we be able to name both ourselves and the world, count on ourselves for the evidence that the world gives us"; it assumes the "general necessity" that we be able to "count on ourselves for the 'truth' of our senses" (de Bolla, 2001, p. 108).

The girl, however, cannot or will not explain in adult terms how she arrived at this sum. Her unwillingness or inability to name and count in accordance with the adult lies at the center of the poem's dramatic staging of what de Bolla sees as the distance between knowledge and acknowledgment. In de Bolla's experience of the poem, the adult's knowledge is rooted on the side of certainty, reality, the referent, and mutual understanding. Here, language founds sense and experience. Here, life and death are two absolutely separate worlds delineated by an absolute boundary with no space of passage between. Here, nothing confuses the math, and the addition comes out "right": the girl and her siblings are five.

de Bolla locates acknowledgment elsewhere in the rarified atmosphere of incommensurability, interpretation, breakdowns in communication, movement/sensation, the fraying of identity, and relationality. But, de Bolla insists, in such spaces between emotion and cognition, acknowledging the limits of knowledge is itself a form of knowing.

In the space between emotion and cognition, sensation has ontological priority over language and knowledge. Here, life and death do not fit snugly up against an absolute, definitive boundary. Here is the nether world, where math is excessive. Here, the girl and her siblings *are* seven. We hear the girl's voice echo in the interval between life and death. It reverberates in the space between senses, in the absence of math, where poetry itself is possible. What is at stake in this poem, and indeed in poetry itself, de Bolla says, is whether language as a tool for referencing consensual knowledge already made about the world will allow a space between what it knows of the world and the world itself — a space for the reverberation of sensation as a way of knowing. If the adult's use of language would dare allow for such reverberation, what quickly becomes an issue for language, if not its crisis, is when and where that reverberation will come to a stop.

The poet describes speaking to the girl as "throwing words away," as in discarding language itself. The poem implies, in de Bolla's reading, that the girl has gone astray of language, of naming and numbering. Naming and numbering dead people in the same fashion as those alive constitutes a "lesion" on language's power to reference a "real" and "consensual" world. As he asks: "What should a poem know of death?" de Bolla says: "I cannot fail to register the spectral impression left by the odd thought that there might be a continuity between the world I inhabit and some other place, named in another poem by Wordsworth (after Milton) as the 'nether world,' in which persons dead and alive might feel one another's presence" (de Bolla, 2001, p. 105). If such a nether world of sense making were acknowledged, de Bolla says, where would the rupture in our ability to count on language ever come to an end?

The crisis that the poem and, therefore, language create for knowledge and that neither can resolve, de Bolla says, is brought on by the poem itself. It does not and cannot know the answer to its own question: "How many may you be?" It seems somehow improper to ask the poem itself to resolve the question of "how many may you be," says de Bolla, because such a request would be an embarrassment to poetry itself. The "answer remains unknowable, and not only to … the reader" (de Bolla, 2001, p. 123). Yet, even as the poem itself does not know how or if to count the dead, it still asks the question. This is the "harm" that it does, and this is poetry's irritation — its ability to present a shock to language's function as a tool for counting and naming. de Bolla's reading of the poem's dramatic struggle between knowledge and acknowledgment (de Bolla, 2001, p. 110) suggests that the child's refusal to take on board the adult's description of the state of affairs might not be a result of ignorance or immaturity after all. Rather, it might be a demand to accept that…

> …there might be a way of knowing unknown to both the adult and the child, a form of knowing that is not susceptible to the mechanics of exchange that pertain in this case.

Some knowings cannot be conveyed through language. They fall in the spaces between the fixed positions on the grids of grammar, definition, and syntax. They fall between states that we "fix" retroactively out of our experiences, states such as "life" and "death." The poem cannot know the answer, yet it implicitly asks: "What does it mean that there are things we can't know or share through language, the very tool we have for exchanging knowledges already made?"

The poem's "answer" is to invite us to acknowledge the existence of forms of knowing that escape the efforts of language to reference a "consensual," "literal," "real" world. Such knowings lie beyond language's explanation; yet, by living through his aesthetic experience of this poem, de Bolla comes to sense, and accept as a way of knowing, the limits of the knowledge that language *is* capable of exchanging (de Bolla, 2001, p. 110). Because it lies beyond language, this other way of knowing is a form of knowledge that cannot…

> …become common property, yet in coming to know that I do not give up on the sense that if this were a form of knowing it must also

be within the orbit of things knowable and therefore shareable with others. This might be termed the burden that art reveals, or the distinctiveness of the aesthetic.

As a scene of pedagogical address, might *We Are Seven* constitute a pedagogical masterpiece?

If learning takes place in the movement/sensation of the self in dissolution, if the experience of learning lies beyond articulation through language, then this poem has acknowledged and addressed something of the experience of the learning self. It has sensed the limits of knowledge and has acknowledged meaning and sensation as a way of knowing, but what might this knowing be *of*? What value might such a knowing have for educators? What might we, as educators, do with or make of such a knowing? de Bolla suggests a *way of knowing* that appears to be unknown to both the adult and to the child of *We Are Seven*. It is a way of knowing that is not susceptible to explanation and thus cannot be made common property through teaching as explanation or through the scaffolding of cognition. This realization does not lead de Bolla or Wordsworth to abandon their sense that acknowledging the limits of knowledge *is* a form of knowing and that it might be "taught" through an encounter with this poem. By virtue of being a form of knowing, such an acknowledgment is "within the limits of things knowable and therefore shareable with others."

Art bends under its chosen burden of *trying to make shareable a knowing that cannot be explained*. Art assumes the burden of a knowing that is anything but literal and will not be reduced to the explainable through socially encoded grids of categories, names, and numbers. de Bolla clearly counts this poem as a work of genius for the way that it carries its distinctively aesthetic burden. Although it lies beyond language, *what the aesthetic knows* can be painted, sculpted, danced, or sensed in and through music, moving images, architecture, and poetry. What poetry "knows" is a way of knowing rooted in the movement of our learning selves as they pass into and through the space between the literal and the figurative and *experience one reality passing into another*.

The Drama at the Heart of Education

As a scene of pedagogical address, this poem's battle between knowledge and acknowledgment sets the stage for the drama at the heart of education. That drama takes place in the distance between what might be known in and to the experience of the learning self and what might be tellable of that knowing in language and through knowledge as a thing made. The drama of the encounter between the adult and the child, de Bolla implies, lies in the unanswerable question of the experience of the learning self.

The proximity of two unanswerable questions — that of aesthetic experience and that of the experience of the learning self — has made the partnership between art and education simultaneously uneasy and invaluable. Like an experience of the learning self, aesthetic experience holds the potential for the coming of a knowing, available only through acknowledgment and inaccessible through explanation. Explanation is simply unable to bear the weight of the "knowings" that are aesthetic experience or the experience of the learning self. Explanation's failures in these realms are of huge consequence for both art and pedagogy.

The failure of explanation in *We Are Seven* points up some of those consequences. In de Bolla's experience of this poem, the question of explanation is at the heart of the distance between its two voices. The pathos of that distance, he says, is constructed around ending, coming to an end, coming to a rest. The poem seems to need to figure out for itself what it might be to "acknowledge that words come to their resting place in explanation, as they would if the child were to accept the inquisitor's meaning of the words 'we are seven,' in other words, to accept the gift of adult sense" (de Bolla, 2001, p. 126). It is the gift of coming to rest in "certainty," and it is one that the adult retreats into after he encounters the child's story and the "weight of being" that it carries (de Bolla, 2001, p. 111).

The adult is not safe in his retreat, however. In the absence of an explanation from the girl, which would "end" the poem's conflict and its drama, the reverberation of her words continues — and it must, because, if this poem allowed words "to come to rest in explanation, then a certain loss or sorrow would result since such a resting point or ending would signal the foreclosure of sense, or of sensing" (de Bolla, 2001, p. 126). For de Bolla, this is another kind of death (de Bolla, 2001, p. 126):

> This is why the adult's sense of ending, of ending as sense, is anathema to the poet....
>
> Poetry, for Wordsworth, must continually ask itself the question of its own knowing, constantly probe the truth it knows yet struggles to reveal. This process cannot end, be in the house of adult certainty; that this is so is one of the axioms ... of being: precisely the admonishment from art that we learn ... to be at one with that knowledge.

By refusing to answer its own question, the poem acknowledges that it is incapable of expressing, in language, what language cannot tell or explain. It acknowledges and assumes the burden that it can never put down: the burden of a knowing that escapes the making of sense. The poem's refusal to interpret or explain the drama that it itself unfolds is not an act of weakness or cowardliness on the part of its poet. The poet has not given up his artistic authority; rather, he has assumed responsibility for poetry's power and gift as an aesthetic practice: to bear the burden of never coming to a rest so that de Bolla's own aesthetic response may formulate, and hear, its own questions (de Bolla, 2001, p. 123).

The measure of this poem's genius as a scene of pedagogical address is evident in de Bolla's descriptions of his aesthetic responses. He does not describe an experience of coming to rest in his own certainty. He describes instead being set in motion. As he reaches for language capable of "fluidfying" his accounts of his responses to this poem, he speaks in terms of feeling a physical register to his response, of being "cued," of sensing the somatic as it responds in its own terms, on its own account. He describes sensing the passage of time — at one moment sensing one response, at another moment sensing something else altogether. He says he senses resonances, places, callings to mind, comings upon, perceptions of one material form seeming to transmute into other material forms. He finds himself in "particular states" and along itineraries of response. Senses arise. Occurrences take place (de Bolla, 2001, pp. 144–145).

de Bolla's attempts to acknowledge a knowing that escapes explanation creates a confusion between making sense and being sensate. It is this confusion that puts him in motion. This is the movement/sensation that is anathema to endings, explanations, and knowledge as a thing made. All of these, of course, are anathema to a pedagogy that would invite the experience of the learning self to "formulate and hear" its *own* knowledge in the making.

I have worked here with a number of anomalous places of learning that reference death in various ways (de Bolla's aesthetic experience of *We Are Seven*, the U.S. Holocaust Memorial Museum, Maya Lin's memorials, designs for the site of New York City's twin towers, Shimon Attie's projections, Anna Deavere Smith's performances). I do not believe that memorials or memorialization have any special relationship to our experiment in thinking pedagogy, but I do believe that the places of learning I have worked with here exemplify a particular force of pedagogy. They site themselves within ideas, events, histories, and memories that are predicated upon highly traumatic or provocative divisions between self and other, us and them, inside and outside, and then they attempt to turn those seemingly absolute boundaries into places of learning by rendering them porous, fluid, and palpable.

I have been drawn to the places of learning that engage death in part because the binary life/death puts tremendous pressure on the idea that has been central to our experiment — namely, that all binaries are exceeded by spaces between and around their terms. The binary life/death, whose terms seem to be absolutely bounded, puts tremendous pressure on the idea that each of the terms that makes up a binary exists in relation to its own outside — which is a space of passage, movement, and potentiality capable of unhinging binary logic. This idea would make death to be the space of life's passage, movement and potentiality. It would make life to be the space of death's passage, movement, and potentiality. Furthermore, the binary life/death sets the issue of the limits of knowledge and the concept of the unknowable in their starkest relief. And, finally, death — as embodiment's outside — presses most forcefully and directly on how we might think of the body, its continuity, and the emergence of embodied experience. Nevertheless, I believe that the same limits to pedagogy and to knowing that were provoked, for example, by the permanent exhibit of the U.S. Holocaust Memorial Museum assert themselves in relation to the most mundane curricular content. What is at issue is not the meanings of life or death for pedagogy; at issue are the meanings of explanation's cohabitation with movement/sensation in the experience of the learning self. What will pedagogy make of that fact?

I Know But I Can't Explain How I Came To Know This

I have used de Bolla's reading of *We Are Seven* to set up a tension between explanation and movement/sensation, and I have placed explanation in the service of knowledge as a thing already made and in the service of the grids of positionality. But, we have also seen explanation as existing in a tense cohabitation with another way of knowing: the knowing that skirts the limits of explanation and sets us in motion through the gaps between positions, identities, categories, and already achieved knowledges. None of the ideas we have considered suggests that we can do without explanation or that educators and pedagogy must now stop teaching curriculum "content." Explanation as knowledge already made is "our way of dealing with the plethora of sensations, vibrations, movements, and intensities that constitute both our world and ourselves, [it is] a practical exigency" (Grosz & Eisenman, 2001, p. 171). I do suggest, however, following Grosz, that explanation may be "indeed perhaps only one mode, not a necessary condition, of our acting in the world" (Grosz & Eisenman, 2001, p. 171), and there is also de Bolla's reminder of the "dark interior secret of knowing otherwise, a stark outpost of the resistance to propositional knowledge" (de Bolla, 2001, p. 145). The knowing that is an acknowledgment of the limits of knowledge, de Bolla says (2001, p. 144), is…

> …a different species of knowledge, a way of knowing that does not lead to certainties or truths about the world or the way things are. It is a state of mind, of being with the world and oneself that … colors all that we know we know.

With this, de Bolla shows us a way out of the explanation/sensation binary and beyond the paradox that plagues liberal education and the practice of pedagogy as a strategy of liberal rule. Because education must deal in and with "knowledge," it must repeat and foster recognition of congealed, formulated, predictable thought forms and cultural forms. Doing so, it conserves a facet of the past and always risks "reducing the future to a form of repetition" because knowledge as a thing that makes the world recognizable even as it is continuously unfolding is always at risk of "tying the new and the never-conceived to that which is already recognized" (Grosz & Eisenman, 2001, p. 103). Yet, for education to avoid becoming propaganda or coercion, it must be open to difference, to the unthought — "it must abandon itself to the force or pull of a future that it cannot secure and which may, at any moment, serve to reverse its thrust" (Grosz, 2002, p. 103).

de Bolla's "knowing that colors all we know we know" moves us out of this paradox because it is not *opposed* to explanation and certainty; rather, *it encompasses them within sensation/movement.* This different knowing circumvents explanation and certainty with sensation/movement. Its skirting movement creates a distinction between explanation/certainty and stasis/movement, but it is not the distinction of a logical binarism; rather, according to Brian Massumi (2002, p. 8), it is a distinction that...

> ...follows the modes by which realities pass into each other. "Passing into" is not a binarism. "Emerging" is not a binarism. They are dynamic unities. The kinds of distinction suggested here pertain to continuities under qualitative transformation.

Our experiences of emergence, movement, and the sensation of skirting or being in passage between fixed points of knowledge and certainty can color how we "hold" our adult certainty. By cultivating acknowledgments and awarenesses of experiences of our learning selves, we might become capable of relating to certainty not as its own guarantee but as an emergent quality of movement/sensation. We may no longer need to stage the drama of pedagogy in liberal education as the struggle between explanation and poetry, rational deliberation and emotional sensation, facts and feelings, a codified curriculum and the lived, singular experience of an exhibition or event. We may recognize instead that the value of aesthetic experience to education is that it moves us out of such binary oppositions. In aesthetic experience and in the experience of the learning self, explanation and poetry pass into and out of each other. Rational deliberation passes into and out of emotional sensation. Facts and feelings, codified curriculum, and singular, unrepeatable, ephemeral experiences of moments of learning pass into and out of each other. Art is the "sensational performance" of the passages of such realities into and out of each other (Massumi, 2002, p. 252). Art foils the opposing, static face-off between these realities that has debilitated liberal education for so long.

The work or gift of aesthetic experience within and to education is not that it will *teach* us this different species of knowledge — this knowing that encompasses explanation. While art gives the potential for us to experience this other way of knowing, our experience of it does not come to rest in any certain knowledge or learning of it. As de Bolla's discussion of

We Are Seven shows, artworks do not know the answers to the many questions that this different species of knowledge raises, and this is the source of its pedagogical power. The pedagogical power and burden of the aesthetic is that it allows us to form and hear our own questions about this knowing. Artworks set us in the midst of knowings that are not tellable, but those knowings *are* "sense-able." What artworks know is how to invite experiences that allow the realities of propositional knowledge to "pass into" acknowledgment of other realities that exceed propositional knowledge, and back again. In this way, aesthetic experience is like the experience of the learning self.

So we arrive at the question of pedagogy's specificity. In the many ways we have been exploring, aesthetic experience is like the experience of the learning self. Both access and put to use the spaces-between culturally constructed significations. Both take place in and through transitional space. Neither can be told, explained, or known as propositional knowledge. Both are sensations/movements of passage and of qualitative transformation. But, art is not education, and an artwork is not a pedagogy. The experience of the learning self is not an aesthetic experience. So what is the difference? What is pedagogy's uniqueness?

Aesthetic experience "speaks" as if to say: "I know, but I can't explain what I know through propositional language. Let me 'tell' this knowing through paint, sound, metaphor, media, built forms, sensation, emotion, or silence." The experience of the learning self "speaks" as if to say: "I know, but I can't explain how I came to know this. I came to know this in a nonconscious time/space. What I now 'know' happened in the interval, in the continuous space of crossing from one way of knowing to another. I can't decompose my movement/sensation of that crossing into an explanation of it, but I can gesture toward the coordinates of its passage and invite you along an itinerary — a pedagogy — designed to open an interval for you to fall outside of what we already know. If that interval opens for you, and if you fall, my itinerary will be transformed by yours as it emerges, in the making, and on the way to a destination uniquely your own."

This is the burden that pedagogy bears. What it knows of the experience of the learning self cannot be shared through telling, explanation, or propositional knowledge, but what it knows of the experience of the learning self can be shared in other terms. What makes for a pedagogical masterpiece is how it bears this burden.

Pedagogy's Burden

We Are Seven, the U.S. Holocaust Memorial Museum, Smith's performances, Wodiczko's projections and critical vehicles, *Bravehearts: Men in Skirts*, and the other anomalous places of learning that we have encountered here open the potential for thinking of pedagogy in new and experimental ways because of how they acknowledge pedagogy's burden. We can now state that burden clearly: *Pedagogy teaches but it does not know how it teaches.*

Places of learning bear this burden masterfully when they bend explanation under its weight. As places of learning twist and draw explanations outside of themselves under the weight of their own impossibility, their pedagogies inflect explanation's stasis and linearity toward learning's movement and obliqueness. If they do this masterfully, they do it without abandoning propositional knowledge, literal language, or knowledge as a thing made, because, Grosz says, these are not faults to be unlearned (Grosz & Eisenman, 2001, p. 174):

> We could not function within this teeming multiplicity without some ability to skeletalize it or diagram or simplify it … the object is that cutting of the world that enables one to see how it meets my needs and interests.

In this respect, says Grosz (2001, p. 181), knowledge as a thing made is like technology, and it is especially like digital technology. Like technology, knowledge…

> …carries within it both the intellectual impulse to divide relations into solids and entities, objects or things, ones and zeroes, and the living impulse to render the world practically amenable. Digitization translates, retranscribes, and circumscribes the fluidity and flux by decomposing the analog or the continuous — currents — into elements, packages, or units, represented by the binary code, and then recomposing them through addition; analysis then synthesis.

This, in effect, is what curriculum is in relation to pedagogy. Curriculum, when staged as education's content, cuts relationality, plural interconnections, swarming complexity, the fluidity of the world into "subject matter," "facts," "timelines," "diagrams," "textbooks." Then it asks pedagogy to put these elements or units back together into the living, breathing continuity of the experience of the learning self. It attempts to do this through, for example, project-based learning and constructivist approaches to teaching. But, pedagogy, when approached as a process of recomposition, loses something in that process even though it may reproduce subject matter, facts, and models perfectly (Grosz & Eisenman, 2001, p. 175):

> We cannot help but view the world in terms of solids, as things. But we leave behind something untapped of the fluidity of the world, the movements, vibrations, transformations that occur below the threshold of perception and calculation and outside the relevance of our practical concerns.

Pedagogy as recomposition of the experience of the learning self in the making loses the "sweep and the spontaneity of the curve." To illustrate what is lost in the transfer from analog to digital, Grosz points to the musical performance whose "fullness of the real" is diminished when it is "represented only through the discrete elements of the score" (Grosz & Eisenman, 2001, p. 181). The analog continuum that is the reality's fullness is broken down and simplified when it is digitized into musical notation on a page. "What is lost in the process of digitization, in the scientific push to analysis or decomposition, is precisely the continuity, the force, that binds together the real as complexity and entwinement" (Grosz & Eisenman, 2001, p. 181).

What is lost in the recomposition of learning through the discrete parts of the curriculum are the sweep and the duration, the dramatic arc of the movement of the experience of the learning self as it skirts already given positions on the grid of knowledge. The indecomposable continuity of the arc of movement "disappears into its reconfiguration as measurable and reconfigurable space, object, or movement" (Grosz & Eisenman, 2001, p. 182) — as test scores, assignments, or portfolios, for example. What must be belied and disavowed in order for a thing made to assert itself, is its own making. The substitutions we make for that undivided movement of the passage from one knowing to another become the grid of "fixed points" in the culturally constructed significations of knowledge. They become curriculum.

As I said earlier, however, knowledge made is not left for dead in the places of learning that we have been exploring here. Knowledge as explanation or as a thing made is honored, but the reason it is honored is both peculiar and powerful. It is honored precisely *because* it is merely half-living. Its inadequacy for life is exactly what makes it useful and valuable as a potential provocation to action. In "masterful" places of learning, knowledge is honored for the way that it can be made to function as a "*promise*, as that which, in the future, in retrospect, yields a destination or effect, another thing" — another knowing (Grosz & Eisenman, 2001, p. 169). Knowledge as a thing made is honored to the extent that it gives itself up to being remade to suit the here and now.

So it turns out, Massumi tells us, that knowledge as a thing made *can* potentialize — it can open the future — but only indirectly (Massumi, 2002, p. 141). We must make knowledge keep its promise to provoke us to actions that will revitalize it and make it contemporaneous with this moment's needs and potentials. It is our experimental and ultimately destructive reception of knowledge already made that sets it in motion.

The Job of Pedagogy Is To Aggressively Tear Knowing Out of the Past

Pedagogy's job is to declare knowledge already made to be merely half-living — unable to sustain life. Pedagogy's job is to tear learning selves away from curriculum's static objects of mourning, out of their loyalties to knowledges that are inert, noncontemporaneous, and already configured. Allegiance to theories or knowledge already arrived at runs the risk, Winnicott warns us, of "becoming a compliant act, of pre-empting the personal and the unexpected" (Phillips, 1988, p. 54).

If pedagogy is to be creative and not compliant, it must have what Winnicott called an "aggressive component" (Phillips, 1988, p. 109). The job of pedagogy is to destroy knowledge in order to acknowledge the experience of the learning self. This is the risk-filled time and space of pedagogy. Pedagogy takes place at the turbulent point of matter crossing into mind, experience into knowledge, stability into potential, knowledge as promise and provocation into bodies in action, doing and making.

The time and place of such a pedagogy brings us up against the limits of "we" as a thing made. It brings us up against the limits of knowledge as a social enterprise. The anomalous pedagogies we have considered here are not for everyone. If learning selves are going to be open endedly noncompliant, if they are to be able to destroy knowledge in order to revitalize it, a scene of pedagogical address must necessarily remain open and vulnerable to learning selves who might misuse it, reject it, hate it, ironize it, find and exploit its limits, and even ridicule it.

The questions of pedagogy, therefore, are not "What knowledge is of most worth?" or "Whose knowledge should be taught?" or "Which practices will be the most efficient in teaching these knowledges?" Rather, the question of pedagogy is the question of how to use what has already been thought as a provocation and a call to invention.

At stake is nothing less than what a teacher is to do. Our experiment in thinking pedagogy has brought us to a place where the work shared by teachers and students can be seen as the work of subverting the space of arrested thought positioned as and within knowledge and making it possible to open up spaces of passage for self and others to face the continuation of their own experience. Pedagogy must face and address the "space of continuing experience" (Massumi, 2002, p. 192). It must do this so that those who have not participated in its history — in making the knowledges already arrived at — may participate in making its future.

The job of teachers is to infuse each step taken along the grids of knowledge and identity and self/other already in place "with a potential for having been otherwise directed" (Massumi, 2002, p. 192). The teacher becomes an opener of the future — one who reinvigorates dead knowledges (as things made) with life through use. Teachers and students become co-discoverers of the limits of our knowledges and of what we can do (next) at those limits. That is why pedagogical designs must address us to and from their own limits of teaching and knowing. They must present us with the irritation of the limits of our (and their) own knowledge.

As teachers, we cannot know how we learn and thus how to teach more effectively and efficiently. No one can know what is "inside" the learning self, and that means that no one can teach to that self. The learning self is inviolable and materially so. Any attempt to know it is also an attempt to violate its inviolable space of emergence. Such attempts are not only invasive; they are also wrongheaded because of the impossibility of knowing the learning self. All they accomplish is to provoke the learning self to erect walls of defense and evasions of compliance. What we end up finding out about the learning self by trying to measure it, assess it, and prescribe to it is not the learning self, but the terms of its defensive compliance or evasion.

When we use pedagogy to create potential fields of emergence for learners and for teachers, we risk creating a potential field of emergence for education itself. When we construct and inhabit pedagogies that hold our knowledge as teachers in ways that are responsive to the fact that a learner is an open system — we engage the fact that, as a human practice, education itself is an open system. This fact might seem obvious, yet so much of education's energies go toward denying or delaying that fact. So much of public education as institution, infrastructure, profession, and civic endeavor is predicated on acting as if we can predict, control, measure, and track the experience of the learning self. So much of what constitutes public education as a practice acts surprised that everything about it must be perennially remade, that the process of learning how to teach and what to teach is interminable, and that the cycles of education's trends and fads that promise successful closure to the learner as an open system are mere repetitions under the guise of breakthroughs, reforms, and revolutions — repetitions made necessary by the inevitable failures of attempts to close learning's open system.

What if we, as educators, started from the reality of teaching and learning that so many educational approaches expend so much energy denying? What if we started from the reality that the experience of the learning self cannot be grasped by knowledge as a thing made? What else might we do, as educators, with all of the time, energy, and resources that such an acknowledgment would reallocate?

Pedagogy and the Unreachable Learning Self

If there is one "human universal," a fact of shareable knowledge that is accessible to everyone across all human experience … it is the fact of embodiment. We all experience that indirectly shareable fact. We all inhabit that shared knowledge in and through the fact that we are bodies. At the same time, we all experience the fact of embodiment in absolutely singular, unique, unrepeatable, and, significantly, *unshareable* ways. Along with the fact of embodiment comes the fact of movement/sensation, which is one way to name the universal and shareable fact of being in relation. As living, moving, sensing bodies, we all exist only and always in relation even as our individual experiences of relationality are singular and unshareable.

Everything we "know," everything that is "tellable," emerges out of the time and place of this embodied movement/sensation — which is also a time and place of self-dissolution. Everyone experiences self-dissolution in his own unique ways. It is a fact that is simultaneously shared by everyone yet unshareable in our singular experiences of it. None of us has the power to perceive the time and place of self-dissolution directly because we come to consciousness of it only in the midst of our experiences of being dissolved, in relation, and in the interval between separation and connection. No one, no "I," can access this place of dissolution because what we experience as "I" emerges from it. This is why we cannot explain "how" we have come to a knowing. This is why pedagogy teaches but does not know how it teaches. We come to a knowing only as we emerge from a realm of sensation/movement that is ontologically prior to cognition. We come to the time and space of speaking about a learning only after it has already taken place in a time and space that language cannot name. Language *follows* that which it would name.

Yet, we *all* experience the realm of sensation/movement that escapes description through the static, fixing categories that compose what we take to be the "literal" in language. This is what we share, universally. It is a peculiar commonality, indeed, to share a knowledge that we all have something in common and that each of us experiences it in an absolutely singular way that we can never share. It is in this way that we are simultaneously separate from and connected to each other. In this way, we are at the same time profoundly alone and profoundly connected to one another (Rajchman, 2000b, p. 13):

> What we have in common would in these terms not be a fixed essence, but on the contrary, an irreducible plurality of "difference" in the arrangements and spaces in which we find ourselves at a particular time and place, exposing them to new forces and so to experimentation; pragmatism would involve an active belief or ethic that our common being is never given or found but always in the making.

Any attempt to "find" this moving self in language — to stop it and name it — threatens to become a "founding," a "pre-emptive intrusion." In that threat we can see the shadow of pedagogies of compliance, in which students are diagnosed, interpreted, named, and "known" in exploitative ways — in ways, for example, that use students as evidence for accountability in the name of politically motivated educational "reforms." Paraphrasing Adam Phillips, we can recall scenes of pedagogy where there is a "primary and enforced attentiveness to the needs of the teacher. And this, according to Winnicott, is a scene in which the [complying] self always lacks something, and that something is the *essential element of creative originality*" (Phillips, 1988, p. 133).

Winnicott spoke of children as being masters of various techniques for indirect communication that they use to hide their vulnerable selves in the making from the impositional teacher or parent and as a way to use language without complying with it (Phillips, 1988, p. 148). Winnicott thought that when children invented and used indirect communication they showed that they had much in common with artists. Children, he thought, share artists' "urgent need to communicate and the still more urgent need not to be found" (Winnicott, quoted in Phillips, 1988, p. 151).

To better understand how some pedagogies use media and architecture to release and hold experiences of the learning self, we do not need to "find" the learning self and "know" it through theoretical or conceptual elaboration on such pedagogies. The radical singularities of anomalous places of learning defeat such attempts. Instead we need, according to de Bolla, "further elaboration *within* these experiences" (de Bolla, 2001, p. 130).

I believe that this is precisely what the pedagogical innovations we have been looking at do. They elaborate our understanding of pedagogy from *within* experiences of the learning self. They give "voice" to those experiences indirectly and poetically — not as artworks do through language, sculpture, paint, or music (at least not through these alone) but through abstract, poetic, metaphorical assemblages of movements/sensations in and through processual paths, landscapes, and buildings in real or imagined use, performance, juxtaposition, and thought as it is sensed. Their elaborations of pedagogy from within the experience of the learning self show us that while the experience of the learning self is unknowable and inaccessible to propositional knowledge and literal language … it is, nevertheless, of this world. The experience of the learning self is simultaneously what is universal and what is singular in the experience of human embodiment.

Pedagogy does not need to "find" children or learning selves in order to "teach" them. Instead, it can master practices of indirect but explicit communication — practices that circumvent naming, counting, and the literalness of language while gesturing explicitly to knowledge in the making. The environments, experience, and events that we have looked at here use media and architecture as indirect forms of communication to point out oblique itineraries to the learning self. They "correlate to the intellect" but not as the maker of things and concepts that leave behind the "real out of which they were drawn and simplified" (Grosz & Eisenman, 2001, p. 179); rather, the anomalous pedagogies we considered here correlate to the capacity of the mind/brain/body to be aware of two things at once: the continuous unfolding of the world *and* the continuous unfolding of the intellect as it draws out and simplifies its own and the word's emergences into things and knowledges made.

The Sensation of the Learning Body

It seems appropriate to illustrate several of the claims I have just made by returning to one of the most popular of the Bell Science Lab animated educational films, *Hemo the Magnificent*. *Hemo* gives the body the last word, but paradoxically so, by mastering an indirectness of communication that addresses the learning selves of children without presuming to know where and who they are and reminds adults of pedagogy's need to creatively destroy knowledge in order to engage learning selves in knowledge in the making.

In 2002, the Games-To-Teach Project (now called The Educational Arcade), a research collaboration between Microsoft and the MIT Comparative Media Studies Program, cited *Hemo the Magnificent* (1957) as one of its inspirations. In their website (http://www.educationarcade.org/gtt/), they called the Bell Labs Science Series a "zenith" of educational filmmaking. "Even by today's standards, [the series] stands as an effective model for the use of educational media."

The terms that adults use to share their memories of watching *Hemo* when they were school children are telling. We might take them to be efforts to give voice to the experience of the learning self, and we will use them here in our efforts to elaborate our understandings of pedagogy from *within* the experience of the learning self.

Hal Erickson offers the following description of *Hemo the Magnificent* on the MSN Entertainment website (http://entertainment.msn.com/movies/movie.aspx?m=36735):

> The second in a group of full-color Bell Science Specials produced, written, and directed by the legendary Frank Capra, *Hemo the Magnificent* is an hour-long combination of animation and live action, explaining in the most entertaining manner possible the human circulatory system. Shakespearean scholar Dr. Frank Baxter again appears as "Dr. Research," with Richard Carlson as "The Fiction Writer." After establishing that "haemo" is the Greek word for blood, Dr. Research introduces The Fiction Writer to Hemo the Magnificent, a muscular animated figure with a transparent body, allowing us to see the entire blood stream from the heart on down. For the amusement of his animal friends (and, incidentally, the home audience), Hemo demonstrates just what makes him tick, with the help of such characters as Professor Anatomy, The Dispatcher, and The Pacemaker. The highlight is a cartoon segment showing how the brain and heart are interchangeable and inextricable, with UPA animation director Bill Hurtz depicting Man's Inner Workings as a huge, high-pressure factory, replete with whistles, warning buzzers, and conveyor belts. The winner of an Emmy award for best cinematography, *Hemo the Magnificent* was rebroadcast several times and later became a staple on the classroom audio-visual circuit.

Recently, a number of the films from the Bell Labs Science Series were re-released on DVD, provoking a flurry of postings from consumer reviews to

Amazon.com's website (http://www.amazon.com/exec/obidos/tg/detail/-/ 6302182484/102-1757921-2243344?v=glance). Again, the terms in which *Hemo*'s viewers speak of their experiences of the film are telling:

> The most cherished education film from our elementary days, December 25, 2001
> Reviewer: ... Duluth, MN
>
> It is nice to know our childhood memories are being preserved even if we do not remember how many times we were shown "Hemo the Magnificent" or any of the other films in the Bell Science Series.... My clearest memory of this video is that the film broke or we had to change reels after Dr. Frank was challenged by Hemo to prove he knew about the origins of blood. The answer (yes, I saw you had your hand up) is "Sea Water." I do not know what else I remember from elementary school in New Jersey, but I know that blood has its origins in sea water.... "Hemo the Magnificent" is one of my fondest movie memories from my youth.

> An ingenious blend of art and science, January 27, 2000
> Reviewer: A viewer from Aiea, Hawaii USA
>
> "Hemo the Magnificent" is a story of a scientist trying to convince a skeptical Greek god and his forest friends about the reality and wonder of how the heart works. And in so doing we are convinced; we find ourselves awestruck over the ingenuity and beauty of nature.... One of the great things about "Hemo" is that it takes a fairly complex subject matter and makes it understandable and entertaining. I can imagine even a pre-schooler learning something from it.... I first saw this film in grade school in the late '60s, and lastly in college while getting my health science degree. It never seemed dated even though it was made in the '50s.... Educational films today seem dry and unemotional in comparison, as if producers were ashamed to show more than an academic view of their subject. It is unfortunate that no one makes films today the way Frank Capra and the Bell Science series did.... Even today when I hear Beethoven's *Eroica* symphony (which was its soundtrack), my first thought is of that great film. I would recommend this to anyone, especially to parents and teachers.

> Best educational film EVER!, June 8, 2003
> Reviewer: ... from The Great Northwest
>
> HEMO is the best educational film EVER. This movie has inspired and continues to inspire generations of health professionals. Imagine today's Doctors, Pharmacists, Nurses, Dentists, Paramedics as 6th graders sitting on the floor in their Toughskins watching HEMO

for the first time. Nobody teaches the LUBDUBS like HEMO [it's all in the valves]! HEMO also shows us why we breathe, why we faint when we stand for too long, why we stretch each morning, how boxers get knocked out, vagal and sympathetic systems, and MUCH, MUCH MORE! When I watch HEMO as an adult health professional, I am amazed at how well it stands up and how much solid info is packed into this 55-minute masterpiece!

Hemo's the greatest, October 30, 2002
Reviewer: A viewer from Philadelphia, PA

Hemo the Magnificent made biology come alive for many children. I still love watching this film today and I use it extensively to simplify the heart and circulatory system as I teach in an allied health post secondary school.... *Hemo* is as fresh and pertinent to science students today as it was 45 years ago.

Hemo the Magnificent, April 1, 2002
Reviewer: David from Texas

As a child I marveled at the way the circulatory system was shown in "Hemo." Now as a teacher I still marvel at its simplicity and timeless delivery. As a nurse, I see a way to educate people, again in a timeless form. Patient and student education is much easier because of it.

My own memories of watching the Bell Lab Science Series are some of the most vivid of my childhood. I know that my fascination with all things scientific began while I sat on the gray metal folding chairs that the janitor had set up on the polished floor of the grade-school gym and gazed at the movie screen on a tripod in the center of the stage high over our heads. While I have indelible memories of specific scenes and images of capillaries and of animated workers who diligently opened and closed the valves of an animated heart with just the right rhythm, my most vivid recollection of those films is not composed of images or factoids about hemoglobin. My most vivid recollection is of a sensation/emotion. The sensation part of that recollection is a full-body memory of being very close to the movie screen, right up in front of it as if there is no distance between the screen and me at all. It is not as if I am *in* the movie; it is more like I am pressing my nose against a window to get a better look at something inside — or is it outside? No, a better description of that sensation is that it is as if I am hovering above our chairs, above our heads, right in front of the screen — so that it fills my entire field of vision, my entire field of attention. Hovering like a hummingbird, I can (and I do!) move in closer or back off farther, slide left or right, not to see what is happening on the screen better — I can see fine — no, this hovering allows me to *meet* what is on the screen, to *dance* with it and go with it to wherever it and I might be going. Of course, my body was not hovering and it was never that close. It was in a chair somewhere in the first several rows of the gym because I would have been in second or third grade.

As I write these words, they strike me as attempts to give body to some of the abstract concepts that we have been experimenting with throughout this book: transitional space, the space between, emergence, and self-dissolution. The emotion part of the sensation/emotion that I recall as I watched these films is an emotion I experience today when I am in the midst of an experience of "my" learning self. It is an emotion that I recognize and associate today with those times and places when I am not being a compliant adult. It is a constellation of feelings/thoughts that include eager anticipation, an impending sense that something is changing but not knowing what it will change to, excitement, pride and satisfaction in following a complicated, unfamiliar "story" as it unfolds on the screen. "Following" but not in a compliant way, because there is also a deep sense of trust that where I and the pedagogy are going will be surprising to both of us because our "destination" is somehow getting made up as we go along. There is also a sense of enjoyment of not having gotten there yet and of not even being eager to do so because the suspension between new and old ways of being is in and of itself a very pleasant and engrossing one.

What is it about *Hemo the Magnificent* that can make viewing it feel like noncompliance? How can an educational film, probably one of the most nonanomalous, "closed" pedagogical texts that we have looked at, unfold in a way that seems to precede its own determination? This film is far from poetic. All of its elements, including its story and animations, are geared toward explanation — the very thing I have identified as being anathema to the learning self's experience of noncompliant knowledge in the making. Maybe this film is considered by so many to be a pedagogical success because it has figured out how to explain without imposing compliance. It has managed somehow to make explanation metaphorical and nonliteral. It has somehow managed to take explanation back even as it offers it.

The "heroes" of *Hemo the Magnificent* and of people's memories of the films are Hemo and the teacher/narrator, Dr. Research, but they are peculiar heroes. Hemo is portrayed as a muscle-bound Greek god named after blood. His power comes from his ability to give life, but he is an incomplete (uneducated?) hero in that he does not know who he is. He knows his power but he does not understand it. He cannot name himself or speak his own meanings. It is up to Dr. Research to teach Hemo (and us) his significance. But, Dr. Research is a peculiar scientist, perhaps because, while he represents himself in the film as a researcher, he was in real life Dr. Frank Baxter, a Shakespearean scholar at the University of Southern California. Maybe that is why his explanation of scientific principles enlists the help of Edgar Allen Poe, the Bible, and narratives that stage stories of scientific inquiry as dramatic detective stories or heroic tragedies.

While it is Dr. Research's job to explain Hemo, he is the first to admit that he does not have all the answers. Most importantly, he admits that even science may *never* know all the answers, especially to the question of life. This admission triggers the film's curious religious references at its end. Rhetorically, those references function as an acknowledgment of the limits of human knowing and the limits of science itself. Dr. Research takes up his role as the teacher, yet he does so in a way that seems to bracket all of his statements. It is as if he flags each explanation or assertion with a caveat: "This is what we think, now. But what we think we know about how the heart works or what makes it work — what we know about the big questions — is not 'real,' it's our interpretation, it's temporary, it's a metaphor."

The metaphorical status of Dr. Research's explanations of blood and how it sustains life is underscored by the film's interweaving of animation and live-action footage. The animation gives what we are being taught the obvious status of interpretation. The animated switchboard operator in the brain of the man undergoing a heart operation who frantically sends messages to capillaries is not "real." The film cuts seamlessly between microscopic images of actual blood cells passing, cell by cell, through tiny capillaries and the animated Hemo looking at himself through the microscope and insisting, thunderously and indignantly, that who he is and what he means cannot be reduced or decomposed to what he sees through the lens. He insists that he cannot be and is not captured by the film's explanation.

Scientific knowledge, Dr. Research implies over and over, is not a thing made because science is incapable of making complete sense. As Dr. Research comes to a key conclusion or to the end of an extended explanation for The Fiction Writer (the student within the film who poses all sorts of questions to Dr. Research), The Fiction Writer expresses a gleeful "Aha!" or "So that's how it works." Dr. Research, however, comes right back with a version of "not so fast" as he proceeds to complicate the story even more and to reveal just how many even bigger questions remain.

In stark contrast to Dr. Research's partial and incomplete explanations stands the animated Hemo, who is continuity, who is life. The discrete facts and definitions that Dr. Research provides simply cannot add up to Hemo. The math does not come out right: As Hemo insists, and as we ourselves are invited to see in the live-action film of a beating heart during open-heart surgery, Hemo is more than Dr. Research's explanations. Hemo may not be able to articulate what he is, though: Even he cannot explain life. But, he moves, he senses, and he knows it in a way that explanation cannot. Hemo knows, but he does not know how he came to know it, and as a result he cannot teach it to Dr. Research. Like the little girl in *We Are Seven*, Hemo cannot show the work of how he arrived at a "knowing," at a life, that exceeds explanation.

The rhetorical job of The Fiction Writer in this film is to find the limits of Dr. Research's knowings. He subverts Dr. Research's pedagogical function, pointing out where the pedagogy, the explanation, and the curriculum break down. He keeps asking why, who, what, and how do you know until Dr. Research comes to the end of his explanatory powers. When the writer's questions and skepticism force Dr. Research to the limits of his knowledge, the writer is not triumphant in his skepticism nor is Dr. Research humiliated by his limits. Instead, they stand side by side, peering into what is unknowable to both of them. They both stand in wonder.

It is in that place that The Fiction Writer learns the greatest lesson — that at the heart of his learning self lies something that is unknowable. Dr. Research seems almost joyful at arriving at the limits of his own knowledge, because paradoxically that limit point becomes a pivot point into a vast spaciousness. Suddenly, there is space for the many doctors and nurses who are actively seeking answers to questions about disease. Suddenly there is space for the future. Most importantly, there is a space between knowledge already made and knowledge in the making for the children to formulate and to hear — out of wonder, not out of compliance — their own questions.

Pedagogy's Continuous Emergence

When I think of *We Are Seven* as a scene of pedagogical address, I wonder what look is on the adult's face as the little girl insists, without explanation but with descriptions of her embodied experiences of her continuing being in relation with her brother and sister, that "we are seven." Is it the look that I have referred to as connoting the experience of the learning self? Or, is it a look similar to that of the silent visitors to *Bravehearts: Men in Skirts* — that look of apprehension, dread even, at the possibility of seeing something that does not make sense, of feeling something that cannot be named, of sensing a presence or a reality that is neither real nor unreal? Or, is the look on the adult's face that of a looming impositional pedagogue who detects a wrong answer he must correct, a difference that he must — with the best intentions — make conform?

Whose risk is it to acknowledge that a teacher could never find or found the experience of the learning self that brought the little girl to her knowing that "we are seven?" What should we educators know of the experience of the learning self? What should we know of its indecomposable arc of movement? Our experiment in thinking pedagogy has brought us to this question, but it is a question that pedagogy must never answer of itself. If it did, it would be the end of pedagogy. The good news is that pedagogy can never answer the question of how it teaches — so its provocation will never end — but we *can* elaborate our understanding of pedagogy from within our experiences of its masterpieces, and there pedagogy is excessive. It is a monstrous gift from the outside of all that we presume to know.

What will we make of the continuous emergence of pedagogy? What will we make of pedagogy's inexpressible involvement in the continuous emergence of the experience of the learning self? The power of our work as educators and as designers of places of learning is that it takes place in the midst of pedagogy's continuous, unstoppable emergence. Why do we so often give up this power to teaching "strategies" that seek to stop the movement of the learning self by knowing pedagogy as a thing made? The world gives pedagogy the gift of its continuous unfolding and qualitative transformation, its endlessly open potential for qualitative change and augmentation. In the midst of pedagogy's continuous emergence, it is the work and play of teachers to keep the flow of difference, movement, sensation — and their destinations — open and undetermined. This is not always the work of happy creative invention. Democracy, Phillips reminds us, requires conflict. It would only make sense that the teacher's job would include finding ways of sustaining the conflict that democracy requires. It would only make sense that teachers would find ways of making classrooms and other places of learning points of rendezvous and envelopes of passage for the difficult, uncomfortable, sometimes dangerous conflicts engendered when conflict is refused and suppressed elsewhere.

What is the place of the teacher to the time and space of the learning self? It is to be in the place of pedagogy's continuous emergence, a "zone of historical indetermination" that allows for surprising and audacious experiences of the learning self. Audacious learning selves in the making will risk relationality with the social body that surrounds them, but only if their emergence is met by a particular look on the teacher's face: the look of a teacher in the midst of the experience of her own learning self in the making.

References

Bahovec, E. (1993, Winter). Turning the screw of *Sentimental Education* [review of the book *Sentimental education: Schooling, popular culture and the regulation of liberty*]. *New Formations*, 165–172.

Baldwin, J. (1963/1988). A talk to teachers. In R. S. S. Walker (Ed.), *Multi-cultural literacy* (pp. 3–12). Saint Paul, MN: Graywolf Press.

Beam, A. (1988, June 29). Venerable Building 20: A building with soul. *The Boston Globe* (retrieved on February 29, 2004, from http://web.mit.edu/newsoffice/tt/1996/oct30/42944/42938.html).

Benedikt, M. (1987). *For an architecture of reality*. New York: Lumen Books.

Benjamin, J. (1998). Shadow *of the other: Intersubjectivity and gender in psychoanalysis*. New York: Routledge.

Bollas, C. (1999). *The mystery of things*. New York: Routledge.

Bruinsma, M. (1998, Winter). Trial and error. *Eye, 30(8)* (retrieved on February 29, 2004, from http://www.xs4all.nl/~maxb/eye30edit.htm).

Buckingham, D. (Ed.) (1998). *Teaching popular culture: Beyond radical pedagogy*. London: UCL Press.

Butler, J. (1997). *Excitable speech: A politics of the performative*. New York; London: Routledge.

Careri, F., Pla, M., Piccolo, S., & Hammond, P. (2002). *Walkscapes: El andar como práctica estética (Walking as an aesthetic practice)*. Barcelona: Editorial Gustavo Gili.

Caruth, C. (Ed.) (1995). *Trauma: Explorations in memory*. Baltimore, MD: Johns Hopkins University Press.

Civic Alliance To Rebuild Downtown New York. (2002). *Listening to the city: Report of proceedings* (retrieved February 29, 2004, from www.listeningtothecity.org).

Copjec, J. (1996). *Radical evil*. New York: Verso.

Dannatt, A. (1995). *Architecture in detail: United States Holocaust Memorial Museum*, London: Phaidon Press.

Dannatt, A., & Hursley, T. (2002). *United States Holocaust Memorial Museum: James Ingo Freed*. London: Phaidon.

de Bolla, P. (2001). *Art matters*. Cambridge, MA: Harvard University Press.

Donald, J. (1992). *Sentimental education: Schooling, popular culture, and the regulation of liberty*. New York: Verso.

Dunne, A. (1999). *Hertzian tales: Electronic products, aesthetic experience and critical design*. London: Royal College of Art.

Ellsworth, E. (1997). *Teaching positions: Difference, pedagogy, and the power of address*. New York: Teachers College Press.

Felman, S. (1983). *The literary speech act: Don Juan with J.L. Austin, or seduction in two languages*. Ithaca, NY: Cornell University Press.

Felman, S. (1987). *Jacques Lacan and the adventure of insight: Psychoanalysis in contemporary culture.* Cambridge, MA: Harvard University Press.

Felman, S. (1995). Education and crisis, or the vicissitudes of teaching. In C. Caruth (Ed.), *Trauma: Explorations in memory* (pp. 13–60). Baltimore, MD: Johns Hopkins University Press.

Felman, S., & Laub, D. (1992). *Testimony: Crises of witnessing in literature, psychoanalysis, and history.* New York: Routledge.

Flax, J. (1993). *Disputed subjects: Essays on psychoanalysis, politics, and philosophy.* New York: Routledge.

Goldberg, M. (1997). The Holocaust and education: An interview with Michael Berenbaum. *Phi Delta Kappan, 79(2),* 317–319.

Graeber, L. (2002, November 20). A journey into art. *The New York Times* (retrieved on February 29, 2004, from http://www.cmom.org/articles/index%20articles.htm).

Green, B. (1998). Teaching for difference: Learning theory and post-critical pedagogy. In D. Buckingham (Ed.), *Teaching popular culture: Beyond radical pedagogy* (pp. 177–197). London: University College London Press.

Grosz, E. A., & Eisenman, P. (2001). *Architecture from the outside: Essays on virtual and real space.* Cambridge, MA: MIT Press.

Halprin, L. (1997). *The Franklin Delano Roosevelt Memorial.* San Francisco, CA: Chronicle Books.

Hapgood, F. (1993). *Up the infinite corridor: MIT and the technical imagination.* Reading, MA: Addison–Wesley.

Heller, S. (1998). *Edwin Schlossberg and his seriously playful learning machines* (photocopy).

Heller, S. (2002, May). Big fun cool things. *Metropolis* (retrieved May 2002 from http://www.metropolismag.com/html/content_0502/sch/).

Heller, S., & Pettit, E. (1998). *Design dialogues.* New York: Allworth Press.

Holmes, M. (2002, November). Getting inside the exhibit: 'Art Inside Out' at children's museum. *Education Update Online* (retrieved on February 29, 2004, from http://www.educationupdate.com/archives/2002/nov02/issue/mus_artinsi.html).

Keenan, T. (1997). *Fables of responsibility: Aberrations and predicaments in ethics and politics.* Stanford, CA: Stanford University Press.

Keenan, T., & Caruth, C. (1995). The AIDS crisis is not over: A conversation with Gregg Bordowitz, Douglas Crimp, and Laura Pinsky. In C. Caruth (Ed.), *Trauma: Explorations in memory* (pp. 256–271). Baltimore, MD: Johns Hopkins University Press.

Kennedy, B. M. (2003). *Deleuze and cinema: The aesthetics of sensation.* Edinburgh: Edinburgh University Press.

Laclau, E. (1996). *Emancipations.* New York: Verso.

Lacy, S. (1996). *The roof is on fire.* (Retrieved October 2003 from http://arts.endowment.gov/Archive/Features2/Lacy.html).

Lacy, S., & Wettrich, A. (2002). *What it takes: A catalogue essay.* Co-Lab: New Generations, Fine Arts Gallery, San Francisco State University (retrieved February 29, 2004, from http://www.suzannelacy.com/pubwhatit.htm).

Lanzmann, C. (1995). The obscenity of understanding: An evening with Claude Lanzmann. In C. Caruth (Ed.), *Trauma: Explorations in memory* (pp. 200–220). Baltimore, MD: Johns Hopkins University Press.

Lin, M. Y. (2000). *Boundaries.* New York: Simon & Schuster.

Linenthal, E. (1995). *Preserving memory: The struggle to create America's holocaust museum.* New York: Viking Press.

Lusted, D. (1986). Why pedagogy? *Screen, 27(5),* 2–14.

Marshall, B. K. (1992). *Teaching the postmodern: Fiction and theory.* New York: Routledge.

Massumi, B. (1995). Interface and active space: Human machine design. In *Proceedings of the Sixth International Symposium on Electronic Art,* Montreal (retrieved on February 29, 2004, from http://www.anu.edu.au/HRC/first_and_last/works/interface.htm).

Massumi, B. (2002). *Parables for the virtual: Movement, affect, sensation.* Durham, NC: Duke University Press.

Mayne, J. (1993). *Cinema and spectatorship.* New York: Routledge.

MIT School of Architecture and Planning. (2000, Winter). Helping Hiroshima heal: Krzysztof Wodiczko's latest work. *PLAN Newsletter, 53* (retrieved February 29, 2004, from http://loohooloo.mit.edu/plan/plan_issues/53/wodiczko2).

Morgan, R. (1993). Transitions from English to cultural studies. *New Education, 15(1),* 21–48.

Morrish, W., & Brown, C. (1999). Infrastructure for the new social covenant. In The Architectural League of New York (Ed.), *The productive park: New waterworks as neighborhood resources* (pp. 2–22). New York: Princeton Architectural Press.

Muschamp, H. (1993, April 11). Shaping a monument to memory. *The New York Times*, Section 2, pp. 1, 22.

Muschamp, H. (2002a, September 8). Don't rebuild. Reimagine. *The New York Times Magazine*, Section 6, pp. 46–58.

Muschamp, H. (2002b, November 10). For all you observers of the urban extravaganza. *The New York Times*, Section 2, p. 34.

Muschamp, H. (2003a, December 20). A skyscraper has a chance to be nobler. *The New York Times*, p. A1.

Muschamp, H. (2003b, January 28). A goal for ground zero: Finding an urban poetry. *The New York Times*, p. E1.

Muschamp, H. (2003c, June 8). Zaha Hadid's urban mothership. *The New York Times*, Section 2, pp. 1, 30.

Nightingale, V. (1996). *Studying audiences: The shock of the real*. New York: Routledge.

Ockman, J. (Ed.) (2000). *The pragmatist imagination: Thinking about "things in the making."* New York: Princeton Architectural Press/Temple Hoyne Buell Center for the Study of American Architecture.

Phelan, P. (1993). *Unmarked: The politics of performance*. New York: Routledge.

Phillips, A. (1988). *Winnicott*. Cambridge, MA: Harvard University Press.

Phillips, A. (1994). *On Flirtation: Psychoanalytic essays on the uncommitted life*. Cambridge, MA: Harvard University Press.

Phillips, A. (2002). *Equals*. London: Faber & Faber.

Phillips, P. C. (2003, Winter). Creating democracy: A discussion with Krzysztof Wodiczko. *Art Journal*, 33–47.

Probyn, E. (1992). Technologizing the self: A future anterior for cultural studies. In C. Nelson, P. A. Treichler, & L. Grossberg (Eds.), *Cultural studies* (p. 509). New York: Routledge.

Rajchman, J. (2000a). *The Deleuze connections*. Cambridge, MA: MIT Press.

Rajchman, J. (2000b). General introduction. In J. Ockman (Ed.), *The pragmatist imagination: Thinking about "things in the making"* (pp. 6–15). New York: Princeton Architectural Press.

Richardson, L. (1997). *Fields of play: Constructing an academic life*. Piscataway, NJ: Rutgers University Press.

Rothstein, E., Muschamp, H., & Marty, M. E. (2003). *Visions of utopia*. New York: Oxford University Press.

Rybczynski, W. (2003, July 8). More perfect union of function and form. *The New York Times*, p. 1.

Schlossberg, E. (1998). *Interactive excellence: Defining and developing new standards for the twenty-first century*. New York: Ballantine.

Simonson, R., & Walker, S. (1988). *Multi-cultural literacy*. Saint Paul, MN: Graywolf Press.

Smith, A. D. (2000). *Talk to me: Listening between the lines*. New York: Random House.

Sorkin, M. (1993). The Holocaust Museum: Between beauty and horror. *Progressive Architecture*, 2, 74.

Speigelman, A. (1995). Interview on National Public Radio January 27 (retrieved on July 5, 2003, from www.npr.org).

Story, L. (2002, September 18). Encouraging innovation by ending isolation. *The Boston Globe* (retrieved on February 29, 2004, from http://web.mit.edu/newsoffice/tt/1996/oct30/42944/42938.html).

Szollosy, M. (1998). Winnicott's potential spaces: Using psychoanalytic theory to redress the crises of postmodern culture. Paper presented at the 1998 MLA Convention, San Francisco (retrieved on March 1, 2004, from http://psychematters.com/papers/szollosy.htm).

Templeton, D. (1999, September 23–29). Weird science: Are Dr. Frank Baxter and those wacky Bell Science films ready for a comeback? *The Sonoma County Independent* (retrieved February 29, 2004, from http://www.metroactive.com/papers/sonoma/09.23.99/bellscience-9938.html).

Thompson, D. (2003). Is race a trope?: Anna Deavere Smith and the question of racial performativity. *African American Review, 37(1)* (retrieved February 29, 2004, from http://www.findarticles.com/cf_dls/m2838/1_37/100959606/p1/article.jhtml).

Ulmer, G. L. (1989). *Teletheory: Grammatology in the age of video.* New York: Routledge.

Upton, D. (2002). Architecture in the everyday. *New Literary History, 33,* 707–723.

Weinberg, J., & Elieli, R. (1995). *The Holocaust Museum in Washington.* New York: Rizzoli International Publications.

Wieseltier, L. (1993). After memory: Reflections on the Holocaust Memorial Museum. *New Republic,* May 3, pp. 16–26.

Williams, P. J. (1991). *The alchemy of race and rights.* Cambridge, MA: Harvard University Press.

Winnicott, D. W. (1989). *Playing and reality.* New York: Routledge.

Winship, F. (2002, October 29). Artists create works for children's museum. United Press International (retrieved on February 29, 2004, from http://www.upi.com/view.cfm?StoryID=20021029-113514-2218r).

Wodiczko, K. (1999). *Critical vehicles: Writings, projects, interviews.* Cambridge, MA: MIT Press.

Young, J. E. (2002). The Holocaust as vicarious past: Restoring the voices of memory to history. *Judaism* (retrieved February 29, 2004, from http://www.findarticles.com/cf_dls/m0411/1_51/85068473/p10/article.jhtml?term=).

Young, R. (1994). Potential space: Transitional phenomena. In *Mental space.* London: Process Press (retrieved February 29, 2004, from http://www.shef.ac.uk/~psysc/mental/chap8.html).

Index

DEMCO